ATE DU

Philosophical
Approaches to Literature

Philosophical Approaches to Literature

*New Essays on Nineteenth-
and Twentieth-Century Texts*

Edited by William E. Cain

Lewisburg
Bucknell University Press
London and Toronto: Associated University Presses

© 1984 by Associated University Presses, Inc.

Associated University Presses
440 Forsgate Drive
Cranbury, NJ 08512

Associated University Presses
25 Sicilian Avenue
London WC1A 2QH, England

Associated University Presses
2133 Royal Windsor Drive
Unit 1
Mississauga, Ontario
Canada L5J 1K5

Library of Congress Cataloging in Publication Data

Main entry under title:

Philosophical approaches to literature.

Bibliography: p.
1. English literature—History and criticism—
Addresses, essays, lectures.   2. Literature—
Philosophy—Addresses, essays, lectures.   3. Philosophy
in literature—Addresses, essays, lectures.
4. American literature—History and criticism—
Addresses, essays, lectures.   I. Cain, William E.,
1952–
PR409.P48P54   1983   820'.9   82-48652
ISBN 0-8387-5055-9

Contents

Acknowledgments

I want, first of all, to thank my contributors for writing essays especially for this collection; I am grateful for their labor and also for their patience. For supporting the manuscript and helping to see it through the Press, I am obliged to Harry R. Garvin, James M. Heath, and Cynthia R. Fell. During difficult moments I greatly benefited from the advice and encouragement given to me by Alan Wilde and Barbara Leah Harman. I wish also to thank Eric Sundquist—both for his insights and for his good humor. Finally, for a key term in my Introduction, I am indebted to the title of Richard Poirier's stimulating study of Robert Frost, *The Work of Knowing* (New York: Oxford University Press, 1977).

Preface

In a stimulating essay Frederic Will remarks that "noticeably lacking to the whole American critical movement, even in its theoretical phase, is a philosophical underpinning."[1] Will's essay was written in the early nineteen-seventies, and it is fair to say that the situation has changed since then. A firm and final "underpinning" for our critical work has yet to be agreed upon, and in view of the range and number of theories, schools, and methodologies, it is unlikely that a consensus will emerge anytime soon. But the question of where such a philosophical "underpinning" might be located is now at least a subject for serious debate and dispute. Literature and philosophy are studied together, and the practice of criticism is no longer seen as essentially hostile to "theorizing."

Such a generalization ought not to be made too quickly. The antagonism between literature and philosophy dies hard, as George Watson makes clear when he complains that "literary critics of a fashionable stamp are inclined to wear second-hand philosophical clothes with an air of chic. It is as if they had shopped in charity bazaars for goods marked down as 'Nearly New.'"[2] And if one is to believe George Steiner, the "current scene" is so "ludicrous" that the only general truth that can be uttered about criticism today is that it is in a state of total confusion and "dishevelment."[3] But it nevertheless is the case, I think, that in the past decade literary criticism has begun to incline toward and merge with philosophy, pushed in this direction by the keen (and sometimes frenzied) interest in structuralism, poststructuralism, and deconstruction. To understand the terms, ideas, and issues that have changed the course of literary criticism, one is obliged to read Jacques Derrida, Paul Ricoeur, and other philosophers. For better and for worse, philosophy, self-critical reflection about method, theoretical analysis, and abstract thinking occupy the center of contemporary discussions about literature.

As this collection demonstrates, my own bias is a literary one: I teach literature (and not philosophy) in most of my classes, and my literary background and concerns manifest themselves in my writing on problems in critical theory and philosophy. In gathering the essays included here, I have been attentive to the facts of my own expertise, training, and commitments. The reader of my introduction will also discover that while I share with my contributors a special interest in the new work being done today in literary theory and philosophy, I continue to admire critics and to endorse methods and values that the *new* New Criticism may appear to have passed by; in one or two places, my reader may be surprised by the writers that I cite.

I have chosen contributors whose writings I respect and have learned from. Most are young critics, trained during the period when the pressure of philosophy on literary analysis first began to be felt. In this collection and elsewhere, their work is shaped and guided by what they have studied in philosophy. I have also included essays written by critics whose careers signal a shift from the New Criticism or historical scholarship to a form of philosophical inquiry. The questions that they ask about texts, the authorities they cite, their conception of their job as critics—all these have changed, and their writing has thus taken new directions.

In putting together this collection I had little hope of representing all the kinds of work now being done, but I have tried to give as much breadth in approach and subject matter as possible. Several of the essays focus on poets and novelists; others deal with philosophical influence, genre, literary periods and movements, critical theory, and the phenomenon of Derrida and deconstruction. I have examined the relevant scholarship on literature and philosophy before the Romantic period, and much of it is of course interesting and important. But in my judgment the best work is being done on nineteenth- and twentieth-century writers and texts. There are exceptions, but to represent the best work means that I have to limit the field.

I hope that this collection will serve, in one sense, as a review of literary criticism as it came to be formed and practiced during the past decade. But it is also intended to be suggestive, and to mark out new possibilities for study and analysis. Rather than rehearsing the familiar story of the conflict between literature and philosophy, which dates back to Plato, I am concerned to inquire and wonder about what lies ahead. The "new" is, however, often difficult to describe and articulate clearly—which leads me to a major theme of my introduction.

Notes

1. Frederic Will, "The Motive of Literary Criticism," in *The Knife in the Stone: Essays in Literary Theory* (The Hague and Paris: Mouton, 1973), p. 17.

2. George Watson, *The Discipline of English: A Guide to Critical Theory and Practice* (New York: Barnes and Noble, 1978), p. 37.

3. George Steiner, "Critic/Reader," *New Literary History* 10 (Spring 1979):437, 451.

Introduction

In his famous critique of F. R. Leavis's *Revaluation*, René Wellek noted that the book "teems with acute critical observations and brilliant interpretations of texts" but is not adequately grounded in philosophy.[1] Leavis, he contends, fails to grasp the "Romantic philosophy" that informs the verse of Shelley and others, and so he misunderstands and undervalues their poetry. Still more disturbing, adds Wellek, is Leavis's failure to provide an explicit account of his own terms and assumptions: he gives us a suggestive "practical criticism," but not the "theory" that would explain and justify it.

Leavis, in replying to Wellek, paid some attention to the point about Romantic philosophy, but he was more concerned to stress the sharp difference between the tasks of the critic and philosopher. "Literary criticism and philosophy," he asserts, "seem to me to be quite distinct and different kinds of disciplines—at least, I think they ought to be."[2] "No doubt," he concludes,

> a philosophic training might possibly—ideally would—make a critic surer and more penetrating in the perception of significance and relation and in the judgment of value. But it is to be noted that the improvement we ask for is of the critic, the critic as critic, and to count on it would be to count on the attainment of an arduous ordeal. It would be reasonable to fear—to fear blunting of edge, blurring of focus, and muddled misdirection of attention: consequences of queering one discipline with the habits of another.

The critic's duties are challenging enough in their own right, and in Leavis's view the study of philosophy and the "philosophical" probing of one's method will likely confuse and jeopardize them.

Leavis is one of the most controversial modern critics; as John Harvey remarks, opinions about him "have been so fiercely divided that most discussions . . . could hardly be called debate."[3] But I think it is generally true that until recently more critics have been on his side in this exchange than on Wellek's. Criticism has been resolutely "practical" and "literary," opposed to theory and wary about mixing up the critic's job of work with

11

the tools, terms, and ideas of philosophy. Like Leavis, critics have sought to "vindicate" their discipline, and one way of doing this is to enclose literature and criticism within a particular set of boundaries. Or, to put it another way: critics define and secure their discipline by resisting whatever threatens to encroach on it. We must be concerned with the "critic as critic"—which is indeed a potent tautology—not with the critic as philosopher, historian, theorist, or anything else. While there are exceptions (Eliseo Vivas, for instance), nearly all of the major critics of this century have been "practical"—close readers of specific texts who are dubious about the value of theory and philosophy. Critics must be critics, and that's that.

But beginning in the nineteen-sixties this situation began to change. The New Criticism lost its prestige, as critics, teachers, and their students objected to the separation of the text from social, political, historical, and other contexts. At Johns Hopkins, Yale, Cornell, and other universities, structuralism and continental theories of literature were accorded a sympathetic hearing, and became the focus for debates about the assumptions and proper methods of criticism. No longer were critics able to maintain the division between literature and philosophy that Leavis so insists upon, and their work started to shift in orientation away from the text itself and toward the various "approaches" through which it might be interpreted. The authority of the New Criticism did not disappear; indeed, it is still an influential, however flawed, technique in pedagogy. But as the New Critical movement weakened, critics stopped assuming that only by being a "critic as critic" could a literary person define himself or herself. Simply to dismiss theory and philosophy, and thereby to dodge or ignore all questions about method, was to claim the right, as most critics came to recognize, to continue to do something for which there might not be any need or warrant. And so the discipline of criticism grew intensely self-aware and self-scrutinizing, in the process crossing over from literature to philosophy, from "practical" studies to theory.

Few would deny that we have gained a great deal. "The separation of philosophy from literary study," as Geoffrey Hartman has recently observed, "has not worked to the benefit of either." "Without the pressure of philosophy on literary texts," he explains,

> or the reciprocal pressure of literary analyses on philosophical writing, each discipline becomes impoverished. If there is the danger of a confusion of realms, it is a danger worth experiencing. Since the era of the German Romantics, however, and of Coleridge—who was deeply influenced by the philosophical criticism coming from Germany around 1800—we have not seen a really fruitful interaction of these "sister arts." Yet the recent revival of philosophic criticism, associated with such names as Lukács, Heidegger, Sartre, Benjamin, Blanchot, and even Richards, Burke, and Empson, is like a new dawn that should not fade into the light of common day.[4]

The New Criticism, Hartman argues, narrowed the range and function of criticism, cutting off literature from a rich and necessary relation with philosophical texts. We are now witnessing a "revival" of a more expansive, exploratory style of criticism, willing to risk abstraction and treat issues that were once described—that is, stigmatized—as "philosophical." If we do not foster such a "revival," we can expect that criticism will return to being a diminished thing; as Hartman points out, its powers will be limited, and it will be isolated from the other disciplines, severely reduced in its methods and canon of texts.

The names that Hartman cites, especially his first group, might be said to constitute a new structure of "philosophical" authority in criticism today. Along with certain nineteenth-century figures, such as Hegel and Nietzsche, and other significant modern writers, including Derrida and Ricoeur, these are the authorities most frequently referred to and discussed in critical books and articles. In assessing this state of affairs, some have suggested that criticism has lost its identity altogether and has surrendered to the fashions of the moment. As Denis Donoghue dryly notes, "it is now widely, though not universally asserted that a serious literary criticism is responsive to issues which are ultimately philosophical. The critics who are proffered to our attention are philosophers, philosophical historians, and linguists; they are literary critics only betimes."[5] We are, it appears, literary critics in name only; we borrow methods from philosophy and other disciplines, and we justify our continued existence through them.

Why does philosophy have such an appeal for literary critics? And why has Leavis's stress on the "critic as critic" been so dramatically overturned? Philosophy holds out, first of all, the promise of exactness and precision in the use of terms: assumptions are explicitly stated and reflected upon; the "given" (the notion of the "text itself") is subjected to scrutiny; critical objectives are specifically declared; and in general, the attempt is made to know the nature of one's analytical acts and the field of inquiry within which they occur. Philosophical study, then, promotes the investigation of theory and method, and hence places the critic in a more self-critical relation to his or her work. In simplest terms, it encourages us to be self-conscious about what we do and why we do it, forcing us to inspect the very things that literary criticism has always assumed and presupposed (the "objectivity" of the critic, for instance). Philosophy also seems, to many people, to engage issues—being, knowledge, truth—that are more essential that those regularly addressed in literary criticism. The treatment of imagery and metaphor, character, and plot has its fascinations and rewards, yet does not lead the critic "beyond" or "outside" the work itself. Criticism strains at being restricted to the words on the page, to the text-as-object, and it seeks expanded horizons; reading the literary text closely and carefully, attending to its themes and patterns, is felt not to be enough. In fact, in Jonathan Culler's judgment, these kinds of "close readings" are no longer necessary: we have too many such readings as it is, and additional ones merely duplicate what we already know.[6] Not everyone agrees with Culler's attack on interpretations of individual texts; but his argument does signal a dissatisfaction shared by many critics, who also believe that we must go beyond readings of texts to questions of theory, method, and philosophy.

But one has to be honest and recognize that the situation is perhaps less lofty and high-minded—and is certainly more complex—than this account suggests. Critics also go to philosophy out of fear—fear that the foundation for literary criticism is not firm enough to justify the writing and teaching that they practice. As Hartman and others have pointed out, the New Critics made claims for the autonomy of the literary text, insisting that it was *not* history, sociology, philosophy, anthropology, or anything *but* literature. But just what this meant was not quite clear. While the New Critics affirmed the specialness of literature, they were never able to define precisely what that specialness consisted of. And part of our legacy from the New Critics is, as Hartman states, that many of us know that we "do" something and fulfill some sort of useful purpose, but are not exactly sure what it is and whether it is enough to keep us in business.[7] Few critics feel comfortable about quoting Matthew Arnold these days, but his words about the "function of criticism," however pious they may sound, are what we usually fall back on to defend ourselves. Anxious to make a more persuasive case for our labors, we then turn to other disciplines, hoping to find in them a more authentic ground than literature itself appears able to supply. And so we manufacture, for example, speech-act theories of literature, and even organize deconstructive "schools" of criticism. Our discipline, it seems, can found itself even on (or is it over?) the abyss that deconstruction reveals.

Nor can one deny the powers and pressures of the academic marketplace. Culler's proposal is drastic, but it is nevertheless true that it is hard to say new things about texts. What will be accomplished by one more reading of *The Waste Land* or *The Great Gatsby*? Texts can be interpreted only so many times before the law of diminishing returns sets in. But interpretation must proceed apace: the economics of the profession requires the process to move forward. By interpreting texts, a person gets a job, hopefully keeps it, and continues on the path to tenure and promotion. And so there is an inevitable drive to uncover new ways of reading texts, new strategies for interpretation. It is not so much an expression of cynicism as it is an understanding of the power of the academic institution that leads me to agree with Gerald Graff's point about our interest in "keeping the market moving."[8] Inflation has hit criticism as hard as everything else, and so the momentum builds for the production of still more books and articles. Enterprising scholars and critics turn to Derrida, Heidegger, or Nietzsche to locate new tools for analysis; and other, possibly even more adventurous souls argue for a major expansion of the category of texts, an expansion that will open up the texts of philosophy themselves for "close reading." Philosophy thereby delivers more texts to be studied as well as giving us new techniques for interpreting the literary texts that we feared had been exhausted.

I am not persuaded that this surge—one is tempted to say, this tor-rent—of publications is the sign of an intellectual corruption at the center of criticism. Or maybe I should say that if criticism is as misguided and undisciplined as some contend, then it shares this condition with other forms of institutional life in America. For good and ill, we work within an academic *institution*, and it is naive to expect that we can escape the social, political, and economic aspects of institutional practice. As markets expand and competitive pressures intensify, the "institution" of criticism, like other institutions, will enlarge its domain and seek new territory to col-onize. Some will find this to be a chilling prospect, one that promises an even more crippling loss of our identity than that envisioned by Donoghue. But it is going to happen, whatever we may feel about it, precisely because the institution is such a powerful, wide-ranging entity. I do not want to oversimplify a complex situation, but I think it is worth hazarding the suggestion that the institution largely controls and orders us, and not the other way around. We need to define ways of living within it, and of accommodating ourselves to its authority without becoming its slaves. This is surely easier said than done, but it is one of the crucial tasks of criticism to deal with the question of the ways in which *our* authority as critics and teachers exists within (is part of) the authority of institutions, and here philosophy can help us.

Philosophy means many different things, and it is not my intention to survey and disentangle these multiple meanings in this brief introduction. But for me, it chiefly implies the forms and work of knowing—what it means to "know" a text; what texts we are able to "know" and in what ways; and the kinds of knowledge that texts give and the kinds that they conceal or repress. In this collection I have included several essays, particu-larly those written by Eric J. Sundquist, Alan Wilde, and Evan Carton, that address these issues, exploring the forms of identity and representation that texts enable us to know. But when I refer to the forms and work of knowing, I am also alluding to the study of how the institution defines and controls the texts that we criticize and teach our students. Such a disci-plined study aims, in a word, to know the conditions (and also the bound-aries) of power and authority in our work. I call this the "philosophy of institutions," and would point to Michel Foucault, Edward Said, and Stan-ley Fish as writers who have, in their very different ways, done interesting research along these lines. Philosophy not only demands that we make our assumptions explicit, but also prompts us to reflect upon the "critical" manner in which we labor and the institutional setting within which we are situated. We will continue to "read" texts closely, and the insights that we have acquired from Derrida, Ricoeur, Wittgenstein, and others can assist us. But we also need to develop terms and methods for "reading" the institution, for connecting our teaching and criticism to our society, and for perceiving the connections that already exist, sometimes to our profit and sometimes not.

A passage from Antonio Gramsci's writings is illuminating in this context:

> What must . . . be explained is how it happens that in all periods there co-exist many systems and currents of philosophical thought, how these currents are born, how they are diffused, and why in the process of diffusion they fracture along certain lines and in certain directions. The fact of this process goes to show how necessary it is to order in a systematic, coherent and critical fashion one's own intuitions of life and the world, and to determine exactly what is to be understood by the word "systematic," so that it is not taken in the pedantic and academic sense. But this elaboration must be, and can only be, performed in the context of the history of philosophy, for it is this history which shows how thought has been elaborated over the centuries and what a collective effort has gone into the present method of thought which has subsumed and absorbed all this past history, including all its follies and mistakes. Nor should those mistakes themselves be neglected, for, although made in the past and since corrected, one cannot be sure that they will not be reproduced in the present and once again require correcting.[9]

Studying the history of philosophy encourages us, as Gramsci implies, to examine forms and orders of knowing, and to understand how these are embedded in our institutions. We can "think" some things and not others, make certain types of statements and not others. As Gramsci makes clear, the history of "thought" that has led us to our present position is dense and complicated. It is only because we still cling to the mystique of humanism, which makes us the site and center for interpretation, that we forget how powerfully our "thinking" is systematized, produced, represented, controlled. From this point of view philosophy pushes us in the direction of describing the "politics" of our interpretive acts.

Many, I know, bristle at the kind of language I am using here. Criticism, it is said, is one thing, and politics another, and for many members of the profession, speaking about the "institution" threatens to drag in political concerns where they do not belong and cannot be handled. To insist on working toward a philosophy of institutions, and to advocate the analysis of the "politics," power, and authority of what we know, may indeed seem like trespassing on forbidden ground. The old orthodoxy persists in some quarters: critics exist to interpret and teach literary texts; they are neither philosophers nor politicians, and ought to remember just where they should be focusing their attention. This is an attitude that many teachers and critics cherish, and it has been stated concisely by Louis D. Rubin in a recent essay:

> The best criticism of literature, so long as it is criticism *of* literature, will have to be that which starts with the text and, no matter how far it may stray or whatever it brings to the text, will find its validity in the text. . . . Because somebody is always going to say, eventually, after the New Historical Scientist or the structuralist or the Marxist or reader-psychologist or whatever has erected his glittering paradigm or simulacrum or manifesto or document or who knows what: "Yes, but how do you *know* it's so?" And the only convincing response will have to be "Let's look at the text."[10]

Like Samuel Johnson kicking the stone to refute the subjective idealism that vexed him, Rubin believes that he is saying something so obvious that no sensible person would presume to quarrel with him: to prove what we objectively "know," we go to the objective text. But this statement is more a dream than a bedrock reality. Rubin imagines a text that is distinct from our interpretive assumptions, a place to which we can return after we have drifted away into philosophies, psychologies, and politics. But the dream is for more than a secure, authoritative text. It is also expressive of a desire for a purity in our work that will enable us to avoid knotty debates about theory, ideology, power. When we "look at the text," we will not be looking at worldly realities that may be intensely painful and problematical. What is, on the one hand, an insistence on looking at the text is also a refusal to contemplate the history that truly informs and shapes it.

Rubin's statement is naive, but I should admit to a certain sympathy for it, despite my discomfort with its antihistorical bent. As teachers and critics, most of us remain loyal to "literature," whatever our problems in defining what "literature" is; and we are not quick to endorse a philosophical project that might deform and disfigure it. It is also true that the practical implications of a commitment to the "philosophy of institutions" seem hard to visualize; and when they do come into view, they strike many as threatening, as leading to an awkward entry of politics into the classroom and perhaps to a new forcing of conscience. Though I admire the Marxist critic Richard Ohmann's writings, I cannot bring myself to accept his proposal that we teach literature "with revolution as our end."[11] This may testify to a failure of courage on my part; but it also reflects my own uneasiness about a classroom practice that gravely risks sliding away from understanding and moving toward indoctrination. I do not deny that, in some capacity or other, our teaching always conditions the minds of students. But it is important to remember that young minds are particularly vulnerable, and are all too prone to being exploited and manipulated in ways that our rhetoric can lead us to justify to ourselves.

There are, of course, critics working today whose writings include a politicized vocabulary. Many are deconstructionists, followers of the French philosopher Jacques Derrida, and they see their analyses as "radical" and "revolutionary" subversions of Western metaphysics, tradition, society, culture. For the most part, I find this spectacle depressing, because the analyses are so exclusively textual. The area of investigation, nearly always, is limited to the "texts" into which all other categories dissolve. It is to Gayatri Spivak's credit that in her essays in this collection and elsewhere she resists easy answers and opposes the tendency to "apply" Derridean insights simply to generate more readings of literary texts; she is also wary about letting catch-phrases from Derrida and other philosophers serve as substitutes for real political study and action. But the same cannot be said for others in the ever-growing deconstructive movement. Deconstruction is a hot commodity; it is in demand, and one suspects that it attracts and fascinates many critics because it gives the thrill of political talk without the problems and responsibilities that any actual politics would bring. As Christopher Lasch states, the poststructuralist fads "provide for timid but fashion-conscious intellectuals an easy escape not only from painful contradictions of all sorts but from politics itself."[12]

Where then does one look for terms and models? There is an urgency to the question, yet one can perceive answers only in flashes, for the field is just coming into existence. Foucault, Fish, Said, and in this collection, Daniel O'Hara, have begun to "know" and chart the contours of this philosophical critique of institutions. In part, their writings can be understood as efforts to know the forms that interpretation takes—its powers, influence, relationships. But I also see their work as justifying, as well as explaining, the value of critical inquiry and interpretive work. Because we live in a troubled economy and are in jeopardy as teachers and critics, unsure of ourselves and what the wider world thinks of us, we will feel especially hard-pressed in the coming years to define ourselves and reform our conception of our role. Faced with a society that is angry about the inability of students to write well, we will be asked—and in some cases, no doubt ordered—to remedy this defect. And this likely will shift our attention, at least in our teaching, away from analysis, criticism, and interpretation and toward the skills required to produce "expository" papers. My distinction is of course drawn too sharply, but I do believe that in a general sense we will indeed be confronted by social pressures against "doing" criticism when, it will be argued, we ought to be teaching writing. And so it grows all the more necessary, I think, to define the important goals and projects that interpretation involves; we need to justify the activity in order to preserve it. By being reflective about the critical work and study we are practicing now, and by learning to read and interpret the institution that forms our work, we will be taking crucial first steps toward elaborating a coherent "philosophy" of what we do and why we do it.

In his review of contemporary criticism Rubin senses that something is wrong with our discipline, but his proposal—that we return to the text—has been tried before and does not lead us in the right direction. From one point of view, the text does seem to be the natural focus for our interpretive energies; it gives order and organization to our work, and functions as our norm and arbiter. But to ground our discipline (and thereby seek to legitimize ourselves) on the text is too limited and confining; and here Rubin is oddly in league with the deconstructionists, who, whatever their obvious differences, also see the text as the place where interpretation begins and ends.

We will always be interpreters of texts, but to renew our discipline and sense of ourselves, we ought not to confine our attention to the text alone. Instead we should attempt, I believe, to realize larger, if more demanding and risky ambitions. Terms and models are, again, difficult to apprehend. But while I cannot declare with full confidence and clarity what they are, I can at least suggest some guidelines that can help direct the forms of our work of knowing. The first is, in Donald Marshall's phrase,[13] "committed thinking," and it means that we hold our views seriously and willingly defend them against challenge. To say this much seems glaringly obvious, but it is a fact that both teachers and students often surrender their positions when faced with questioning or resistance. It is easier to give up or to consign one's views to the category of opinion—as though no judgment could ever be more than a statement of opinion, or ever pretend to claim more than merely personal validity. No one wants to appear to be forcing judgments on others; and no one wishes to brutalize and coerce students into accepting the teacher's authority. But while these are legitimate fears, they have led to the belief that judgments ought not to be made at all and may not in fact even be possible. Opinion then reigns, all commitments are withdrawn as soon as they are hazarded, and we persuade ourselves—and give the impression to our students—that "thinking" expends energy but is without serious point or purpose, that criticism cannot truly issue in enabling judgments and decisions, and that self-conscious interpretive work is confined to the classroom or scholarly journal.

"Making value judgments," as Maria Ruegg has recently argued, is "precisely the *function* of criticism."[14] We believe in making judgments, and in ordering and discriminating what we know, because our "thinking" is committed—committed in ways that motivate our writing and teaching, and that those in our classes can emulate and practice outside the classroom. No sane person underestimates the threat of an intellectual tyranny; but the threat should not lead us to deny that we can indeed commit our acts of mind to articulating and defending certain positions. As Marshall suggests, borrowing from William James, we can be "committed thinkers" yet also be accepting of "pluralism," which will help ward off any tendency of judgment to turn into domination. And by "pluralism," neither I nor

Marshall intend to imply an empty and uncritical acceptance of any and all views. Instead, it connotes something more positive and focused, more critically reflective and inquiring. In Marshall's words, it means a "residual resistance to totalization that keeps actual the possibility of alternatives."[15] Put in this form, the "pluralism" that will guide and modify our commitments will be deeply critical, suspicious of "totalizing" philosophies, theories, judgments. Making real commitments, in both our teaching and criticism, does not signal a closing off of exchange and debate, but rather implies that these judgments be made and tested, affirmed and extended. We make statements and take action on the basis of what we know, aware that we do not know everything and recognizing that we need to examine, reflect upon, and perhaps qualify what we know. We may even discover that we were wrong—which will be wholly self-subversive only if we had blinded ourselves to this possibility before.

I began this introduction by referring to Leavis's unwillingness to bring together literary criticism and philosophy. The two, he emphasized in his quarrel with Wellek, are radically different in their terms, objects of study, and goals, But for all his hostility toward the merging of criticism and philosophy, Leavis's own work, I believe, engages philosophical issues in powerful ways. In *The Living Principle* and other books written in the later part of his career, Leavis describes his method as a flexible, ongoing means of inquiry. It is, in my judgment, philosophical in attitude and scope, and literary critics and teachers can profit from studying it. I cannot nominate Leavis as a final authority, nor can I feel confident that his method is a true model for the "committed" and "pluralistic" thinking that I have attempted to chart. He is too problematical a critic; his polemics are too often self-serving; he is too absorbed in D. H. Lawrence and so misses what other writers can teach him; and while he argues for openness in critical debate, his practice is intolerant and dismissive. But for all his faults and shortcomings, Leavis remains a critic that I admire; in a collection devoted to the relations between literature and philosophy, I think that referring to Leavis in favorable terms makes an apt, if ironic, kind of sense.

In *The Living Principle,* as in his earlier books, Leavis asserts that philosophy ought not to intrude on the critic's work. He does cite Michael Polanyi, Marjorie Grene, and others approvingly, and concedes that "the presence of philosophy in the university" will benefit the "discipline" of English. But he stands opposed to "seminars on Wittgenstein for literary students," and to anything else that obscures the strength and purity of criticism *as criticism.*[16] These, I should stress, are views that I cannot share, for they require that the category of texts stay too narrowly "literary." Texts have dense and complex histories, and they get connected in many different relationships of power and authority. There is indeed a category of *literary* texts that criticism studies, but it is a changing category; the existence of the literary canon is not a fact of nature, but results from institutional decisions and pressures. What counts as "literary" often alters, as certain texts are displaced and others emerge into prominence. Leavis is of course concerned with canon-formation and hierarchies of writers, and he is also greatly interested in the social and cultural institutions (the university, in particular) that maintain them. But he does not seem enough aware of the implications of his own critical practice—that it too is an act of power, that it seeks to make distinctions among groups of texts (placing them in "literary" and "philosophical" categories) that are much more debatable than he seems to recognize.

This is the central difficulty in coming to terms with Leavis, and in citing his criticism as having important "philosophical" value. He is not as reflective and critical about his method as he should be; he does not, that is, perceive the difference between the flexibility and openness implicit in his account of his method and the sometimes rigid and reductive manner of his practice. But despite this serious limitation in Leavis's work, his description of the way in which criticism ideally should proceed retains its point and usefulness. It can give us a fine example of "committed thinking" even as we remember that a "pluralistic" self-scrutiny ought to accompany it, and thereby help to temper Leavis's urge to dominate and totalize.

Criticism, Leavis insists, requires both "analysis" and "judgment":

> Analysis is a process of re-creation in response to the black marks on the pages. It is a more pondered following-through of the process of re-creation in response to the poet's words that any genuine and discussible reading of the poem must be. Such a re-creation entails a diversity of kinds of judgment, and when I emphasize the diversity I am thinking of the different kinds of "value" that we cover with the one word. A judgment is personal and spontaneous or it is nothing. But to say that it is "spontaneous" is not to say that it may not have been prompted by a suggestion from another; and to say that it is "personal" is not to say that it means to be merely that. The form of a judgment is "This is so, isn't it?", the question asking for confirmation that the thing *is* so, but prepared for an answer in the form, "Yes, but—", the "but" standing for corrections, refinements, precisions, amplifications. (p. 35)

This describes how we act and work in knowing a text, and though Leavis himself might disagree, I would call the kind of exchange and "collaboration" (his word) envisioned here to be "philosophical," and profoundly so. To write and teach with this ideal in mind is to engage in a creative and communal activity, a dialectical pursuit of knowledge that depends on articulating and sharing responses. We analyze and make judgments because we are committed to them, and to the value of the discipline. And the judgments are personal yet stated with an extra-personal authority, for we believe them to be true for others as well as for ourselves. But we also recognize that our judgments are made in the expectation of questioning and debate: we resist in ourselves—just as we anticipate that others will resist in us—any sign of what Marshall terms "totalization."

What makes Leavis's account especially stimulating is that while he talks about specific poems, plays, and novels, he does not adopt a rigid or reified view of the text, and he refuses to see it as the "objective" and final authority. For this reason, I feel he can be differentiated from the groups of critics writing today whose interests are, if in opposition on some issues, still first and foremost "textual." In elaborating upon his means of approach, Leavis offers a striking definition of the text—one that moves the emphasis from "the words on the page" to our critical and communal inquiry about them.

> Analysis, then, in so far as it aims at establishing a favourable judgment, is the process of justifying the assumption that a poem which we take to be a real poem stands between us in what is in some sense a public world. Minds can meet in it, and there is so essential a measure of concurrence as to its nature and constitution that there can be intelligent—that is, profitable—differing about what precisely it is. It is neither merely private, nor public in the sense that it can be brought into a laboratory, quantified, tripped over or even pointed to—the only way of pointing to particulars in it is to put one's finger on given spots in the assemblage of black marks on the page—and that assemblage is not the poem. (p. 36)

The text is not an objective structure "on the page" but is instead the process of exchange and disagreement that occurs in criticism. The poem, the text, is the site where "minds meet" and creative responses, testing, argument, and qualification take place. This puts the emphasis on the critic and his or her audience, the teacher and his or her students. For Leavis "English" is truly a "discipline" of "thought," and it involves growth, change, and development within communities. It acknowledges the presence of other minds, and they are far more important than any object that we name, for convenient reference, the text or the poem. The center of our attentive concern is not the "black marks" but the text only as it exists and can be known among us.

In a perceptive essay on Leavis, Lionel Trilling remarks that "it isn't by his freedom from error that we properly judge a critic's value but by the integrity and point of his whole critical impulse, which, if it is personal and committed in the demands it makes upon life and literature, will be as instructive in its errors as in its correct judgments."[17] Leavis erred on many occasions, as when, early in his career, he ruled out the study of philosophy from the work of the literary critic. But the voice that speaks in his criticism is deeply committed and expressive, and it can be admired and learned from today. His method has to be expanded upon and supplemented; it is not the last word, and ought not to keep us from studying, interpreting, questioning the power and authority of the institution within which we might choose to practice it. But in affirming a common ground that is not the objective text, and in promoting acts of inquiry and judgment, Leavis shows us an important form of the relation between literature and philosophy. And it is other ways in which these relations are manifested that I now invite the reader to turn.

Notes

1. René Wellek, "Literary Criticism and Philosophy" (1937), included in *The Importance of Scrutiny*, ed. Eric Bentley (New York: New York University Press, 1964), pp. 23–30, at p. 23.

2. F. R. Leavis, "A Reply" (1937), in *The Importance of Scrutiny*, pp. 30–40, at p. 31.

3. John Harvey, "F. R. Leavis," *Encounter* 52 (May 1979):59.

4. Geoffrey Hartman, "Preface," *Deconstruction and Criticism* (New York: The Seabury Press, 1979), p. ix.

5. Denis Donoghue, "French Structuralist Theories," *Partisan Review* 47 (1980):397.

6. Jonathan Culler, "Beyond Interpretation: The Prospects of Contemporary Criticism," *Comparative Literature* 28 (Summer 1976):244–56.

7. See Hartman's stimulating essay on these issues, "A Short History of Practical Criticism," *New Literary History* 10 (Spring 1979):495–509.

8. Gerald Graff, "Who Killed Criticism?," *American Scholar* 49 (Summer 1980):353.

9. Antonio Gramsci, *The Prison Notebooks: Selections*, trans. and ed. Quintin Hoare and Geoffrey Nowell Smith (New York: International Publishers, 1971), p. 327; quoted in Edward Said, "Reflections on Recent American 'Left' Literary Criticism," *Boundary 2* 8 (Fall 1979):22–23.

10. Louis D. Rubin, "Tory Formalists, New York Intellectuals, and the New Historical Science of Criticism," *Sewanee Review* 88 (Fall 1980):683.

11. Richard Ohmann, *English in America: A Radical View of the Profession* (New York: Oxford University Press, 1976), p. 335.

12. Christopher Lasch, "Politics and Social Theory: A Reply to the Critics," *Salmagundi* 46 (Fall 1979):197. See also Gerald Graff, "Politics, Language, Deconstruction, Lies, and the Reflexive Fallacy: A Rejoinder to W. J. T. Mitchell," *Salmagundi* 47–48 (Winter-Spring 1980):78–94; David J. Gordon, "The Story of a Critical Idea," *Partisan Review* 47 (1980):93–108; Said, "Reflections," pp. 11–30; Michael Sprinker, "Criticism as Reaction," *Diacritics* 10 (Fall 1980):2–14; and Michael Sprinker, "Textual Politics: Foucault and Derrida," *Boundary 2* 8 (Spring 1980):75–98.

13. Donald Marshall, "Teaching of Literature," *Partisan Review* 47 (1980):432–33.

14. Maria Ruegg, "The End(s) of French Style: Structuralism and Post-Structuralism in the American Context," *Criticism* 21 (1979):216.

15. Marshall, "Teaching of Literature," p. 434.

16. F. R. Leavis, *The Living Principle: "English" as a Discipline of Thought* (London: Chatto and Windus, 1975), p. 28.

17. Lionel Trilling, "Dr. Leavis and the Moral Tradition," in *A Gathering of Fugitives* (Boston: Beacon Press, 1956), p. 106.

Philosophical
Approaches to Literature

Philosophy/Literature: The Associationist Precedent for Coleridge's Late Poems

Jerome Christensen

The current Anglo-American defense of criticism against French textual strategies owes its polemical energy in part to the seriousness of the threat deconstruction poses to crucial humanist assumptions about literature: the unity of the literary work, the intending consciousness of an author, and the determinacy of meaning. The defenders perceive that deconstruction is not a criticism at all but instead a comprehensive philosophical program. If it is unresisted, it will not only revise traditional critical assumptions and procedures but also undermine the very presumption of understanding that has been thought to distinguish criticism as a disciplined activity of the mind. In defending itself criticism can also claim to be defending literature by preventing it from being aggrandized as province and product of philosophy, from being mastered by an alien and alienating power.[1]

For the past one-hundred-and-sixty-five years criticism has acted as intermediary between literature and other disciplines; its mission, as Eugenio Donato describes it, has been "to pretend that it philosophically determines the textual, psychological, historical *ground* of a literary representation or fiction."[2] That era can be measured with precision, at least for the English tradition, because it was the brilliant enterprise of Coleridge, particularly in the *Biographia Literaria*, which established the principles and *ethos* of the "philosophical critic,"[3] and which throughout the past two centuries has enfranchised both critical monisms and pluralisms.[4] Deeply impressed by his own experience of the dark enchantments in the labyrinthine passages of metaphysics, Coleridge sought a criticism that would deploy philosophy as illustration and corroboration of the logic proper to poetry as poetry; he aimed to coordinate philosophy *and* literature and perhaps to achieve a philosophy *of* literature, but he resisted all tendencies to derive the literary work from philosophical precedent. The chief philosophy that Coleridge endeavored to coordinate with literature was Kant's, whose metaphysics may have been inadequate to Coleridge's ends (*BL* 1:

99–100), but whose aesthetics represented a benign corollary of the Kantian critique, which served for Coleridge, as it does for the neo-Kantians of today, as a means "of saving the art object from those wishing to absorb it into the realm of determinate concepts of science or ethics."[5]

Deconstruction challenges the Kantian protocol and the principled stance of philosophical criticism with a philosophical "rhetoric of authority" that prescribes not the concepts by which a poem should be judged, but rather the mechanics by which literature is written.[6] The complaint that readings of literary texts according to this prescription are "written mostly for the sake of the theory they are supposed to endorse" expresses by indirection the more fundamental fear that as a consequence of this philosophically motivated "criticism" *theory itself*, not the idealized subject called "author," appears to have written the texts that are so read.[7] The Derridean script of the "already written" de-identifies literature and with it criticism by staging both as characters in a play philosophy has wrought.

I have recalled the Coleridgean matrix not so much to put the current debate in historical context as to refer it to historical precedent. The contemporary defense of a tradition anchored in Coleridge's criticism repeats a defense already conducted by Coleridge himself. He did not formulate his philosophical criticism in a vacuum or even under the duress of the "giant's hand" of Kant (BL 1: 99); he devised it, largely *ad hoc*, in order to defend against the threat of David Hartley's doctrine of the association of ideas. In *Observations on Man* Hartley explains both automatic and voluntary human activity as the mechanical consequence of sensations, which when repeatedly impressed together on the mind produce vestigial ideas of sensation. These ideas will be recalled in turn by the renewal of their associated sensations. The same process of association accounts for the combining of simple ideas into complex ones, for the compounding of sensible pleasures and pains into intellectual ones, and, therefore, for all human knowledge and behavior. Like deconstruction, Hartley's doctrine renders the human as a dynamic nexus of representations ungrounded by a subject ever present to itself. Most pertinently for the critic, association classifies the poetic work, like everything else, as an epiphenomenon of a philosophical mechanism. Coleridge overthrew Hartley's system less by logical argument or by Kantian authority than by the force of what I have described elsewhere as his marginal rhetoric and the appeal of his *ethos* as principled man and critic.[8] But the decisive maneuver by which he contained the projected aggrandizement of poetry occurs in chapter 13 of the *Biographia Literaria*, where the association of ideas is assigned to the "Fancy," which "has no other counters to play with, but fixities and definites," and is thereby apodictically subordinated to the "essentially *vital*" "secondary Imagination," which "dissolves, diffuses, dissipates, in order to recreate" (*BL* 1: 202).

It is one of the clichés of literary history (first vented by Coleridge himself) that Coleridge's descent into the mines of metaphysic marked his death as a poet. It has not been so generally recognized that this supposed death corresponds with his earliest documented speculation on the imagination as the "co-adunating Faculty."[9] The same theory of the imagination that provided the principles of esteem for Coleridge's early poetry (and identified its "essential vitality") also legislated the resolute neglect by later critics of all but a few thematically congenial poems following the valedictory "Dejection"; and it also invited the elegiac tone that has dominated commentary on Coleridge's career. Perhaps Coleridge did die as poet. More power to him. Or, to be more precise, more power to his poems, for poets and poems, as even Coleridge's criticism of Wordsworth nervously attests, are quite different things.[10] It may be that a severe recognition, beyond elegy, of the poet's death and the stilling of his voice is necessary for the poems to be read.

My characterization of the current defense of criticism is part of a strategy to make possible such a reading of the poems. The historical necessity for recovering Hartley can be described in strictly Hartleian terms: the vivid opposition of contemporary schools of criticism and philosophy recalls, in the "memory text" of the transactions among criticism, literature, and philosophy, what Hartley would call a vestigial precedent. That precedent is the exclusion of Hartleian association from the discourse of poetics by Coleridge, whose instrument was the *index expurgatorius* of the imagination. That interdict fell, not at all paradoxically, on Coleridge's late poems as well. Victims of the same interdict, doctrine and poems are linked by association like successive effects of the same cause. That linkage is what Hartley described as "a Clue and Guide to the Invention"—a guide, that is, to the invention of the inquirer and a clue as to the processes of invention itself. The interdict of the imagination seals an association between Hartley's philosophy and Coleridge's poems *and* identifies an excluded, all-but-effaced region of memory, where invention occurs absolved of the *"onerific"* of the conscious will, where a productive process implicates philosophy and poetry in the elaboration of a silent design. I shall try to show how that design itself figures in Hartley's volumes and Coleridge's poems, and do so in two stages: first, by arguing that the inconsistencies in Hartley's system of association do not represent logical contradictions that vitiate its force, but instead demonstrate a process of figuration that is capably inventive; and second, by describing the way that process, thoroughly associationist, does "invent" Coleridge's late poetry, particularly "The Garden of Boccaccio." Hartleian association is a technical philosophy that displays language as a technique of invention by association; and Coleridge's late poems are the figures of that technique, formal accomplishments of the association of ideas. Perhaps because it is technical, Hartley's *Observations on Man* is all but unread and may appear all but unreadable, his unburnished abstractions mute and opaque. But the opacity of the language, as Coleridge proved in the *Biographia Literaria,* is not a historical accident but a philosophical necessity: Hartley's language leaves nothing to the imagination; it is a prose of fixities and definites, fully liable to be turned by the inventive fancy.

This essay aims to let fancy have its turn. What follows will not pursue the analogy between the past and present relations of literature and philosophy, which is still being drawn, nor will it untangle the affiliations of association and deconstruction. By fancifully supplanting one master, deconstruction, with another, association, it should be possible to disarm philosophical mastery without submitting to critical *revanchism.* One can mark a line of succession that connects philosophy/poetry, not by critical coordination or metaphysical subordination but by diacritical association. Coleridge's criticism may have extinguished his imagination, but it did not kill off his poems. They are there to be read by an eye observant of both the philosophical precedent for poetic product and the poetic process of the philosophical mechanism.

I

One of Coleridge's most persuasive objections to Hartley's system bears directly on its supposed capacity to dictate his writing:

> Yet according to this hypothesis, the disquisition, to which I am at present soliciting the reader's attention, may be as truly said to be written by Saint Paul's church, as by *me;* for it is the mere motion of my muscles and nerves; and these again are set in motion from external causes equally passive, which external causes stand themselves in interdependent connection with every thing that exists or has existed. Thus the whole universe co-operates to produce the minutest stroke of every letter, save only that I myself, and I alone, have nothing to do with it, but merely the causeless and *effectless* beholding of it when it is done. (*BL* 1: 82)

If the associationist hypothesis fails to explain out of existence the plain truth of the "I myself" that speaks its authorship of Coleridge's prose, its absurdity is compounded by its inability to explain its own existence: "Association in philosophy," Coleridge comments, "is like the term stimulus in medicine: explaining every thing, it explains nothing; and above all leaves itself unexplained" (*BL* 2: 222).[12] The Kantian critique, that the theory of association can explain everything except for the prior presence of an invariable process of ordering associations, becomes in Coleridge's hands a perfectly empirical challenge that questions the status of the text. The systematic and comprehensive demonstration of association by a philosopher in a text presupposes an organizing power unexplained by the associationist system itself. According to Coleridge's criticism, the associationist text is an *oversight*. By adapting Kant to the problem of self-explanation or self-representation, Coleridge imputes to Hartleian doctrine a version of what Daniel C. Dennett has called *"Hume's Problem,"* which has "bedeviled philosophers and psychologists for over two hundred years." The problem has two aspects: *"First,* the only psychology that could possibly succeed in explaining the complexities of human activity must posit internal representations. . . . But, second, nothing is intrinsically a representation of anything; something is a representation only *for* or *to* someone; any representation or system of representations thus requires at least one *user* or interpreter of the representation who is external to it. . . . Such an interpreter is then a sort of homunculus." Dennett provisionally concludes that, consequently, "psychology *without* homunculi is impossible. But psychology *with* homunculi is doomed to circularity or infinite regress, so psychology is impossible."[13] Although both Hartley and Hume have problems with representation, self-explanation is not quite the same as self-understanding. Moreover, the requirements for a true psychology are not the same as those for a working poetics. Yet it would seem impossible for a system that cannot consistently explain itself, its own representation, to explain consistently a poem. The literal failure of consistency and the figurative success of inconsistency, homunculi and all, will be the burden of my argument.

II

The charge of mechanism leveled against Hartleian association by Coleridge has been so damning within the critical tradition Coleridge fathered that it has been difficult, particularly for the student of Romanticism, to distinguish the formulation of the system in *Observations on Man* from the metaphors, such as the watch and the "Cat harpsichord," Coleridge employed in the *Biographia Literaria* to disparage it. Although Hartley does explicitly describe the association of ideas as a mechanism, he resolutely avoids machine metaphors and actually fetches his figures for the mind from less of a distance than does the organicist. The unitarian organic model grounds itself by the massive metaphorical substitution of something far afield to the pastures within (love of plants = love of self); Hartleian association begins with a metonymic derivation of mind from body, of psychology from physiology. Despite the philosopher's powerful attraction to a monistic solution, his system never degenerates into a crude materialism. As he insists, mind and body remain analytically distinct, though communicative. Superficially, distinctness can be ascribed to a philosophical act of will: Hartley simply refuses to abandon the immateriality of the soul. That religious commitment baffles the materialistic logic of the system, obliging Hartley to resort to several dramatically inadequate devices to acknowledge division and provide for interaction. Most notoriously, he invents speculative entities such as vibrations and an "infinitesimal elementary Body" in hopes of at once maintaining and bridging the gap between body and soul.[14] The help or harm of such fictions is mooted, however, by Hartley's analytical reduction of all association between impressions, sensations, and ideas to the simple and single mode of contiguity. That reduction presupposes an ineradicable spacing that cannot be filled by any invention but that somehow can itself invent. Hartley does not need to insist on a break between mind and body because mind and body are, like all other ideas, analytically contiguous: conceptually adjacent, related metonymically. The result is a conformity and correspondence *between* mind *and* body, not an identity *of* mind *with* body. The so-called break between mind and body need not be so called, because it is actually an association, a macrocosmic version of the contiguity articulate at every level of the mechanism.

Central to Coleridge's critique of empiricism in general and of associationism in particular is, as is well known, his objection to elementarism.[15] He argues that associationist psychology errs in its premise that the senses perceive and the mind records discrete units of impression. "Who ever *felt* a *single* sensation?"[16] Typically, Coleridge's rhetorical question deftly annexes perception to consciousness and imposes qualitative criteria on what for Hartley, if not for Hume, are distinct quantities that have no content in themselves (and so cannot be "felt") but combine into formations so like qualities as to be virtually the same. Of the two ways Hartley chooses to enhance the explanatory power of his quantitative model, one is doubtlessly vulnerable to the Coleridgean criticism. In a conventionally Lockean maneuver, Hartley reifies dispersed quantities into the two affective categories of pleasures and pains, a move that orders quantity by identifying it as either one of two possible motives. Hartley relies on that presumed order to moralize experience optimistically: he proposes the double hypothesis that pleasures generally direct us to good ends and that pains gradually diminish in number; as a consequence, the order of behavioral stimuli can be imagined to design human life as a qualitative progression toward a perfect pleasure that is an ultimate good, a self-annihilation in the deity. Hypothesis and consequence founder because the very premise of order is groundless. Hartley's quantitative model cannot substantiate the essentialist distinction between pleasure and pain; his radical analysis cannot nourish his teleological wish. Hartley's other explanation for the transformation of quantity into quality is both more coherent and more effective. It follows from his consistent representation of the association of quantities as a linguistic system. At the level of perceptions he designates all sensations and ideas, pleasures and pains, by alphabetical letters in lower and upper case. Generally, he describes the associationist mechanism as a language with the formal coherence of algebra: "Since Words may be compared to the Letters used in Algebra, Language itself may be termed one Species of Algebra, and, conversely, Algebra is nothing more than the Language which is peculiarly fitted to explain Quantities of all Kinds" (*OM* I:280). The systematic analogy between algebra and language at once argues that ideas are analyzable into differential quantities and the converse, that quantities combine into substantive ideas, for as "simple Ideas run into complex ones by Association, so complex Ideas run into decomplex ones by the same" (*OM* 1:77).[17] Hartley's assurance of that fit, a key instance of "mutual indefinite Implication" (*OM* 1:71), lies behind his confident application of the linguistic analogy elsewhere: both to confirm the "Coalescence of simple Ideas into complex ones . . . by the similar Coalescence of Letters into Syllables and Words, in which Association is likewise a chief Instrument" (*OM* 1:75) and to synopsize that because "Combinations of . . . Letters represent Combinations of Pleasures and Pains," the words those letters form constitute a "Language [that] will be an Emblem or Adumbration of our Passage through the present life . . ." (*OM* 1:319).

Analogies "twin." If all that is capable of being associated is representable in language, the opposite is also true: *"Words and Phrases must excite Ideas in us by Association . . . and by no other means"* (*OM* 1:268). Words are connected to ideas and to each other by the same contiguity as the ideas they represent are bonded in the mind. Two linked consequences follow. First, though indispensable as the solvent of quantity and quality, language, conceived as a system of signs, does not in itself explain how quantities or letters *move* to coalescence; mere contiguity in space would seem to lack the dynamic power to produce ideas or words. Second, although the linguistic analogy discovers some sense in the variable transactions of quantity, by mutual implication the indeterminacy characteristic of quantitative relations involves whatever sense language finds. No more than the combination of ideas does linguistic coalescence *necessarily* express a determinate logic; the place of language within association may figure as another example of an aboriginally indeterminate analogic. By dint of the singular analogical rapport between it and association, language would seem to lose the quality of meaningfulness that attracts Hartley to it as analogical illustration. Language cannot, in Hartley's words, independently confirm association because it is "not only a Type of these associated Combinations, but one Part of the Thing typified" (*OM* 1:320). The same could be said of all analogies, of course: none of them can fully comprehend association because each of them is ineluctably apprehended by association. The predicament of language highlights once again the deficiency in association's explanatory power. Nonetheless, the recuperation of the type as typified does not completely erase the peculiar movement *to* the type, as if something had, however inconsistently, moved outside the network of association. To notice that barely perceptible movement is to reclaim the strategic prominence of language among all the other illustrative analogies in *Observations on Man,* for only language can account for the movement between part and whole, the variance between type and typified; only language can figure.

The figure is "a Word, which, first representing the Object or Idea *A*, is afterwards made to represent *B* on account of the Relation which these bear to each other" (*OM* 1:291). At best morally ambiguous, the power of the figure to *turn* comes to epitomize for Hartley the corruptive potential of the arts, the perversion of the imagination to the pleasures of gilding vice and diverting the mind from "Devotion, and earnest Concern for our own and future Welfare" (*OM* 2:253–54). Answering Hartley's suspicion of the figurative are both a yearning for a chaste, reliable language of "the real Thing"(*OM* 1:432) and a concern to fix the literal usage of words. The opposition of figurative to literal provides cold comfort, however, for although the associationist can easily define and illustrate the figure, the literal eludes him indefinitely. Since all language is acquired by association, no word can be conceived to be attached to an idea in any given or fixed correspondence. Technically, there is no word that *first* represents "the Object or Idea *A*" because any first representation is already made to represent *A* by means of contiguity, the only relation that signifies, and each representation is intrinsically differential, capable of associating with and therefore representing *B*. Hartley never locates a literal at the first; the best he can do is suggest how an essential idea might emerge among the variable "Particularities, Circumstances, and Adjuncts" (*OM* 1:272). And he can *only* suggest, because although such a notion might satisfy conventional wisdom, the literal so framed is clearly the determination *of* conventions, which are themselves variable formations of particularities, circumstances, and adjuncts.

Despite his inclinations, Hartley's scrupulous respect for the premise that a shift of reference is the fundamental process by which all words first come to signify dictates his concession that a figure need *not* be restricted to resemblance, but can be turned on any relation—"Cause, Effect, Opposition, Derivation, Generality, Particularity"—and predicates the transfer of what was thought proper to only a part of language to "Language itself, [which] by its Resemblances, Oppositions, &c. becomes a new source of Figures, distinct from the Relations of Things" (*OM* 1:292). Once that transfer is made (the figure *necessary* to efface the inconsistency of giving privilege to the literal), language can be conceived as turning on itself with the literal figuratively projected as its perfect coincidence with itself.

The completion of that turn would announce the death of both language and philosophy. The language that says completely what it wants to say has nothing left to say; there can be no "Advancement in the Knowledge of Things" (*OM* 1:315) without association and no association without figurative "Deficiency, Superfluity or Equivocation . . ." (*OM* 1:315). But because the turn is figurative, the projected coincidence can never be attained. Language is saved from itself by the irreducible associative play of the figure in which the idea of the literal is always there alongside as the idea of a governing design, its affective differential:

> Now figurative Words seem to strike and please us chiefly from that Impropriety which appears at first Sight, upon their Application to the Things denoted by them, and from the consequent Heightening of the Propriety, as soon as it is duly perceived. For when figurative Words have recurred so often as to excite the secondary Idea instantaneously, and without any previous Harshness to the Imagination, they lose their peculiar Beauty and Force; and, in order to recover this, and make ourselves sensible of it, we are obliged to recall the literal Sense, and to place the literal and figurative Senses close together, that so we may first be sensible of the Inconsistency, and then be more affected with the Union and Coalescence. (*OM* 1: 429)

Striking/pleasing, impropriety/propriety, harshness/[smoothness], inconsistency/coalescence, figure/literal—although antithesis ostensibly captures and tames the figure, the relation of opposition is, after all, just one of a number of turns possible on mere contiguity. Hartley prescribes and employs it here as a device to refresh the "peculiar Beauty and Force" of the figurative by recalling the figure of the literal. As beautiful as simple space and as forceful as "a certain Kind and Degree of Inconsistency" (*OM* 1: 430) in the idea of anything so simple, the figure is the affective aspect of contiguity. By transferring affect to what is not in literal fact there, the figure *moves* association, turns sensations to ideas, body to mind, visual to tactile, A to B, while maintaining and, indeed, enlivening the differences.

Although Hartley tries to isolate the figure as an instance of imaginative artfulness or deviance, association will have its way; by evading due perception of the mechanism of figurative transference, Hartley ramifies its evidences. The inconsistency of a linguistic model in which the figurative is not balanced by the literal produces theoretical paradises and ethical anodynes which, in their harsh impropriety with Hartley's system, repeatedly recover the peculiar beauty and force of the figurative within that system. That repetition, the discursive movement of *Observations on Man*, simulates progress, for "many or most common Figures pass so far into literal Expressions by Use, *i.e.*, Association, that we do not attend at all to their figurative Nature. And thus by Degrees figurative Senses become a Foundation for successive Figures, in the same manner, as originally literal Senses" (*OM* 1: 292). Whatever there is of necessity in association and whatever there is of coherence in Hartley's stages of imagination, ambition, self-interest, sympathy, theopathy, and the moral sense are typed by that mechanism of contiguity and inconsistency. The recognition that necessity and progress are figurative effectively diverts the mind from Hartley's tendentious illogic and allows one to observe that the capacity of the figurative in association is to turn logical weakness into analogical power; in other words, to turn philosophical inconsistency into literature. Incapable of explaining itself in a self-annihilating literalism, association figures itself in a succession of analogies that place philosophic truth and poetic lies close together, so that we may first be sensible of the inconsistency and then be more affected by the union and coalescence.

III

Kathleen Coburn, general editor of *The Collected Coleridge*, opens her study of Coleridge entitled *The Self-Conscious Imagination* with the epigraph, "A philosophy is an abstraction from an autobiography"—a thoroughly Romantic and an especially Coleridgean proposition.[18] But the precedent of Hartley suggests an alternate hypothesis, that autobiography (including its lyrical expressions) is the figure of philosophy. Coburn's epigraph supervises a learned reconstruction of Coleridge's philosophy from the prodigious resource of his notebooks, "his most private, personal, unguarded, unhistrionic utterance," where he "is meditating on his experiences in the very act of experiencing."[19] The Hartleian hypothesis proposes that we regard the notebooks (and I would include under this rubric, with some qualifications, the marginalia and the letters) not as meditations but as a discursive intelligence, not the utterances of experience but as ideas that involve and counterinvolve one another in "*streamy* association."[20] A method appropriate to that conception would begin not with the presumption that Coleridge's notebooks comprise the book of the soul, ultimately unified by an evolving self-consciousness, but with the observation that they constitute a text in which the ultimate is just another idea amid a host of fixities and definites designed by the mechanics of contiguity and inconsistency. It is in this chartered flow that the majority of the late poems appear. Fragmentary, enigmatic, insistently abstract, a poetry of the fancy in which the mode of memory is the mode of life—the poems, when released from the artificial constraint of the *Poetical Works*, become readable as the union and coalescence of ideas, resonantly articulate in the circulating flow.[21]

Given enough time such a reading could be completed, I believe, but certainly not here and now. One way to anticipate that end, however, is to step as near the horizon of completion as possible in the hope of achieving some perspective on the terrain of the country eventually to be mapped. Coleridge's "Epitaph" is about as near the vanishing point as one can get: both its position in *Poetical Works* and its title announce it as Coleridge's last work. In "Epitaph" autobiographical fact merges with canonical authority to acquit language of figurative vitality by assigning the poet the place of his literal death. That death can be deconstructed, however, as Richard A. Rand has demonstrated in a reading of the poem that puts into play the various transformations of the signature "S.T.C.," which are then chased through sundry lyrics. But even Rand's reckless pursuit of Coleridge's "secret" reckons on a "note in the manuscript."[22] What makes both literal death implausible and deconstruction unnecessary is that there is no "the manuscript"; as the editor's note indicates, "Epitaph" exists as six versions of itself in letters and marginalia.[23] The inconsistency incurred by the figurative transference of the life that was "first" the property of Samuel Taylor Coleridge to the representative letters S.T.C., a variant reading of Coleridge, is recapitulated by the graph of the epitaph as variant texts, none of which has authority over any other, all of which diagram a text in which emblematic definites associate in a chorus of S.T.C.'s. A *silent* chorus. For what seems like death in the epitaph is merely a relinquishment of the voice, the so-calling authoritative speech of an homuncular consciousness that could proclaim its literal coincidence with S.T.C. and identify the true epitaph that in fact marks its death. That voice silenced and beyond recall, the job of finishing off Coleridge is left to his editors. Far from planting Samuel Taylor Coleridge in the literal completion of his work, the epitaph(s) broadcast S.T.C. as a representative idea, which in its vital figurative impropriety can indefinitely succeed itself, as type and typified, in the capacious memory of the text.

The "Epitaph," then, prefigures a full reading of the associated combinations of Coleridge's discursive intelligence by predicating a penultimate turn away from the fatal literalism of the self-conscious imagination. But to extract the inscription from the text as I have done may be to force the turn. In order to give more weight to the burden of associationist self-explanation and thereby to enhance the sense of freedom attained in escaping its incumbency, I would like to examine more fully one of Coleridge's published poems, "The Garden of Boccaccio," which fancies a self-contained space superbly suited for the spatial play of the fancy.

IV

There can be little disagreement that "The Garden of Boccaccio" could be read as a poem *about* the association of ideas.[24] Such a reading would note the way the initial *acedia* of the poet, comparable to the mood at the beginning of "Frost at Midnight," is diverted by the "quiet hand" (13) of a friend, who places before his eyes an engraving of Thomas Stothard's *The Garden of Boccaccio.*[25] The picture steals upon his inward sight with a warmth that is evidently a tactile idea associated with the friend's gesture, and which, as though the touch of an "infant's finger" (26), arouses a chain of visual ideas from the poet's past that end, once again like "Frost at Midnight," with the recollection of an innocent youth. That memory in turn enables the poet to escape the fixity of self-consciousness and by association awake to the higher innocence symbolized by the power of the

"mastering eye" (58) over the visual scene. The movement culminates in a
recognition of Boccaccio that is simultaneously a self-recognition, a realization of the "all-enjoying, all-blending" (101) genial power that has been
active, albeit unawares, all along. Such a reading would conclude that "The
Garden" is about association in the way the conversation poems are, identifying it as a convalescent, slumbrous interlude from which the poet
awakes to the consciousness of a regenerate imagination that has never
been altogether quiescent. Perhaps the most salient problem with such a
reading is that the poem does not close as it should with imaginative
recreation, indeed does not properly close at all. If *about* implies cir-
cumscription, this poem cannot be about association, for the poem ends
not with the restoration of the self to itself but with the "me" (105) still in
the garden that is the poem's design.

The failure of "The Garden" to end as one might expect reflects its
failure to begin as one might have thought. The poem starts off not in the
conversational present but in the past tense, recollecting "one of those
most weary hours" when beginning anything seems impossible, "When
life seems emptied of its genial powers" (1–2). If the past tense seems
appropriate to a "vacancy" (8) so complete that it could not find the words
in which to converse, the past tense raises the question of how anything
was begun, and how, having been begun, the poem can find images for the
vacancy that is its premise. The pivotal shift in tense from past to present
("Thanks, gentle artist! now I can descry/Thy fair creation with a mastering
eye/And all awake!" [57–59]) aggravates the problem of the beginning by
doubling beginnings. The present tense marks out a place where the poet
is here and now, where the poem he writes must begin and which must be
distinguished from where the poem once began. From the vantage of
where the poet is now, where the poem begins, the story of how it began
will take the form of an explanation: the poem's explanation of itself.

To understand the explanation it will help to look at what is to be
explained. After a succession of "nows" the poem ends here:

> Still in thy garden let me watch their pranks,
> And see in Dian's vest between the ranks
> Of the trim vines, some maid that half believes
> The vestal fires, of which her lover grieves,
> With that sly satyr peeping through the leaves!
>
> (105–9)

The poet pictures himself within a scene where he watches, sees, and
apparently peeps. "Apparently," because although the poet is in the garden it is not a simple matter to place him there. The syntax does not make it
clear who is "With that sly satyr": the lover who grieves or the poet who
watches, or whether all three stand together in ocular collaboration. Any

one of the alternatives is possible; the combination of possibilities makes it impossible to locate the poet within the place where he still is. A multiplication of perspectives, this is a place where true grief, knowing slyness, and perhaps a composite of both are compatible responses to the sight of a virgin practicing her rituals unaware, empty of all blemish but observably pitched out of innocent piety by a half-belief.

As the "me" is placed both here and there in the garden scene, so is the past recollected and seen as another place for the "I" within the *hortus inconclusus* of the poem. Insofar as that past is recollected as a time before the poem began or could begin, it must appear as a vacancy. But insofar as that vacancy is recollected as having in some way produced the poem, it will have to be, though empty, placed within the poem as marked by the design of its undoing, as though a sheet of paper that on first sight appears to be blank were, after due perception or a striking stimulus, to divulge vestiges and traces. Difficult to conceptualize at the very beginning, according to the Hartleian system this process is repeated at every transitive moment of perception, each of which is to some degree the beginning of a chain of ideas. Its features are clearest in the transitions between verse paragraphs and especially evident in the movement from the first to the second. When the poet idly gazed at the "exquisite design" (17) visual and tactile sensations summoned a chain of ideas, "all spirits of power" (28), that were latent in the vacant and ostensibly passive mind. Because it initiated the mechanical transformation of "idle eye" (23) into "mastering eye" (58), the *then* into *now*, the stimulus of the design, described as empirically prior to what is on the page, might be said to have produced the poem. But associationist mechanics are not such simple matters of fact. We cannot specify with certainty at this point either the nature of the "design" or the capacity of the agent. The poem is hardly a speaking picture: the images that immediately follow the stimulus do not recognizably imitate those drawn by Stothard. Indeed, the descriptions of the picture generalize it as "Idyll" (17), "silent poesy of form" (18), and "exquisite design" (14), suggesting that this is primarily the stimulus *of* form and implying that the picture may be strictly a formal stimulus. As for agency, the way the prepositional phrase "with silent might" (22) floats between the gazing eye and the stealing picture introduces the syntactical indeterminacy characteristic of associationist formations: it raises the question of whether poet's eye or picture, or both or neither, is or are determinant by linking two contiguous ideas in a dynamic relation that does not depend on the priority of either for its productive power.

But of course there *is* something prior that appears to explain the stimulus. A "quiet hand" (13) placed the picture on the desk. The only visible act of a human agent in the poem, this intercession may be accounted its efficient cause. Perhaps too efficient. Coleridge once complained of "that all-annihilating system of explaining every thing by association/either *conjuring* millions out of 0,0,0,0,0,00—or into noughts."[26] Incapable of truly explaining "all," prodigal association pays its debts by means of a beguiling calculus that makes millions appear as if from nothing. In the good conscience of its recollection "The Garden" evokes the figure of its inconsistency as a *manus ex machina* that conjures millions from the nought of the soul. "All-annihilating" seems, however, a rather bellicose epithet for what is perhaps better described as "whole-halving." Half-seen by the eye of the poet, the quiet hand is "of thine" (13) as the garden is of Boccaccio: not a synecdoche for the whole person but a metonymic representative of the better, silent half: the gesture without the voice, the act without the authority, the design without the designer. The hand compounds with the half-sight in a formal feeling that diverts great pain, that soothes if not solves inconsistency. Eye and touch collaborate in an inadvertence that *composes*, and does so by fancifully putting half the soul of man into activity, finessing thereby the humorless edict of the imagination, which demands the whole soul or nothing. In "The Garden of Boccaccio" Coleridge leads a half-life in which we are invited to half-believe.

As the representative of a designer, the quiet hand succeeds the emptiness that the idea of its touch has relieved. Vacancy that has such success is not nothing. Described as the absence of genial powers, the failure of a call, vacancy is only nought to the mind that reverences the sound of its own voice. Under the gaze of an enlivening eye, however, vacancy appears as a stage on which configure characters, a scene in which "I watch'd the dull continuous ache" (9). Not in the visionary line of the "infinite I AM" (*BL* 1: 202), this "I" is a fixity and definite that observes the fixed and definite. It does nothing but watch and is nothing but a watcher—an I that is wholly an eye. The punning association of "I" with "eye" renders mind and body as neither identical nor dialectical but as dynamically contiguous ideas perceptibly articulated by a glancing variance. The pun enables the reader to prove the association of ideas on his senses as a figure of transference, which in turn prefigures the pattern of movement back and forth between "eye" and "I" that forms the poem. To the idealist, commanding the watchtower of the absolute self, an "I" wholly visualized wrecks dialectical ambitions and invites the damnation of Coleridge's persuasive definition, "the despotism of the eye" (*BL* 1:74). But that curse has no power within the precincts of this garden, where no vision can tyrannize because all seeing is peripheral. Besides, the "I" that we first meet, hardly a despot, cowers over the vacancy that is the signal achievement of the absolutist imagination in Coleridge's career. We read the vestige that survived: an "I" that watched.

The "I" neither oversees nor feels sensation; it watches from alongside. Pain can be seen because "ache" and "I" are transitive representations of sensation, words of the same language, in the same silent poesy. Pain is diverted because the inconsistency of "I" contiguous with "ache" affects associated ideas into more complicated figurative formations. The "I" watching the "ache" half sees the hand deposit the picture and sees by association a palliative warmth in the design. The generous conceit that attributes the warmth to "Boccaccio's spirit" (16) observes the analogic of half-belief, and defers a premature consciousness of coincidence between mind and design that would bring the poem to a halt.

That hypothesis of closure can be derived not only from Hartleian mechanics but also from the subsequent depiction of "Philosophy," a "matron now," whom as a "faery child" the child-poet once wooed, "Though then unconscious of herself pardie, /She bore no other name than Poesy" (46–51). Philosophy is poesy grown to consciousness and poesy unconscious philosophy, philosophy at play in an elfin garden. When the poet comes to the child poesy after a sequence of ideas, he comes to it as innocent and childlike in a poem like a garden. The organization of innocence occurs once again by means of an association of eye and touch:

> Gazed by an idle eye with silent might
> The picture stole upon my inward sight
> A tremulous warmth crept gradual o'er my chest
> As though an infant's finger touch'd my breast.
>
> (23–26)

The touch conjures the picture on the inward sight into pictures from the poet's own past, pictures, that is, touching on himself. That touch, the touch of infant innocence, represents the touch of the child in the poet's own past, the touch of poesy. It is as if by an association of ideas the poet touches himself in an unconscious organization of self *toward* an innocence propaedeutic of the awakening into the "now" of poetry. Whereas the poet once romantically "sought a form for love" (32), his idle gaze has let the form of love find him in an auto-affection that both organizes the self unbeknownst to a censorious consciousness and brings the past in touch with the present in a coalescence unmarred by the scars of time. Because the auto-affection is conducted by representatives and because it remains, no matter how preconsciously intimate, a contiguity of hand and eye, it does not literalize itself in the closure of witless self-pleasure, but figures itself upon the margin of its inconsistency as a coming into oneself in the present of poetic mastery.

The swing into the present hinges on the invocation of a "gentle artist" (57) who has designed the picture and assigned its associations, and whose capable hand is taken as metonymy for the garden in which the poet's eye can "now in fix'd gaze stand/Now wander . . ." (59–60). The appearance of progression involved in the shift from past to present, slumber to wakefulness, idleness to mastery depends on the transfer of the formal power of the mechanism of association to an explanatory source that is the figure of the poem's inconsistency. What has been bound by a designer can be mastered by an observer. The "mastering eye"—coefficient of the artist's hand, the warm touch, and the quiet hand—would seem to portend an ascent to supervision and control, the triumph of the ego over the welter of sensation, but mastery appears as a clear view of the affiliations of the "I" with the design there before it and succeeds to a *realization* of the I-that-watched in a life of sensation. What that life is like, how it represents the "I" and is represented to the eye becomes evident in a scene of narcissistic self-recognition:

> And with that serviceable nymph I stoop,
> The crystal from its restless pool, to scoop.
> I see no longer! I myself am there,
> Sit on the groundsward, and the banquet share.
>
> (63–66)

"I see no longer" elides the sight that, we know from Ovid, is there: eye to eye with myself in the pool. Elides, not suppresses, for the exclamation accurately records the blinding of the mastering "I" that occurs in this (dis)place of self-recognition, where the restlessness of the pool both reflects and deflects what eyes it. The statement that follows, "I myself am there," is a fair translation of Narcissus's *"iste ego sum,"* which, according to John Brenkman's powerful reading of Ovid, marks "the moment in which Narcissus not only recognizes the image as image but also *recognizes himself* (as image). . . ."[27] But the translation does not quite match up with the original, for the symmetry of Narcissus's exclamation becomes an asymmetry in which the psychic redundancy of "I myself" is countered only by the "there." That imbalance magnifies the inconsistency of the scene; it revises what Narcissus says into a sentence that could never be said, even to a mirror, but could only be written in a text. The sentence, moreover, is not itself autonomous, nor is it bound to the stooping at the pool. It links with the scene that follows, recording the moment of self-recognition but eluding its fixity by forcefully displacing the "I" from even its restless imaging to a succession of images with which it associates. The inconsistency of "I" to "I" transfers the "I" *there* to contiguous images in the design—a figuration that enables the "I" to avoid learning the Ovidian lesson of death and instead to succeed itself in representatives that inhabit the "silent poesy of form," *there* to "breathe an air like life" (72). In finding himself in the design before any designer, the poet discharges all masters in the poem, including Boccaccio and the "I myself." By finding itself there in the pretext of the design, represented as a differential idea affecting its successor, the "I" opens the poem to a catholicity of sentiment and an erotic ingenuity unfamiliar in the poetry of Samuel Taylor Coleridge.

V

As his answer to "Hume's Problem" of self-understanding representations, Daniel Dennett borrows a design from Artificial Intelligence research that promises a model of the mind that begs no questions. One begins by breaking an "intentional system into an organization of subsystems, each of which could itself be viewed as an intentional system . . . and hence as formally a homunculus." The result is a flow chart that is "typically the organizational chart of a committee of homunculi. . . ; each box specifies a homunculus by prescribing a function *without saying how it is to be accomplished.* . . . The function of each [box] is accomplished by subdividing it via another flow chart into smaller, more stupid homunculi. Eventually this nesting of boxes within boxes lands you with homunculi so stupid (all they have to do is remember whether to say 'yes or no' when asked) that they can be . . . 'replaced by a machine.' " One gets away "with *lesser* homunculi at high levels by getting their earlier or lower brethren to do some of the work. One never gets *completely* self-understanding representations . . . but all homunculi are ultimately discharged."[28]

Not only is the idea of an artificial intelligence conceptually congruous with Hartleian association, but also its application to gardens, as recent scholarship indicates, has historical propriety.[29] Dennett's particular model will take us some distance through "The Garden of Boccaccio." It enables one to view the poem as an intentional system subdivided into stages (roughly correspondent to the verse paragraphs), each of which posits a governing homunculus, a designer, of considerable sophistication, and each of which can be analyzed into smaller boxes, until one reaches the intellectually stupid but technically skilled association of hand and eye. But at this point I, at least, can see no longer: the analogy fails to comprehend the poem. The reason, I think, is that the representation of hand and eye, their placement in the artifice, remains unexplained and cannot, it would seem, be accounted for without recourse to another and yet another intentional system: the author whose hand and eye must be combined to design this design, his author, and so on. One cannot discharge the homunculus of the designer in the manner proposed by Dennett because the question one puts in regard to the poem is not the same that one poses for the mind—"How does it perform or function?" Rather, it is more like what one asks of the design for the mind drafted by the Artificial Intelligence researcher: "Let it be given that this prescribes a mechanism of self-understanding or at least self-governing representations; then how do you explain that the design is there on the page?" One wants to know, that is, not how representations are self-understanding, but how self-understanding representations come to be represented.

To ask that question returns this essay to the place where the discussion of the poem began, at the question of "The Garden" 's beginning. To refer all the apparent action of the poem to hand and eye knots more tightly the problem of its recollected beginning. How *did* "I watch'd an ache" appear on a mind thought empty? How did a poem appear on a page thought blank? An answer may be formulated by replacing the sublimatory and hierarchical mechanism of discharge from high to low with the Hartleian mechanism of displacement, driven by contiguity and inconsistency.

Because the "whole Powers of the Soul" may be referred to the "Memory" (*OM* 1: 382), the recollection of the past that appears within and that may be said both to begin and have begun the poem has in itself no temporal priority. In fact, the recollection takes place within a memory where the difference between past and present is wholly diacritical. Trains of ideas, juxtaposed in mutual indefinite implication, are identified as past or present because of more or less vivid imagery (*OM* 1: 374–79) and marked as such by arbitrary spacing or the visible signs of tense. Past and present are both *there* in the design as differentials of contiguous ideas. Hence the failure to fully recreate and bring the poem to a close is not, as the censorious imagination might view it, an evasion of the moral consequences of a pagan holiday, but the direct expression of both the scene itself (which belongs to no one, not Stothard, Boccaccio, Ovid, or, least of all, Coleridge) and its place in the exquisite design. Rather than closing, the scene works by juxtaposing. Alongside one another are half-believing virgin, grieving lover, and peeping satyr—among whom troupes the "I" in a dramatic association that is always displaced from identification by the affective inconsistency of the "I" with any single representative, and that relieves the overt eroticism of any egoistic freight that could curtail the restless fancy by repression or consummation.

This scene, where the "I" still is (if we let it be there) and the poem begins, remarks on the place where the poem began. The "beginning" and "end" of the poem, contiguous but for the ideas of "silent might" that their proximity excites in the articulate space between them, coexist in a mutually indefinite implication whereby the former serves as genetic explanation of the latter and the latter as the dramatic shape of the former. The image of an emptiness capable of beginning is aroused by the vivid image of the maid, to her mind alone, half believing in her ritual virginity. The scene of "I" and ache that appears on the emptiness is the vestigial correspondent of the peeping satyr and the grieving lover. Conversely, the "I" is able to represent itself in that final scene, to watch and apprehend the half-belief, grief, and sly peeping by association with the pretext of a beginning that has conducted it there. Each scene is the precedent of the other and designed by that which it makes possible. The pretext of design is therefore both thoroughly necessary and absolutely inessential. I would epitomize that relation with the proposition that Boccaccio's Garden is the design of the "I"—not in order to state either cause or coincidence but to release all the speechless inconsistency proper to that "of"—preposition and genitive in intimate contiguity—a grammatical and philosophical inconsistency that yields not an explanation but a poem.

Such an epitome does not discharge the homuncular *I*. On the contrary, it finds the "I" there alongside itself, a conductor that will amiably pass the pink slip along in an indefinite digression at once toward and away from its intended object. It is as if one were by chance to come upon a circle of figures in the middle of an empty field (Salisbury Plain would do), choose one to ask "Who is responsible for this circle?", and be answered not by Miltonic declamation but with a sidelong glance and gesture pointing to the next man and repeated by him and the next man and so on, round and round. "Sonority" may be "disqualified in favor of diagram," but one does not as a consequence end "gaping at monumental inscriptions"; one continually begins reading an indefinite reinscription.[30] My artificial intelligence will not explain "the full complex of human activity," nor will it pay back its cognitive debts; it begs question after question. But under the benign dispensation of the fancy and guided by the precedent of association we can enjoy only half the soul of man being put into activity, can, capably deaf to the puritanical admonitions of ancestral voices, build a garden on paper by deficit spending, and can hope to turn question-begging into a fluent rhetoric, a still exquisite design.

Notes

1. See Wayne Booth, *Critical Understanding: The Powers and Limits of Pluralism* (Chicago: University of Chicago Press, 1979), pp. 229–32, 347–49, and *passim* for a recent and formidable defense of critical understanding from the challenge of deconstruction. For a splendid overview of the theoretical controversy aroused by poststructuralism and a characterization of Jacques Derrida's "deconstructive project" as a philosophical formalism, see Frank Lentricchia's *After the New Criticism* (Chicago: University of Chicago Press, 1980), pp. 157–77. Lentricchia discusses the aggrandizement of literature and criticism by philosophical premises most fully in his discussion of Paul De Man (pp. 283–317). On that topic see also Gerald Graff, "Deconstruction as Dogma or 'Come Back to the Raft Ag'n Strether Honey!'," *The Georgia Review* 34 (Summer 1980):407. Jonathan Culler remarks on the unsettling effects of Derrida's "mastery" in his essay on Derrida in *Structuralism and Since,* ed. John Sturrock (New York: Oxford University Press, 1980), pp. 155–57.

2. Eugenio Donato, "The Idioms of the *Text:* Notes on the Language of Philosophy and the Fictions of Literature," *GLYPH* 2 (Baltimore, Md.: Johns Hopkins University Press, 1977):3.

3. Samuel Taylor Coleridge, *Biographia Literaria,* ed. J. Shawcross (1907; reprint ed. Oxford: Oxford University Press, 1967), 1:62. Hereafter cited in text as *BL*.

4. The *locus classicus* of this convergence in American criticism is R. S. Crane's "The Critical Monism of Cleanth Brooks," *Critics and Criticism,* ed. R. S. Crane (Chicago: University of Chicago Press, 1952), pp. 83–107.

5. Charles Altieri, "The Hermeneutics of Literary Indeterminacy: A Dissent from the New Orthodoxy," *New Literary History* 10 (Autumn 1978):91.

6., The tag "rhetoric of authority" is applied by Frank Lentricchia to the criticism of Paul De Man (*After the New Criticism,* p. 283).

7. Denis Donoghue, "Deconstruction Deconstructed," *New York Review of Books* 27 (June 12, 1980):41.

8. See Jerome C. Christensen, "Coleridge's Marginal Method in the *Biographia Literaria,*" *PMLA* 92 (October 1977):928–40.

9. The phrase and the fancy-imagination distinction first appear in a letter from Coleridge to William Sotheby, five months after the verse epistle that would become "Dejection: An Ode" was sent to Sara Hutchinson and two months after selections of that epistle had been sent to Sotheby himself (*Collected Letters of Samuel Taylor Coleridge*, ed. Earl Leslie Griggs [Oxford: Oxford University Press, 1956], 2:865–66, 790–98, 815–18).

10. Wordsworth could be altogether too fanciful for Coleridge. For an acute discussion of Wordsworth's poems of the fancy see Frances Ferguson, *Wordsworth: Language as Counter-Spirit* (New Haven, Conn.: Yale University Press, 1977), pp. 53–68.

11. Criticism that argues for a strong and continuous associationist influence on poetics during the eighteenth and nineteenth centuries characteristically excludes Hartley as too "extreme" and therefore unrepresentative. See, for example, Walter Jackson Bate, *From Classic to Romantic: Premises of Taste in Eighteenth Century England* (New York: Harper Torchbooks, 1961), p. 100, and Ralph Cohen, "Association of Ideas and Poetic Unity," *Philological Quarterly* 36 (October 1957):465. An exception is Robert Marsh, who in *Four Dialectical Theories of Poetry* (Chicago: University of Chicago Press, 1965) subsumes Hartley in a larger dialectical tradition that also includes Coleridge (pp. 87–128). In "Language and Hartleian Associationism in *Sentimental Journey*," *Eighteenth Century Studies* 13 (Spring 1980):285–312, Jonathan Lamb does impressive work in applying the Hartleian system to Sterne's novel. His essay may be consulted as one that cites the same Hartley as I but to different ends. Paul De Man provides a suggestive reading of the place and power of figuration in Locke, Condillac, and Kant in "The Epistemology of Metaphor," *On Metaphor*, ed. Sheldon Sacks (Chicago: University of Chicago Press, 1979), pp. 11–28.

12. The comment is in "On the Principles of Genial Criticism" and is directed to "Alison, &c." or associationists in general.

13. Daniel C. Dennett, "Artificial Intelligence as Philosophy and Psychology," in *Brainstorms: Philosophic Essays on Mind and Psychology* (Montgomery, Vt.: Bradford Books, 1978), pp. 119–22.

14. David Hartley, *Observations on Man, His Frame, His Duty, and His Expectations*, 2 vols. (1749; reprint ed. New York: Garland Publishing, Inc., 1971), 1:11–34. Hereafter cited in text as *OM*.

15. See M. H. Abrams, *The Mirror and the Lamp: Romantic Theory and the Critical Tradition* (New York: Norton Library, 1958), pp. 160 ff. and 171 ff.

16. *The Notebooks of Samuel Taylor Coleridge*, ed. Kathleen Coburn (New York: Bollingen Foundation, 1961), 2:2370.

17. See Walter J. Ong, "Psyche and the Geometers: Associationist Critical Theory" in *Rhetoric, Romance and Technology: Studies in the Interaction of Expression and Culture* (Ithaca, N.Y.: Cornell University Press, 1971), pp. 213–36, for a shrewd discussion of the quantitative basis of associationist theory. The differences between Ong's view and my own may be indicated by the fact that Ong quotes only the first half of Hartley's comparison of language to algebra, ignoring the crucial converse—symptomatic of his neglect of the solvency of language in Hartleian associationism (p. 223).

18. The epigraph for Coburn's collection of her Riddell Memorial Lectures of 1973 quotes Sir Russell Brain, *The Nature of Experience*, *The Riddell Memorial Lectures, 1958* (*The Self-Conscious Imagination* [London: Oxford University Press, 1974]).

19. Coburn, *The Self-Conscious Imagination*, pp. 2–3.

20. Coleridge, *Notebooks*, 1:1770.

21. The only extended study of Coleridge's late poetry, Edward Kessler's *Coleridge's Metaphors of Being* (Princeton, N.J.: Princeton University Press, 1979), does affirm that the poems are a species of note (pp. 4–6), but that affirmation serves an ontological premise that dictates a critical practice in which the conventional distinctions and priorities between notes and poems are enforced

22. Richard A. Rand, "Geraldine," *GLYPH* 3 (Baltimore, Md.: Johns Hopkins University Press, 1978), p. 94.

23. *The Complete Poetical Works of Samuel Taylor Coleridge*, ed. E. H. Coleridge, 2 vols. (Oxford: Oxford University Press, 1912), 2:491–92. The editor comments that from "the letter to Mrs. Aders it appears that Coleridge did not contemplate the epitaph being inscribed on his tombstone, but that he intended it to be printed 'in letters of a distinctly visible and legible size' on the outline of a tombstone to be engraved as a vignette to be published in a magazine,

or to illustrate the last page of his 'Miscellaneous Poems' in the second volume of his *Poetical Works*."

24. "The Garden of Boccaccio" is reprinted by permission of the publisher from *The Complete Poetical Works of Samuel Taylor Coleridge*, ed. E. H. Coleridge, 2 vols. (Oxford: Oxford University Press, 1912).

Cf. Humphrey House's description of "Frost at Midnight" as a "poem *about* the movement of the mind" in *Coleridge: The Clark Lectures, 1951–52* (London: Rupert Hart-Davis, 1969), p. 151.

25. Coleridge's poem and F. Englehart's engraving of Thomas Stothard's picture appeared in *The Keepsake for 1829*, ed. Frederic Mansel Reynolds (London: 1829), pp. 282–85. For a discussion of the poem within the context of Coleridge's overall "approach to Boccaccio" see Herbert G. Wright, *Boccaccio in England from Chaucer to Tennyson* (London: Athlone Press, 1957), pp. 337–43. All quotations of the poem are from Poetical Works, 1:478–81.

26. Coleridge, *Notebooks*, 2:2093.

27. John Brenkmen, "Narcissus in the Text," *The Georgia Review* 30 (Summer 1976):316.

28. Dennett, "Artificial Intelligence," pp. 123–24.

29. See Ronald Paulson's discussion of the "poetic garden" in *Emblem and Expression: Meaning in English Art of the Eighteenth Century* (Cambridge, Mass.: Harvard University Press, 1975), pp. 19–34, and John Dixon Hunt's description of Shenstone's garden at The Leasowes as the " 'perfect picture of his mind' and poetic fancy" in *The Figure in the Landscape: Poetry, Painting, and Gardening during the Eighteenth Century* (Baltimore, Md.: Johns Hopkins University Press, 1976), p. 191.

30. Ong, "Psyche and the Geometers," p. 236; Jonathan Culler, *Structuralist Poetics: Structuralism, Linguistics and the Study of Literature* (Ithaca, N.Y.: Cornell University Press, 1975), p. 134.

The Garden of Boccaccio

Samuel Taylor Coleridge

Of late, in one of those most weary hours,
When life seems emptied of all genial powers,
A dreary mood, which he who ne'er has known
May bless his happy lot, I sate alone;
And, from the numbing spell to win relief,   5
Call'd on the Past for thought of glee or grief.
In vain! bereft alike of grief and glee,
I sate and cow'r'd o'er my own vacancy!
And as I watch'd the dull continuous ache,
Which, all else slumb'ring, seem'd alone to wake;   10
O Friend! long wont to notice yet conceal,
And soothe by silence what words cannot heal,
I but half saw that quiet hand of thine
Place on my desk this exquisite design.
Boccaccio's Garden and its faery,   15
The love, the joyaunce, and the gallantry!
An Idyll, with Boccaccio's spirit warm,
Framed in the silent poesy of form.

Like flocks adown a newly-bathéd steep
Emerging from a mist: or like a stream   20
Of music soft that not dispels the sleep,
But casts in happier moulds the slumberer's dream,
Gazed by an idle eye with silent might
The picture stole upon my inward sight.
A tremulous warmth crept gradual o'er my chest,   25
As though an infant's finger touch'd my breast.
And one by one (I know not whence) were brought
All spirits of power that most had stirr'd my thought
In selfless boyhood, on a new world tost
Of wonder, and in its own fancies lost;   30
Or charm'd my youth, that, kindled from above,
Loved ere it loved, and sought a form for love;
Or lent a lustre to the earnest scan
Of manhood, musing what and whence is man!
Wild strain of Scalds, that in the sea-worn caves   35
Rehearsed their war-spell to the winds and waves;
Or fateful hymn of those prophetic maids,
That call'd on Hertha in deep forest glades;
Or minstrel lay, that cheer'd the baron's feast;
Or rhyme of city pomp, of monk and priest,   40
Judge, mayor, and many a guild in long array,
To high-church pacing on the great saint's day:
And many a verse which to myself I sang.

That woke the tear, yet stole away the pang
Of hopes, which in lamenting I renew'd: 45
And last, a matron now, of sober mien,
Yet radiant still and with no earthly sheen,
Whom as a faery child my childhood woo'd
Even in my dawn of thought—Philosophy;
Though then unconscious of herself, pardie, 50
She bore no other name than Poesy;
And, like a gift from heaven, in lifeful glee,
That had but newly left a mother's knee,
Prattled and play'd with bird and flower, and stone,
As if with elfin playfellows well known, 55
And life reveal'd to innocence alone.

Thanks, gentle artist! now I can descry
Thy fair creation with a mastering eye,
And all awake! And now in fix'd gaze stand,
Now wander through the Eden of thy hand; 60
Praise the green arches, on the fountain clear
See fragment shadows of the crossing deer;
And with that serviceable nymph I stoop,
The crystal, from its restless pool, to scoop.
I see no longer! I myself am there, 65
Sit on the ground-sward, and the banquet share.
'Tis I, that sweep that lute's love-echoing strings,
And gaze upon the maid who gazing sings:
Or pause and listen to the tinkling bells
From the high tower, and think that there she dwells. 70
With old Boccaccio's soul I stand possest,
And breathe an air like life, that swells my chest.
The brightness of the world, O thou once free.
And always fair, rare land of courtesy!
O Florence! with the Tuscan fields and hills 75
And famous Arno, fed with all their rills;
Thou brightest star of star-bright Italy!
Rich, ornate, populous—all treasures thine,
The golden corn, the olive, and the vine.
Fair cities, gallant mansions, castles old, 80
And forests, where beside his leafy hold
The sullen boar hath heard the distant horn,
And whets his tusks against the gnarléd thorn;
Palladian palace with its storied halls;
Fountains, where Love lies listening to their falls; 85
Gardens, where flings the bridge its airy span,
And Nature makes her happy home with man;
Where many a gorgeous flower is duly fed
With its own rill, on its own spangled bed,
And wreathes the marble urn, or leans its head, 90

A mimic mourner, that with veil withdrawn
Weeps liquid gems, the presents of the dawn;—
Thine all delights, and every muse is thine;
And more than all, the embrace and intertwine
Of all with all in gay and twinkling dance!   95
Mid gods of Greece and warriors of romance,
See! Boccace sits, unfolding on his knees
The new-found roll of old Maeonides;[1]
But from his mantle's fold, and near the heart,
Peers Ovid's Holy Book of Love's sweet smart![2]   100
O all-enjoying and all-blending sage,
Long be it mine to con thy mazy page,
Where, half conceal'd, the eye of fancy views
Fauns, nymphs, and winged saints, all gracious to thy muse!

Still in thy garden let me watch their pranks,   105
And see in Dian's vest between the ranks
Of the trim vines, some maid that half believes
The vestal fires, of which her lover grieves,
With that sly satyr peeping through the leaves!

[1] Boccaccio claimed for himself the glory of having first introduced the works of Homer to his countrymen.

[2] I know few more striking or more interesting proofs of the overwhelming influence which the study of the Greek and Roman classics exercised on the judgments, feelings, and imaginations of the literati of Europe at the commencement of the restoration of literature, than the passage in the *Filocopo* of Boccacio, where the sage instructor, Racheo, as soon as the young prince and the beautiful girl Biancofiore had learned their letters, sets them to study the Holy Book, Ovid's Art of Love. 'Incomincio Racheo a mettere il suo [officio] in esecuzione con intera sollecitudine. E loro, in breve tempo, insegnato a conoscer le lettere, fece leggere il santo libro d'Ovvidio, [!!S.T.C.] nel quale il sommo poeta mostra, come i santi fuochi di Venere si debbano ne' freddi cuori con sollecitudine accendere.' ["Deeply interesting—but observe, p. 63, ll 33–5 [loc.cit.] The *holy Book*—Ovid's Art of Love!! This is not the result of mere Immorality:—

> Multum, Multum
> Hic jacet sepultum."

MS. note on the fly-leaf of S. T. C.'s copy of vol. 1 of Boccaccio's *Opere*, 1723.]
(*Poetic Works*, 2:478–81)

Tennyson's Philosophy:
Some Lyric Examples

Timothy Peltason

Tennyson's bad reputation as the painfully sober and discursive metaphy-
sician of "The Higher Pantheism" has made all talk of his philosophy
suspicious. He wrote poetry and not philosophy, of course, but this
truism, applied to Tennyson, becomes a form of serious qualification or
even dismissal, another echo of W. H. Auden's famous slap: "He had the
finest ear, perhaps, of any English poet; he was also undoubtedly the
stupidest; there was little about melancholia that he didn't know; there was
little else that he did."[1] Tennyson's is indeed a poetry of darkened moods
and subtle meters, and in insisting on its philosophical interest I am not
denying this or redirecting attention to some neglected and anomalous
part of the canon. My examples are among Tennyson's best-known and
most widely admired poems, and, in reading them as philosophical exer-
cises, I do not intend to upset received opinion, at least not the opinions of
Tennyson's admirers, but to make my own addition to it, trying as well to
stand back and talk explicitly about the critical values that underlie an
inclination to take Tennyson and his moods seriously. This is to claim for
mood its own philosophic dignity and for Tennyson's evocations of mood
a strenuous thoughtfulness.

"Tears, Idle Tears" has been blamed and praised for its exclusive attentiveness to a particular mood or state of mind, blamed for the exclusiveness
and praised for the attentiveness, but hardly pinned down as to the precise
quality and significance of the mood itself. And this is curious because so
much of what the poem has to offer it offers so immediately and insistently:

> Tears, idle tears, I know not what they mean,
> Tears from the depth of some divine despair
> Rise in the heart and gather to the eyes,
> In looking on the happy autumn-fields,
> And thinking of the days that are no more.

Fresh as the first beam glittering on a sail,
That brings our friends up from the underworld,
Sad as the last which reddens over one
That sinks with all we love below the verge;
So sad, so fresh, the days that are no more.

Ah, sad and strange as in dark summer dawns
The earliest pipe of half-awakened birds
To dying ears, when unto dying eyes
The casement slowly grows a glimmering square;
So sad, so strange, the days that are no more.

Dear as remembered kisses after death,
And sweet as those by hopeless fancy feigned
On lips that are for others; deep as love,
Deep as first love, and wild with all regret;
O Death in Life, the days that are no more.

F. R. Leavis, in his largely dismissive commentary, reads the poem as a skillful piece of nostalgia, a feeling cheap and familiar and uncritically indulged. Leavis is discussing Tennyson under the heading "Thought and Emotional Quality" as a writer in whom the latter crowds out the former entirely. There is no thought in the poem, according to Leavis, because "there is no attitude towards the experience except one of complaisance; we are to be wholly in it and of it."[2] And this is true, I think, except for the seriously misleading assumption that the poem records a single, local experience of a kind that we might have at one moment or another of our lives. Rather than offering us "no attitude," I should say that the poem is all attitude, and that its project is to describe precisely the situation, the placement, that is, of human consciousness in time. The poem's most articulate admirers—I think particularly of Cleanth Brooks, Graham Hough, and Harold Bloom—have all pointed toward this fact, or perhaps proceeded from it, in praising the universality of feeling that the poem achieves. But it is not a matter of feeling alone.

Certainly, the poem begins in the unabashed emotionalism of those tears. But their idleness is directly a challenge to thought: In what sense idle and are tears ever otherwise? And they are the products of thought as well, of "looking on the happy autumn-fields" that the poem attends to only in that quick pathetic fallacy, and of "thinking of the days that are no more." As in "Break, break, break," where the poet's surging feelings are carefully named as "the thoughts that arise in me," Tennyson here insists on the union of heart and head in the full human experience of inwardness. At the same time, taking the shift from looking to thinking as its premise, the poem quickly steps free of its origins in idiosyncratic perception and attempts to document another order of experience, something urgent and firsthand, yet not circumscribed by the conditions of a single person, place, or time. The first-person singular appears in the poem only as the baffled interpreter of the first line. The object of interpretation and meditation is a phenomenon strangely impersonal, the tears of "some divine despair," with the vagueness of "some" and the largeness of "divine" only reemphasized by the oddly categorical mention of "the heart" and "the eyes." The poem was written at Tintern Abbey, Tennyson reports in the *Memoir*, "filled for me with the memory of bygone days,"[3] but neither the place nor any particular memory evoked by it occupies the poet's attention, and he does not present himself in relation to the landscape or even begin to record the significant details of his experience there. Instead, the poem becomes a second-order meditation that does not think about the days that are no more, but thinks about thinking about them. It is not an account of memories, but of memory, the mysterious and equivocal presence of the past. And yet the past and memory are not really the subjects of the poem either, not at least if the past is taken as something that can be separated out from the present and located and observed and not if memory is the faculty or operation of mind that does the locating and observing. The poem describes no act of will or recovery, but rather a condition of being. It reads finally as if written in answer to the question of the philosopher, or, more precisely, of the phenomenologist: "What does consciousness feel like?" Or, to give the question a Heideggerian turn and to take those tears more fully into account, "What is the mood of consciousness?"

For present consciousness really is the exclusive object of the poem's regard. The poem employs no past tenses, depicts no past scenes, never interests itself in the days that are no more as they exist, or existed, independently of consciousness, but only as they appear to consciousness now. The beams that glitter on the sails of otherworldly boats are not fresh or sad in themselves, out there on the horizon, but in our experience here at the center of consciousness. The phrase itself, "the days that are no more," oddly evades naming the past as past, as if such a conception were outside the realm of interest or possibility, just as the idea of falsehood is so alien to Swift's Houyhnhms that they can refer only to "saying the thing which is not." What the straightforward grammar of "the days that are no more" insists on for Tennyson is that paradox of philosophers and poets both, the presence of absence, and this paradox appears ultimately in the poem as "Death in Life," a phrase that wants only a few hyphens to have the true Heideggerian look. But the feel here is thoroughly Tennysonian, and these phrases, along with the adjectives and the gorgeous series of similes that illustrate them, separate out and examine anew the conclusion of "Break, break, break," the rising thought that that poem finally brings itself to utter:

But the tender grace of a day that is dead
Will never come back to me.

Where "Break, break, break," however, is movingly personal and records the struggle of a deeply feeling individual to reconcile himself to loss, "Tears, Idle Tears" takes place on the far side of reconciliation and risks its composure only in the surprising "Wild with all regret" of the penultimate line. It does not offer the progress of personal consciousness, but the progressively sharpened and deepened portrait of consciousness in its perpetual present tense. Thus, its tears gather but do not fall and, thus, there is no horizontal movement across its imagined sea, but only the rising and sinking at the horizon. Even these movements are not described, but inferred from the still image of the boat on the far horizon, a single image for the boat that comes and the boat that goes. None of the final three stanzas of the poem is even a complete sentence, and each of them seems to start over again, to throw onto the screen of consciousness a new image and a new set of adjectives that attempt to capture the present experience of the days that are no more. In spite of our talk of inwardness, projection does seem the apt metaphor here rather than insight, for it is an exemplary inwardness that the poem presents us with and not a glimpse into the merely private inner visions of the speaker.

But these exclusively visual metaphors are truly adequate only to the image of stanza two. There the poem imagines time as space and present consciousness as an expanse that just contains the past, but only in its moment of appearance or of disappearance. There is no horizontal motion across that sea of consciousness, but there is the gaping horizontal distance between here and the horizon that is the image of an inner emptiness, of the space across which consciousness feels itself stretched thin. The next stanza offers us not a simple picture of the space of consciousness, but a narrative situation. The days that are no more are as sad and strange as first light and first bird-song must be to the eyes and ears of a dying man. The images of this stanza are finely adjusted to the portrayal of liminal states, of first things and last. These dawns are still dark, stabilized only by the intrusion of "summer." The birds are just waking and just singing, the light of nature is just dawning as the light of sense hovers on the verge of extinction, and both these lights are evoked in the image of the glimmering square, an image of brightening and fading at once. Illumined by the rising sun, the casement window is growing lighter, but is also flattening out into a mere square of light instead of a window to the world outside. The days that are no more in this stanza render consciousness more tenuous still, both more strangely vivid and more fearfully empty, harder than ever to describe and to place. The consciousness of this stanza is not located precisely inside the dying man, who is never named or pictured, not evoked as a full presence, but in the event that connects the dying senses to the strangely distinct call of the bird. To be conscious in time is to be slipping away perpetually from experience into extinction, to be always just sensing and always just losing what is most real and alive. The poem fills out and presses upon us its apprehension of the days that are no more as an urgently present absence by combining ever more vivid imagery with less and less palpable imagined objects. The boat of the first stanza was already less than it seemed, not a boat, but a sail, not even a sail, but a glittering beam. In each of the next two stanzas new intensities of feeling are gleaned from an ever-more-marginal experience of consciousness, as the poem approaches and then passes beyond the boundary of death.

In the final stanza the present is an after life and the past is more vividly and delusively present than ever, the past and the present more deeply and distressingly intimate. Earlier they have been connected, but also separated by the clear distance between here and the horizon or by the less clear, but still estranging, distance between the dying senses and the sounds of earliness that reach them. The past is now like a kiss, but only a remembered kiss, and the objects of memory slip finally away into the virtual existence of the imagined. The poem's desire to see the past only as it lives in the present of consciousness makes it, on the one hand, a fact of consciousness, yet reduces it to the impalpability of all mere facts of consciousness that are not facts of perception as well. And perception has been left behind in the first stanza. Consciousness is never the simple act of looking on the world, but always the linked and complex awareness of "thinking of the days that are no more." And such thinking does not assure the continuing vitality of the past, but fills the present with delusive images. The kisses of actual experience, once that experience is past, cannot be distinguished from the kisses of fancy. The past exists only in the experience of the present, while the present surrenders its fullness, its presence, to the beckoning memories of the past. Experience itself feels tenuous, stretched thin. The poet's self, drawn out at first to the autumn fields, doubles back to the world within, a shared and expansive inwardness, but an inwardness nevertheless. And now the past is "deep" and "wild," adjectives that absorb it entirely into consciousness, as Cleanth Brooks has noted.[4] The erotic longing of the last stanza and the placement of the past at precisely the depth of first love finally identify the inevitable and frustrated reaching out of consciousness to its own past with the most primal and urgent reaching out to others.[5] The "Death in Life" that the poem ends by lamenting is, among other things, the inner vacancy of Romantic desire, and the poem's wild regret is for all the possible forms of connection of which Tintern Abbey would be a potent reminder. But Wordsworth's poem at this spot is so much more mobile and various and ambitious that it can hardly serve as a foil. Tennyson's wild regretfulness can be compared more helpfully and pointedly with the absolute sufficiency of consciousness evoked by Keats's "To Autumn," a poem that

Harold Bloom has convincingly identified as the nearest poetic source of "Tears, Idle Tears."[6]

The attitude of consciousness in "Tears, Idle Tears" is introspective and retrospective, and the mood of consciousness is strange, sad, and urgent. Keats's beautifully different meditation on happy autumn fields shares with "Tears, Idle Tears" its conception of the present moment as the repository of the past. For Keats, as John Jones has remarked, "Ripeness is a kind of simultaneity,"[7] and the past endures in the present and fills it up. The fullness of Keats's arrested present and the emptiness of Tennyson's are oddly congruent, but perfectly opposed in mood and attitude. Keats locates his images of fullness scrupulously outside himself in the plants and animals of the observed or imagined scene and in the spirit of Autumn that he insists on presenting in the full externality of personification. And when he thinks of the past and the songs of spring, he assigns even that thought to the objects before him and then quickly brushes it aside. Tennyson, blinded by the tears that have gathered to fullness and that will be his only harvest, hardly sees the world at all, and his poem makes no show of resisting the acknowledgment that its mood is a human imposition and a fact of human consciousness. Keats's is the greater poem, and for reasons to which Leavis's dispraise of Tennyson points the way, but in saying this I intend to give up very little of my claim for Tennyson and not at all to give way to Leavis's contention that their is something emotionally unhygienic or intellectually limited about "Tears, Idle Tears." A mood piece need not be slack or self-indulgent, and a mood piece as beautiful and successful and exemplary as "Tears, Idle Tears" advances the collective human project of consciousness by making available for our examination and for the pleasure of recognition one precisely evoked way of being in the world.

I have referred to the question of mood as Heideggerian. In the first volume of his recently translated lectures on Nietzsche, Heidegger defends the conception of mood as a necessary philosophical category, as a way of describing the situation in which man finds himself in the world:

> Here it is essential to observe that feeling is not something that runs its course in our "inner lives." It is rather that basic mode of our Dasein by force of which and in accordance with which we are always already lifted beyond ourselves into being as a whole, which in this or that way matters to us or does not matter to us. Mood is never merely a way of being determined in our inner being for ourselves. It is above all a way of being attuned, and letting ourselves be attuned, in this way or that way in mood. Mood is precisely the basic way in which we are *outside* ourselves. But that is the way we are essentially and constantly.[8]

It is this respectful conception of mood which, along with my high estimate of Tennyson's linguistic energy and resourcefulness, underlies my conviction that "Tears, Idle Tears" is a great poem and not an indulgence of mere feeling. Of course, I first read and admired Tennyson without any explicit philosophical rationale, and I do not intend now to glamorize or legitimize Tennyson by this appropriation of Heidegger, still less to claim influence or mystical affinity. I do intend to suggest that more than coincidence links the recent surge of interest in continental philosophy among Anglo-American students of literature with the growing prestige of, say, Harold Bloom's great tradition, with its honored place for Tennyson, as over against F. R. Leavis's.

Pairing these names is likely to offend all parties, but I think that the two bodies of work, Bloom's still in progress and on an uncertain course, may reasonably be likened in ambition, if not in achievement. Both represent sustained, coherent, self-assured, and boldly judgmental attempts to rewrite literary history, so affirming the immediate significance of great poetry and the linked and urgent relevance of the act of judgment that distinguishes the great from the less great. Emerging in league with a suddenly lively interest in Kierkegaard, Nietzsche, Heidegger, Derrida, and others, Bloom's criticism is not therefore an intellectually broader and more sophisticated alternative to Leavisian insularity, but neither is it therefore the evidence of a new enthusiasm for obscurity and mere theorizing. Such easy prejudices will do justice only to the lesser disciples of either critic. And, of course, there are more than two critics to choose from, more choices to make than those among critics, and more to one's own reading of literature, or to Leavis's or Bloom's, than the single act of choice. Criticism does not simply vote yes or no on either Tennyson or on philosophy. Leavis himself, in the same volume that reprints his remarks on "Tears, Idle Tears," expresses great admiration for the philosophy of Marjorie Grene and for her book *The Knower and the Known*, a book that repeatedly declares its affinity with the phenomenological regrounding of philosophy in the experience of persons.[9] And Christopher Ricks, both in his complete edition of Tennyson's poems and in his critical study of 1972, demonstrates brilliantly the possibility of admiring Tennyson from within the tradition of Leavis.

Nevertheless, patterns of allegiance and judgment do emerge. Ricks, in his book on Tennyson, is rather quick with "Tears, Idle Tears" and declares its limitations in ways that seem to me a Leavisian mistaking of its nature.[10] A less qualified admiration for "Tears, Idle Tears" and for other of Tennyson's most famous evocations of mood is likely to coincide with an enthusiasm far greater than Leavis's for the nondramatic generality of philosophical examination. Reading and responding to Tennyson's poetry myself, I am quite consciously under the influence of Bloom, although I read his work with frequent disagreement and incomprehension, and I doubt that he would read mine with any pride of paternity. And this influence presses me to consider what Tennyson's poetry does, as well as what it says, and to consider also the way in which each of his poems assumes or defines an attitude toward human and poetic possibility. Like Bloom, I find much of the interest and value of Tennyson's poetry in the relationship between the achieved intimacy of his style and the careful distance of what Bloom would call his stance, his way of locating the poem in literary history as well as between his consciousness and that of the reader. And the judgment of this act of locating goes outside the poem to place it in a context that is not merely psychological or sociological or historical, but philosophical.

A little earlier in the discussion from which I quoted above, Heidegger says that "the will cannot directly awaken or create a countermood: for moods are overcome and transformed always only by moods." An exciting and sympathetic account of *In Memoriam* might take that remark as its guide, but I am interested now in reading "Ulysses" and "Tithonus" as mood and countermood, as poems that amplify and enrich one another and that help to fill out a brief account of Tennyson's philosophy. Another way to phrase part of Leavis's objection to "Tears, Idle Tears" might have been to say that the poem contains no suggestion of its own countermood, a suggestion that I tried to make in the introduction of Keats. Of course, the quickest answer to Leavis would be to point out the immediate context of "Tears, Idle Tears" in *The Princess* and to show the title character herself making just his objections to the lyric, objections that the rest of the poem attempts in turn to answer and surround. But one would refer anti-Tennysonians to *The Princess* only with reluctance, and very few among pro-Tennysonians find its blank verse narrative an adequate complement to the lyrics that interrupt it. "Ulysses" and "Tithonus," however, are evenly and productively matched.

Tennyson wrote "Ulysses" in 1833, a decade or more before "Tears, Idle Tears," and he began "Tithonus" in the same year, although it was not completed and published until 1860. He called "Tithonus" a "pendent" to "Ulysses,"[11] so I follow the poet's own lead, as well as that of many subsequent critics, in examining the two together. And even without Tennyson's comment to point the way, one would hardly miss the purposeful contrast between the two poems. They are matched and opposed as the utterances of Greek and Trojan, victor and vanquished, hero and victim. Surely no reader would miss or mistake the opposition between the upright, active resolve of Ulysses, embodied in the plump assertiveness of a rhetoric that is, like that of Shakespeare's Henry V, a continuing favorite of politicians, and the luxurious passivity of the dying cadences of Tithonus. Yet many readers have perceived as well an odd similarity that makes these contrasts seem misleading or superficial and that makes it hard to distinguish with final clarity and assurance between the moods of the two poems. Robert Langbaum, for instance, hears in both poems, "a certain life-weariness" that is, for him, the true signature of their author,[12] and one must take into account this Tennysonian common denominator without blurring the distinctions between the two poems, distinctions that are too obviously intentional and too important a part of any reader's experience to be merely superficial. One possibility is to consider the subversive still-ness of "Ulysses" and the deceptive stillness of "Tithonus" as features of what I have been trying to establish as Tennyson's philosophic attitude.

Tennyson's interest in Ulysses and Tithonus is not an interest in character or dramatic circumstances, and he provides none of the density of social or historical detail that would characterize a monologue by Brown-ing. Rather, these two speakers are cut free from the mythological narra-tives that suggested them and present in their fixity two ways of being in the world. For Goldwin Smith, a nineteenth-century critic, Ulysses "merely intends to roam, but stands forever a listless and melancholy figure on the shore."[13] And for Christopher Ricks, to whom I am indebted for the Smith quotation, the poem and its speaker reveal an odd and underlying ambivalence toward the future in their curious failure to em-ploy the future tense,[14] a failure that recalls the avoidance of the past tense in "Tears, Idle Tears." Both these poems and "Tithonus," too, are search-ing out the experience of life from within the present moment and can hardly imagine the past and the future as places actually to find oneself. Nor can they imagine a point of view outside the present moment from which it is just one point in a line. "Tithonus" immobilizes consciousness in a relationship to time and the world quite outside the order of things and by means of the kind of extravagant hypothesis of which some schools of twentieth-century philosophy are fond. And "Ulysses" is not so much a report on an episode in its hero's life as an expansion of the moment in his story that can figure forth an attitude toward all the moments of our own lives.

> Yet all experience is an arch wherethrough
> Gleams that untravelled world whose margin fades
> For ever and for ever when I move.
>
> (19–21)

It is like Ulysses and like Tennyson to offer this single image for "all experience," an image that incorporates movement but does not move. Dante's Ulysses approaches the straits of Gibraltar and then leaves them behind in the space of five lines. He tells his story from outside history and the world. Tennyson and his hero share the urgency of a self-consciousness that cannot take for granted its place in the order of things, but must discover, articulate, and so maintain it. Ulysses and Tithonus do not represent for Tennyson significant idiosyncrasies of human character in action, but compelling apprehensions of the situation of human con-sciousness, and our readings need to discover just what, in their two poems, that situation is.

Tennyson said of "Ulysses" that it expressed, in the dark days after Hallam's death, his sense of the need of going forward, but it would perhaps be more accurate to say of both "Ulysses" and "Tithonus" that they express the desperate necessity of having someplace to go forward to, of being able to imagine a future. At the same time, both poems respond to the pressures of the past, not merely an abstraction here, but the sum of personal, lived experience that challenges or mocks the present. The importance of establishing some vital connection with the past reflects for these speakers an anxiety over the continuity of personal identity that is quite unlike the objectless regret so brilliantly evoked in "Tears, Idle Tears." For Tithonus, too, existence is posthumous, but the transcendental subjectivity of "Tears, Idle Tears" has only a generalized past and nothing like a personal history. Both Ulysses and Tithonus can say with Tiresias, a third classical monologist of this phase of Tennyson's career, "I wish I were as in the days of old." For Ulysses, the admission of personal loss works to confirm a continuing strength of identity: "though/We are not now that strength which in old days/Moved earth and heaven, that which we are, we are" (65–67). Tithonus makes the same admission in a tone of quietly despairing wonder:

> Ay me! ay me! with what another heart
> In days far off, and with what other eyes
> I used to watch—if I be he that watched—
>
> (50–52)

Tithonus here expresses a new and radical concern for the contingency of the self. In other of Tennyson's poems, in "Tears, Idle Tears" and also in "Mariana" and "The Lady of Shalott" and others, the experience of time has provoked the sense of continuous and unfulfilled desire, of an emptiness and a need within. But in each of those poems, the world has somehow failed the self. Now Tennyson assumes the mask of age in order to look back over a long life and wonder if it is not the very self that fails.

Ulysses blames his failure to be himself on circumstance:

> It little profits that an idle king,
> By this still hearth, among these barren crags,
> Matched with an aged wife, I mete and dole
> Unequal laws unto a savage race
> That hoard, and sleep, and feed, and know not me.
>
> (1–5)

Whatever the precise tone of this dismissal and whatever praise or blame attaches to it, it does make clear the terms of Ulysses' dissatisfaction with his subjects: they "know not me." Yet surely the citizens of Ithaca do know their king, and the statement can only mean that Ulysses in Ithaca is not "me," not his truest self. In a new verse paragraph, in a rhetoric grand and assertive, Ulysses defines the self to which he would remain true.

> I cannot rest from travel: I will drink
> Life to the lees: all times I have enjoyed
> Greatly, have suffered greatly, both with those
> That loved me, and alone; on shore, and when
> Through scudding drifts the rainy Hyades
> Vext the dim sea. I am become a name;
> For always roaming with a hungry heart
> Much have I seen and known,—cities of men
> And manners, climates, councils, governments,
> Myself not least, but honored of them all,—
> And drunk delight of battle with my peers,
> Far on the ringing plains of windy Troy.
>
> (6–17)

Ulysses defines himself as a man of action and now must struggle to live up to his self-definition, to realize the full significance of being himself. And action, for Ulysses, is taking and giving at once, voracious appetite and profuse self-expenditure. His hungry heart will consume experience, converting all that he meets into his grand sense of himself. Yet he can reverse this flow, too, and say "I am a part of all that I have met."[14] He wants more and more of life, but he will not have the self a mere storehouse of past experience:

> Life piled on life
> Were all too little, and of one to me
> Little remains; but every hour is saved
> From that eternal silence, something more,
> A bringer of new things; and vile it were
> For some three suns to store and hoard myself,
> And this gray spirit yearning in desire
> To follow knowledge like a sinking star,
> Beyond the utmost bound of human thought.
>
> (24–32)

Ulysses has earlier scorned the hoarding of his subjects, and he now finds that to stand watch over them is to hoard himself as well. Both in rejecting such husbandry and in discovering such a coincidence of experience between his subjects and himself, Ulysses distinguishes himself from the consciousness of "Tears, Idle Tears." There the world and the self stood in clear opposition, the realm of looking and the realm of thinking, one happy and one sad. The self was precisely an inner storehouse, painfully empty of all but its images, but still a kind of space to be mapped and described. For Ulysses, however, consciousness does not hold itself from the world, but leans into it, and intensest consciousness is a perpetual process of relationship, extracting from every hour the maximum value by investing in every hour all the energies of the self. Ulysses requires both to know and to be known, and he can be known only in actions that are themselves knowledge-seeking. He is not himself and consciousness is not itself while enthroned on an island, set over against a world of brute facts and mechanical processes.

Whether such a view of the kingship of Ulysses does justice or not to Penelope and Telemachus and the citizens of Ithaca is almost, if not entirely, beside the point. The poem evokes enough of Homer and dwells enough on Telemachus to introduce the possibility of social judgment. But this is the bad conscience and not the true consciousness of the poem. The reduction of Ulysses' kingship to an epistemological paradigm goes beyond the prudent limits of paraphrase in order to reach toward the philosophical understanding that the poem bespeaks. And this is essentially an understanding of what Husserl's phenomenology names as the intentionality of consciousness, its directedness toward the world.[15] The mind and the world are not separately conceivable, but are joined by the temporal activity of consciousness, which is always consciousness of something and never merely the self-awareness of an enclosed container. Marjorie Grene, writing in a tradition distinct from but sympathetic to phenomenology, phrases the matter finely and in language that recalls Tennyson: "But if reason, if self-consciousness, is essentially temporal, then knowledge is never finished, never at rest in 'manifest truth.' We are always beyond ourselves in the venture of knowing, the task of finding and giving as best we can significance to our world, the world which is always beyond us at the horizon, but whose concrescence, whose interpretation, whose meaning we are."[16] So, for Ulysses, the sense of personal history is generated by the interplay of knowing and being known, drawing the world into the self and spending the self in the world.

Yet one can hardly distinguish these two activities in practice, and for a consciousness so purified and purposeful as that of Ulysses, the present danger is solipsism. At the cutting edge of experience, knowing and being known amount to the same ceaseless movement, perhaps because Ulysses so vaguely defines the knowledge that he seeks. If he is a part of all that he has met, no wonder then that when he meets his past again in memory, he meets himself:

> Much have I seen and known; cities of men
> And manners, climates, councils, governments,
> Myself not least, but honoured of them all.

> (13–15)

He has drunk delight and he will drink life, but these are only equivocally external. And when he comes finally to describe a truly external scene—

The lights begin to twinkle from the rocks:
The long day wanes: the slow moon climbs: the deep
Moans round with many voices.

(54–56)

—he seems to be conjuring up rather than describing the scene, so dream-ily appropriate is it to his mood. A sensibility that can convert contingency so readily into significance encourages the suspicion that it never truly engages the world at all, but only its own projections. "I am a part of all that I have met" may be less a boast of influence than a confession of inability to see anything beyond the self.[17] Ulysses does not seek a newer world in order to find it, but to find and be himself in the act of seeking.

But to know the world only in relationship to the self is not to be a solipsist. Ulysses, after all, is only a part of all that he meets, and he does know Telemachus and acknowledge him. Knowledge is relationship and Ulysses knows Telemachus by knowing and articulating the differences between Telemachus and himself. This does not seem to me as humanly unattractive as it has seemed to other readers, and it does, in the poem's allegory of consciousness, suggest accurately the relationship between the two senses of consciousness of which Ulysses and Telemachus are the representatives. Telemachus, the agent of assimilation and order and tradi-tion, represents consciousness as content, the aspect of our inner lives that is generated by true, intentional consciousness but also left behind by it as the father here leaves behind the son.

Yet these are a father and a son, and there is a wife here, too. If Ulysses is not solipsistic, he may at least be selfish. Disgusted with Ulysses for his Romantic irresponsibility, W. H. Auden listened exclusively to what I have called the bad conscience of the poem. As a character and as a psychological case, Ulysses is indeed flawed in many ways and could be accused not merely of stasis, as in the remarks of Langbaum and Goldwin Smith, but of regression. The margin that fades forever and forever might as easily be the past as the future, and the desire to pursue it may not be a desire to progress, but rather to repeat oneself. Only a willingness to accept change, to grow perhaps from an adventurer into a statesman, would indicate true progress of the self. And Tennyson himself has given us further encouragement to suspect the heroism of Ulysses by taking as his source Dante's *Inferno*, where Ulysses has been damned for his pre-sumption and reckless leadership, and then by underscoring this infernal connection with echoes of the rhetoric of Milton's Satan.

Writing soon after Hallam's death, Tennyson would indeed have felt a guilty resistance to the urge to move forward, or even to face forward, into the future. This resistance, in fact, is an important subject of *In Memoriam*. But "Ulysses" is not the vehicle of explicit self-examination, just as it is not a psychological case history. Tennyson may have struggled to reach the mood of "Ulysses," and it may be that kings should not leave their wives and sons and duties behind, but the poem itself is not about Tennyson's struggle or about what some king Ulysses should have done. It abstracts itself from these empirical occasions to present a philosophical, which is not to say a bloodless or impersonal or idealized, attitude: not an attitude toward kingship or mourning, but toward being. Subversive readings of the poem cannot and should not undo its assertive rhetorical power, and it is this power, the evident and persuasive feeling of the poem, with which the philosophical reading attempts to stay in touch. Even though it is possible to expose his heroic, ceaseless activity as motion without locomotion, a kind of busy, aspiring stasis, Ulysses does engage the world in a manner sharply different from that of Tithonus. Whatever the status of his planned, barrier-breaking voyage, Ulysses does move ceaselessly through time toward death, and his triumph is to render this curse of mortality a source of imaginative life. To be perpetually "yearning in desire" defined a mortal dilemma for the many Tennysonian—and Coleridgean and Shelleyan and Byronic—victims of romantic desire. The resolution "To strive, to seek, to find, and not to yield" makes of perpetual frustration a form of heroism. Ulysses will not yield to obstacles and, as the order of these celebrated infinitives makes clear, he will not yield to finding, will not make an end until one is made for him.

It is a matter, once again, of mood, of attunement to the world, of the spirit in which one takes up the given situation of consciousness, and this situation includes the fact of death. Saying flatly that "Death closes all," Ulysses does not use constant movement as a defense against this knowledge, but instead uses this knowledge as the incentive to movement. Facing the future, Ulysses faces always toward his death at the horizon, and it is surprising to notice how unemphatically but also how unequivocally he acknowledges this absolute limitation:

> for my purpose holds
> To sail beyond the sunset, and the baths
> Of all the western stars, until I die.

> (59–61)

This achievement of authentic Being-toward-death, to adopt the existential terminology of Heidegger, makes possible the hopeful intensity of the quest. Ulysses longs for an eternity of aspiration and knows at the same time that aspiration can have meaning only in a finite, death-bound world. Only the fact of death imposes on experience the urgency that renders each hour the source of potential value.

At least, this is clearly the wisdom of "Ulysses" and of "Tithonus," too, but can it really be this easy? We know that Tennyson himself had hardly achieved such composure in the face of death and that he achieved it finally only by assuming a faith in the benign immortality of Christianity. And we notice, too, that Ulysses invokes an agnostic escape clause:

It may be that the gulfs will wash us down;
It may be we shall touch the Happy Isles,
And see the great Achilles whom we knew.

(62–64)

Death may be death, or it may be another form of living, and neither "Ulysses" nor "Tithonus" advocates the existential heroism that would renounce this uncertainty in favor of a sure and clear negation. Consciousness cannot stand outside itself and it cannot intend the end of intending, its own nonexistence. That this is so in the case of Tithonus will require some later argument. Ulysses, facing his own death, does not face or desire certain extinction, but he does accept and rely on something he calls death, and this is an acceptance of the world as bounded and given. Consciousness discovers the world, but does not choose it. Death and the horizon, whether or not they bring extinction, mark the limits of our intending, "the utmost bound of human thought." It is not a question of choosing death, but of acknowledging the limits of choice. To inhabit a field of choice unlimited by the constraints of death and the horizon is to be in the position of Tithonus.

Tithonus has discovered the curse of fulfillment, of having his carelessly worded wish come true. He lives where no man ought to live, on the other side of the horizon, the other side of the border that Ulysses could only plan to cross. This results in a terrible reversal of the ordinary conditions of human life, but also in some of Tennyson's most extraordinary writing.

The woods decay, the woods decay and fall,
The vapours weep their burthen to the ground,
Man comes and tills the field and lies beneath,
And after many a summer dies the swan.
Me only cruel immortality
Consumes: I wither slowly in thine arms,
Here at the quiet limit of the world,
A white-haired shadow roaming like a dream
The ever silent spaces of the East,
Far-folded mists and gleaming halls of morn.

Alas! for this gray shadow once a man—
So glorious in his beauty and thy choice,
Who madest him thy chosen, that he seemed
To his great heart none other than a God!
I asked thee, "Give me immortality,"
Then didst thou grant mine asking with a smile,
Like wealthy men who care not how they give.
But thy strong Hours indignant worked their wills,

And beat me down and marred and wasted me,
And though they could not end me, left me maimed
To dwell in presence of immortal youth,
Immortal age beside immortal youth,
And all I was, in ashes.

(1–23)

In the passage from Book 6 of *The Prelude* that Tennyson's opening echoes, Wordsworth describes in nature an "eterne in mutabilitie" beyond the reach of mortal striving:

The immeasurable height
Of woods decaying, never to be decayed,
The stationary blasts of waterfalls.

(1805; 6: 624–26)

For Tithonus, however, the world of nature represents the mortal estate of which he would be part. From the viewpoint of exile, nature and man are joined in their subjection to time. Tithonus, meanwhile, in his passage beyond the horizon, has fallen out of the natural and temporal orders and now finds himself an anomaly, immortal like Aurora, but subject to decay like the objects of nature. Without the prospect of death, he cannot bend toward the future, cannot feel himself moving toward anything. Neither is the past a source of self-confirmation, for his relationship to it is discontinuous. Aging slowly, inexorably into decrepitude, he ought at least to be able to trace through past time the arc of his decline. But the present stands to the past not as one moment to another in the order of a genetic history, but rather as shadow to substance, or ashes to living fire. It is a wholly different and reduced sphere of being. In becoming immortal, Tithonus has ceased to be himself, has sacrificed his mortal identity.

For Ulysses, who is all that a man might be, the past functions as a usable resource, a potent if also a tyrannical source of energy. With all the momentum of his past activity, he must go forward from the place to which past activity has brought him. The present moment gathers together at once all of the past—this is the gathering accomplished by his meditation—and imagines the future as a straight line breaking forth out of the enclosure of the present. For Tithonus, however, no such connection exists. What he glimpses obscurely through the mist and just beyond the horizon is not the future, but the past, the world of his ordinary mortality:

A soft air fans the cloud apart; there comes
A glimpse of that dark world where I was born.

(32–33)

Tithonus has been excluded from history. Linear motion lies behind him and not the past, but, appallingly, the future coexists with the present. Looking ahead, he sees no possibility of the motion or change by which the passage of time can be defined. The future is here and now and the same.

Tithonus, having once emerged into this new temporal order, is effectively without a past or a future. His partial transcendence of the human condition has stranded him in a realm where both the perpetual repetitions of God-time and the progression of human time are turned against the self. His desire to achieve a God-like changelessness has been tragically frustrated. Even that original desire, however, arouses suspicion; the poem does not encourage a sense that all would be well if only Tithonus had retained his youth. Perhaps the sexual energy of his relationship with Aurora would have provided the necessary and perpetual renewal of desire, but the sense remains that stasis rather than withering age is the source of misery. The desire for perpetual youth was itself flawed and regressive, and its frustration reveals the inevitable failure of spatial solutions to temporal problems. Tithonus travels to the land of the dawn, but continues to age. The mere absence of death (although its presence, admittedly, could never be called mere) does not resolve the dilemma of temporal existence. It creates instead a timelessness that is more destructive to the self than the time it seeks to escape. If time threatens to alter the self, then stepping out of ordinary, death-bound time does not stabilize it, but alters it absolutely.

Crossing the horizon and falling out of time, Tithonus confirms by negation the linkage between the temporality and the intentionality of consciousness. Out of time, he is out of the world, a "shadow," a "ghost," a "dream," and he cannot enter into self-confirming relationship either with the world of his birth and his mortality or with the weirdly insubstantial "Far-folded mists and gleaming halls of morn." Aurora herself is real and warm and gorgeously alive, but Tithonus has been reduced to mere spectatorship, and he has no place in the extraordinary erotic drama of the dawn that he describes:

> A soft air fans the cloud apart; there comes
> A glimpse of that dark world where I was born.
> Once more the old mysterious glimmer steals
> From thy pure brows, and from thy shoulders pure,
> And bosom beating with a heart renewed.
> Thy cheek begins to redden through the gloom,
> Thy sweet eyes brighten slowly close to mine,
> Ere yet they blind the stars, and the wild team
> Which love thee, yearning for thy yoke, arise,
> And shake the darkness from their loosened manes,
> And beat the twilight into flakes of fire.
>
> (32–42)

Taunted by these images that he can only describe, Tithonus suffers what the Lady of Shalott would suffer if she could not enter the world and die, but was instead condemned to watch Lancelot reappearing through the ages. "How can my nature longer mix with thine?" Tithonus asks Aurora, and he receives no answer, because it cannot and they are absolutely divided. Tithonus is out of nature, but he is out of this dawn world, too. Aurora speaks to him only through her tears, and these are only the morning dew. Tithonus has none of the privileges of immortality or of mortality, except one. He can speak.

Ulysses, in spite of his rhetoric, knows that he will die, and Tithonus, in spite of his, knows that he will not. What does rhetoric accomplish for these speakers or for their maker, Tennyson? In the case of Ulysses, one has suspected throughout that rhetoric substituted for action. As Arthur Gold has commented to me, the reader often feels that Ulysses' truest quest is to reach the point where he can burst into the majestic eloquence of the poem's last paragraph. Yet how severely ought he to be criticized for this? Is not speech, too, a mode of becoming? "I am become a name." The ambiguity of the verb tense allows this assertion to do double service, primarily to indicate that life has passed already into legend, has already been written, but also to remind us that Ulysses is even now rewriting his own legend, which had mistakenly been brought to conclusion. "I am become a name" joins with "I cannot rest from travel" and "I am a part of all that I have met" in suggesting the constant outward energies of the self. As long as Ulysses is still talking, these energies still flow, and the legend of self remains in vital flux. John Pettigrew has plausibly and perceptively suggested that the poem breaks into an interior and an exterior monologue, that the third and fourth paragraphs "reword for public proclamation" the private meditations of the first two.[18] I find this convincing, but would press further to notice the way in which all of the poem holds open the passage not just between private and public, but between future and past, living potential and dead achievement. The very act of speech combines the taking and giving that characterize Ulysses' progress through the world. As he speaks in the poem, he both reads his past and writes his future, absorbs his own experience through memory and projects it into the imagined future.

Yet speech also defers the future that it struggles to create, and we return to the remark of Goldwin Smith, that Ulysses merely "intends to roam, but stands forever a listless and melancholy figure on the shore." But this penetrating and sensitive criticism goes too far in calling the maker of such heightened speech "listless" and not far enough in seeing only melancholy in Ulysses' posture on the shore. Rhetoric that displaces action may seem to mark a retreat from life. But when action means setting sail at dusk into a glooming, dark, broad sea, the rhetoric that defers it does not retreat from life so much as prolong life in the face of death. The speaker always about to cease speaking and set out offers the same resistance to the death of completion as does the adventurer always preparing to cross the horizon. Like the daughters of Hesperus in "The Hesperides" or the bulbul in "Recollections of the Arabian Nights," Ulysses must sing to sustain the enchantment. But his song is public speech and private consciousness at once, and it does not suspend time, but enters it word by word.

Speech announces presence and life in the face of "that eternal silence" ("Ulysses," 27). For Tithonus, eternity and silence together conspire against being, and his speech in the poem struggles to make a noise and so to emerge from the nighmare of nonbeing that the poem everywhere documents. Tithonus inhabits a "quiet limit," "ever-silent spaces," and has himself faded into insubstantiality: "A white-haired shadow roaming like a dream." Yet he is haunted by memories of a speech magically potent and productive, by gestures of effortless and God-like creativity. He remembers the moment in which his own quick words, "Give me immortality," became sudden and awful reality, and he remembers how Apollo could sing a city into being. Now his own speech cannot bring anything out of the silence.

> Lo ever thus thou growest beautiful
> In silence, then before thine answer given
> Departest, and thy tears are on my cheek.
>
> (43–45)

Tithonus is trying to open a closed case. His story has already been written, in his own request, "Give me immortality," and in the dimly remembered saying, "The Gods themselves cannot recall their gifts." Recorded speech here, speech fixed in time, is the mark of doom. Crossing the horizon, Tithonus has left behind not only time and the world, but the ordinary powers and properties of language. Language now is the agent of fate and not of freedom, something that has happened to Tithonus, a sentence and not a power. His future has been spoken, and his own speech is cut adrift, insubstantial as the shadow from which it emanates and the mists in which it dissolves without effect. Tithonus's desire for the earth is not just a desire for the grave, but for connection and substantiality. The problem is not that language and the self are divided, but that they are perfectly coterminous and disembodied, without a home in time and without effect in the world. "Thou seest all things, thou wilt see my grave." Tithonus tries through this play of speech to invest his own word and wish with Aurora's power. But he cannot, and his speech ends in lovely and hopeless bravery, asserting itself against an inalterably fixed destiny:

> Release me and restore me to the ground.
> Thou seest all things, thou wilt see my grave;

Thou wilt renew thy beauty morn by morn,
I earth in earth forget these empty courts,
And thee returning on thy silver wheels.

(72–76)

But these final lines provoke a few final misgivings and questions. Can we really believe that Tithonus wants to die when his language is so palpably the agent and evidence of a struggle into being and life? And is such language without power altogether, merely because it is without the power to change fate and to move Aurora to action? A. Dwight Culler's summary remark helps us toward some answers: "Both Tithonus and Ulysses want to be released into the human world of Becoming, the world of change, movement, activity, life—and death."[19] Thus Tithonus wants to be dying as evidence that he is alive. And failing that, he can offer in evidence the very fact of his articulated desire. In petitioning Aurora, Tithonus does continue to press himself into the future and against the boundaries of his freedom, and he can do this as long as he holds to any sense of his own being in the world. And he just does hold on, feeling his cold and "wrinkled feet" (67) on the threshold as a late and last evidence of the body and obstinately interpreting the morning dew as the tears of sympathy. So long as the perpetual order of things can be humanized, Tithonus must still be human, able to glimpse his past and to reach into the future. The opportunity to speak offers him a respite, however pathetic, from the contemplation of his changeless fate, and within the space of the poem he can experience temporarily the consolations of teleology. So the paradoxical answer to our questions is that Tithonus must continue to desire death or he will be dead, and he proves his continued desire in his speech.

Speech is all that is left to Tithonus, nearly all that is left of him, and he does not seem in speaking to reach Aurora or to make a noise in his world at all. But this extreme and negative view of his condition finally will not do, because it falsifies our own experience of the poem. We do hear Tithonus, and we hear him because a language out of time and disembodied and dehumanized simply cannot be. Language always has a body and a place in the world and time, or it would not exist for us, and Tennyson's language in this poem imposes on us with all the intensity of Tithonus's imagined need. The mingled pathos and sublimity of "Tithonus," the sense of enervation and intensity at once, testify to the opposed, acknowledged, and fully realized strengths of immovable fate and moving human resistance—a summary that returns us to Ulysses.

Our moods have no power to change the order of things, and "Tithonus" and "Ulysses" describe and emerge from congruent orderings of consciousness, time, and the world. But moods do offer us alternative ways to take up the apprehensions of philosophy in our continuing, lived experience, and the two poems thus address different moments or possibilities of our experience. The situation of Ulysses obviously suggests that of any spirit confronting its own mortality and choosing life in the face of it. Although neither Tennyson nor any of his readers lives with the goddess of the dawn, the situation of Tithonus also has its analogue in the sort of youthful vastation that Tennyson and his sister Emily (and, to a lesser degree, his whole family) suffered in the shock of Arthur Hallam's death, which seemed to empty their lives of all secure points of reference, all happy anticipations. M. J. Donahue, in her discussion of the poem's first draft, cites Emily's letter to Tennyson in 1834: "What is life to me! If I die (which the Tennysons never do)."[20] "Ulysses" and "Tithonus" offer the paired challenges of being in time, of consciousness discovering that it must die and discovering that it must live. In "Tithonus," especially, we can hear the shaken, impassioned, and still disbelieving voice of consciousness, just realizing that it must indeed endure the unendurable. And in speaking, the business of enduring and of living begins.

Ulysses and Tithonus do not alter the given conditions of the world with their language, a privilege that is reserved for the gods, but they do enter and, indeed, constitute a human world with their language and thus enact a philosophical truth. In their attentiveness to the ways of speaking and to the life of speech, Ulysses and Tithonus and, finally, Tennyson himself are brilliantly interested parties, and it may be salutary in concluding to distinguish sharply, if somewhat arbitrarily, between philosophy and literature and to lay stress on the distinctly literary character of Tennyson's achievement. The philosophical value of "Ulysses" and "Tithonus" is to identify language and consciousness by presenting their subjection, or, in another mood, their shared access, to time and the world. The literary value of "Ulysses" and "Tithonus" and of "Tears, Idle Tears," too, is also to identify language and consciousness, but this time by the miracle of style that renders these poems distinct from one another and just as distinctly Tennysonian, and that presses their language and Tennyson's consciousness into time and the world. But we must stop just short of the thrilling conclusion that Tennyson lives in his poems and speaks to us from the other side. The poems themselves invite such a mystification in their urgency and personality of voice and also in their readiness to employ death as a metaphor for some of the possibilities of our conscious lives. But they refuse this mystification as well, separating the metaphorical deaths of consciousness from the stillness of a death that is always beyond the horizon, and also separating themselves from the empirical, lived concreteness of life—of Tennyson's life—by their assumption of the exemplary consciousness of the philosophical attitude. Urgency and personality coexist with the philosophical attitude as final evidence that poetry is the form of philosophy that attends most seriously to the body of its language, so that the poem is always its own most compelling philosophical example.

Notes

All quotations from Tennyson's poetry are taken from *The Poems of Tennyson,* ed. Christopher Ricks (London and New York: Longman, 1969). Reprinted by permission of the publisher.

1. W. H. Auden, *A Selection from the Poems of Alfred, Lord Tennyson* (Garden City, N.Y.: Doubleday, 1944), p. x.

2. F. R. Leavis, *The Living Principle* (Oxford: Oxford University Press, 1975), pp. 78–79.

3. *The Works of Tennyson,* ed. Hallam Tennyson (London: Macmillan, 1908), 4:255.

4. Cleanth Brooks, *The Well Wrought Urn* (New York: Harcourt, Brace and World, 1947), pp. 172–74.

5. See A. J. Ayer's remarks on the analogy between the problem of making statements about the past and problem of making statements about other minds; in *Philosophical Essays* (London: Macmillan, 1954), pp. 188–89.

6. Harold Bloom, *Poetry and Repression* (New Haven, Conn.: Yale University Press, 1976), p. 163.

7. John Jones, *John Keats's Dream of Truth* (London: Chatto & Windus, 1969), p. 217.

8. Martin Heidegger, *Nietzsche: Volume I: The Will to Power as Art,* trans. David Krell (San Francisco, Calif.: Harper and Row, 1979), p. 99.

9. Marjorie Grene, *The Knower and the Known* (New York: Basic Books, 1966). The book is discussed and praised by Leavis at numerous points in his essay "Thought, Language, and Objectivity" in *The Living Principle.*

10. Christopher Ricks, *Tennyson* (New York: Macmillan, 1972), p. 200.

11. *Alfred, Lord Tennyson: A Memoir,* ed. Hallam Tennyson (London: Macmillan, 1897), 1:459.

12. Robert Langbaum, *The Poetry of Experience* (New York: Random House, 1957), pp. 89–90.

13. Goldwin Smith, in *Saturday Review,* 3 November 1855; reprinted in *Tennyson: The Critical Heritage,* ed. John Jump (London: Routledge and Kegan Paul, 1967).

14. Ricks, *Tennyson,* p. 125.

15. The concept of intentionality is explicated many times over by both Husserl and his critics. For the best and clearest account I have found, see Maurice Natanson, *Edmund Husserl: Philosopher of Infinite Tasks* (Evanston, Ill.: Northwestern University Press, 1973), pp. 85 ff.

16. *The Knower and the Known,* p. 91.

17. So Harold Bloom takes it in *Poetry and Repression,* pp. 158–59, citing Vico and Emerson as analogues.

18. John Pettigrew, *Tennyson: The Early Poems* (London: Edward Arnold, 1970), p. 59.

19. A. Dwight Culler, *The Poetry of Tennyson* (New Haven, Conn.: Yale University Press, 1977), p. 98.

20. M. J. Donahue, *Memoir,* 1:135. Quoted by Donahue in "Tennyson's *Hail Briton!* and *Tithonus* in the Heath Manuscript," *PMLA* 64 (1949):385–416.

"The Frightful Co-Existence of the *To Be* and the *Not To Be*": Antinomy and Irony in De Quincey's "Sir William Hamilton"

Bryan Tyson

In an essay whose putative subject is the philosopher Sir William Hamilton, Thomas De Quincey describes an adolescent experience in which he gazes on the corpse of a long-dead woman. His account of that experience concentrates on its disconcerting and contradictory quality. It seems composed of opposites and antinomies:

> Some overflowing of the Dee had exposed to view the secrets of the churchyard. Amongst the coffins in the lower tiers was one which contained the corpse of a woman, particularly blooming. According to my first precipitate computation, she might be rated as one hundred and twenty years old; for she had died in Queen Anne's reign (about 1707, I think) and by the plate on the coffin lid had been twenty-four at the time of death. Yet her face was most blooming, her lips beautifully fresh, and her hair of the loveliest auburn. Ninety-and-three years of the eighteenth century, and two years of the nineteenth, had she spent in the grave; and adding these ninety-five years of rest to the twenty-four of her (doubtless unresting) life, for a moment I fell into the natural confusion of making her a very, very old woman; and proportionably I wondered at the vernal beauty which had not ceased to adorn her in the wintry grave. This special indulgence to a special beauty had been the gift of a soil preternaturally antiseptic. But inevitably the sudden collision of a youthfulness so apparent with an antiquity so historical, caused each idea reciprocally to illuminate the other; so that, for a moment or two, until I had distinguished the elements of this antiquity, and had separated the ninety-five years that did not belong to the young woman herself from the twenty-four that did, I struggled with the impossible and contradictory conception of crazy superannuation incarnated in perfect womanly loveliness. (5: 320)[1]

The passage moves from an immediate, "precipitate" encounter with death, through a process in which a series of balancing categories is created, contrasting "vernal beauty" and a sense of physical freshness and newness to the "wintry grave" and a "historical antiquity." When he has erected these categories, De Quincey seems to suggest that he has completed a task, or proffered a solution to a difficult problem. The acts of having "distinguished" and "separated" elements lead to an almost kinesthetic sense of relief in the cessation of the struggle with a "contradictory conception." The friction caused by the collision of two exclusive qualities creates a spark of clarifying illumination. The balanced quality of the passage's prose, its exploitation of antithesis and repetition, seems determined to repeat and affirm the very act of judgment it describes.

But the situation itself, the confrontation within one unified body of the antinomies of life and death, youth and age, is so uncanny that we find De Quincey's explanation of it too reductive and positive, and at the same time, too evasive. De Quincey's wonder is "proportionable" to his confusion, but the dissolving of his "natural confusion" does not alleviate our own wonder. The resolution seems inadequate to the implications and potential meanings that could be drawn from the situation. We feel that the situation could at the very least become a powerful image, and perhaps in some way it asserts that power by overriding and denying any too-simplistic apprehension of it.

In fact, De Quincey seems aware of this power. The anecdote has been introduced not merely for the sake of its own resolution, but in order to reinforce a pervading atmosphere of melancholy that is a constitutive part of the narrator's situation in the essay. De Quincey may recover from his fall into "natural confusion," but it is a fall that can never be avoided. He moves from the singular "I" to an inclusive "we" as he describes our existence as "tenants" within the space of a generation. When this space is surveyed "through the inverted tube of the present," we appear antinomically, as historical oxymorons, as "present antiquities and relics" (5: 320–21). The pathos here is no longer that of the struggling viewer who must grapple with a "contradictory conception," but rather that of the tenant himself, whose act of self-revelation is frustrated by the contradictory nature of his medium.

As a willful digression from the essay's nominal subject, the anecdote is a recognizable idiosyncrasy of De Quincey's style, but it can also be used to determine the essay's unannounced and elusive aims. Like the corpse it describes, the essay must be disinterred from an intervening century and a half which has buried the name and reputation of its subject, Hamilton, the most famous English philosopher of his day. Moreover, the reader engaged in interpreting the essay soon finds himself assuming the young De Quincey's role, baffled by the contradictory conceptions incarnated in the essay. The piece violates the generic demands of the memoir to present personal recollections of a given subject, presenting instead the narrator's overwhelming absorption in his own voice and situation. The essay's treatment of language and philosophy is equally duplicitous: it uses the figure of Hamilton as philosopher in order to proclaim an ideal language founded upon the authority and privilege of logic, while subverting that ideal through an incessant indulgence in an "unserious" language of puns, tricks, and digressions. De Quincey creates an adversary relationship between philosophical and literary discourse. The literary voice, anxious for its own power and freedom, challenges and exploits an effigy of philosophy in order to free itself. In adopting this uneasy and sometimes aggressive stance, De Quincey approaches the practice of his continental contemporaries in romantic irony.

However, De Quincey's more immediate antecedents are from English literary history. His reference to the "inverted tube of the present" suggests a sudden reversal of perspective: the present generation, aware of itself as full of life and power, is suddenly looked at through the wrong end of a telescope and is reduced to the pastness of death. Such drastic and unsettling reversals of perspective are part of the stock-in-trade of the mid-eighteenth-century poets known as the Graveyard School. The most famous representatives of this morbid, obsessive style of writing are Robert Blair and Edward Young, and in Young's long poem *Night Thoughts* we also find the image of the inverted telescope. Young, who constantly employs paradoxical formulations, notes that all men complain about the tedium and length of life until they are called upon to give it up, when "years to moments shrink, / Ages to years. The telescope is turn'd."[2] Complacent in his absorption in the present moment, blind to the possibility of his own death, man is suddenly betrayed into panic when he confronts his own mortality.

This induced panic is a preliminary but necessary condition for the consolation that Young and writers like him are prepared to offer. That consolation takes the form of a religious apprehension of existence: the Graveyard School of poets all follow orthodox interpretations of experience in which life, on account of its mutability, is denigrated to the status of shadowy illusion. Dispelling this illusion, death cancels out life and deprives it of meaning. However, the reader's understandable discomfort at this spectacle is quieted by Young's substitution of a new world, permanent and immutable, in its place: "All, all on earth is shadow, all beyond / Is substance."[3] Skilled as they are at undoing conventional notions of meaningfulness, the Graveyard poets are more interested in exchanging one idea of meaning or substance for another: spiritual reality fills the gap left by the collapse of physical reality. Constantly urging this new and spirit-centered perspective upon the reader, Young hopes to correct "man's false optics."[4]

De Quincey, also interested in the problems of human, subjective vision, writes in his "Letters to a Young Man" that the "purpose of philosophy is not so much to accumulate positive truths . . . as to rectify the position of the human mind, and to correct its mode of seeing" (10: 78). However, this progress toward a rectified seeing is "not direct, but oblique" (10: 78). Unlike the Graveyard poets, De Quincey cannot engage in an easy rejection of the phenomenal world and a quick substitution of a numinous reality. Questioning any kind of imaginative or rhetorical substitution, the enigma of his graveyard experience lies in the co-presence of contradictory qualities rather than in the triumph of one force over another. Moreover, where the consciousness of death seems, to the Graveyard poets, to give the lie to experience, forcing men to adopt an attitude of quietist withdrawal from life, it frequently gives De Quincey a motive for action. In his *Confessions of an English Opium-Eater*, he remembers the pallid sermons he was subjected to as a child and contrasts them with the impassioned preaching of the seventeenth century. A remembered couplet describes that style: "I preached, as never sure to preach again, / And as a dying man to dying men" (3: 240). Instead of merely refuting experience, death is made the limit and the measure by which we determine the truth and authenticity of experience.

The figure who intervenes poetically and historically between the Graveyard poets and De Quincey is Wordsworth. Wordsworth's encounters with death, recorded in the fifth book of *The Prelude*, move beyond the lugubrious apprehension of the Graveyard School, seeking a more plausible way to interpret death by exploring less straitened and conventional kinds of substitution. The churchyard where the "boy of Winander" is buried "hangs / Upon a slope above the village school," and the boy's story ends in Wordsworth's reflective pause before the blankness and silence of the grave. Wordsworth's story tells of an imaginative education, as the boy, blowing "mimic hootings" to birds "Responsive to his call," is suddenly arrested by "a pause / Of silence such as baffled his best skill."[5] The moment of silence, in which the boy discovers an apparently unresponsive limitation to his song, foreshadows the absolute limitation of death. The baffling pause of silence seems to be repeated in Wordsworth's "mute" stance before the boy's grave. No Christian consolation is forthcoming—instead, Wordsworth unashamedly remembers his own youth and the "race of real children" who will continue to people the spot. He offers no positive statement about death—the graveyard and the school are proximate, but not identical.

De Quincey discussed the boy of Winander with Wordsworth, and his recollections of that talk indicate both his affinities for and differences from Wordsworth's graveyard meditation. He connects the poem to one of Wordsworth's sententious pronouncements: "If under any circumstances, the attention is energetically braced up to an act of steady observation, or of steady expectation, then if this intense condition of vigilance should suddenly relax, at that moment any beautiful, any impressive visual object, or collection of objects, falling upon the eye, is carried to the heart with a power not known under other circumstances."[6] This is what happens to the boy, who, after the silence, finds that "a gentle shock of mild surprise/ Has carried far into his heart the voice/ Of mountain torrents." The "condition of vigilance" is momentarily interrupted, but receives a compensating impression from the torrents that become a speaking "voice." De Quincey standing before the grave is also in a state of vigilant confrontation, but no sudden influx from the natural world releases him from that tension. His elaborate dissolution of an enigma, reflected in his labyrinthine prose, at its best is a deficient evasion of tension, and what is "carried far into his heart" is an insistently antinomic structure that asserts itself within the essay as a model of experience, language, and consciousness.

The physical presence of the body in De Quincey is different from anything in Wordsworth, but we may relate it to the story that follows that of the boy of Winander. The perfectly preserved body cast up by a flood is a situation made melodramatically present to the senses. It hovers precariously between an image of resurrection and the casual catastrophes of Gothic romance, and provokes an anxiety that is absent in Wordsworth. Baffled not by an absence, but by an incarnation that verges on reincarnation, De Quincey's meditation is colored by an analytic attitude that is unsatisfied by the consolations of Wordsworthian meditation, or those of an earlier poet like Gray.

However, Wordsworth does record such an unsettling vision of a dead body and affords us a measure of the distance between his own response and De Quincey's. In the fifth book of *The Prelude*, entitled "Books," he recalls how his reading and exposure to art acted as a prefiguration of and preparation for the experience of discovering a drowned man. As a young boy just arrived in the Esthwaite valley, he spots a man's abandoned clothes on the opposite bank of a lake. The lake is dragged the next day, and "At length, the dead Man, 'mid that beauteous scene . . . bolt upright/ Rose with his ghastly face."[7] However, the boy is not terrified by the "spectre shape," because "my inner eye had seen/ Such things before, among the shining streams/ Of Fairy land, the Forests of Romance."[8] His preparation for the event endows the body with a strange "smoothness," wearing down the potential Gothic terror of the body to lineaments of "ideal grace . . . like the works of Grecian art."[9] The calm with which Wordsworth transforms a gruesome death to the aesthetic perfection of an artifact signifies an extraordinary and unsettling power of will in the face of mortality.[10] The smoothness of the corpse in De Quincey is not the effect of an unnervingly secure vision like Wordsworth's, but a condition that is both natural and a violation of nature. It is the cause of a vision within the essay that lacks Wordsworth's talent for imaginative reduction, but is instead continuously double and doubling.

The posture of the incessant questioner before a grave that seems to mock his questions, and Wordsworth's phrase about his "inner eye," recall another important literary antecedent for De Quincey. Hamlet's cynical contemplation of the "base uses" to which we may return is spoken before an empty grave, only to be displaced into a hyperbolical language of grief at the appearance of the body of a young woman, whose death is connected with flowers. So here, the appearance of a corpse of "vernal beauty" and "blooming" freshness displaces De Quincey's own reductive essay into a hyperbolical language that tries to overcome contradiction while confessing its own inability to do so. Later in the essay, when De Quincey actually does discuss a few problems of logic and philosophy, he revises Hamlet's most famous question. Instead of the ethical, either-or choice implicit in "to be or not to be," De Quincey discusses the logical problem of antinomy, "the frightful co-existence of the *to be* and the *not to be*" (5: 351).

De Quincey begins his memorial essay with the voice of an enervated survivor, a survivor of his own, unspoken experience: "With this brain, so time-shattered, I must work, in order to give significancy and value to the few facts which I possess" (5: 304). This attempt must be effected through memory, but to the speaker, memory, the revivifying of a dead past, is a kind of "martyrdom," creating a corrosive sorrow, "as of some unknown snake-like enemy, in some unknown hostile world, brooding over the fountains of one's own vitality" (5: 305). Lamenting time's power of negation, he longs for "the privilege of one day's secular resurrection, like the Arabian phoenix, or any other memento of power in things earthly and sublunary births" (5: 306). Unable to move from this wish to its fulfillment, De Quincey is forced to incorporate the wish into his essay as a substitute for what he really wants to say. Trying to say everything important about his subject within the limited space of the magazine essay, he finds himself undone by the "expansion of hurry and inevitable precipitancy." As a consequence, he is indebted to the reader and can only offer his wishes in place of repayment: "I had three hundred things, at least, to say . . . I must remain in your debt . . . and my wish, were wishes discountable, would run exactly in that channel [of repayment]" (5: 315–16).

Indebtedness is a term used later in the essay to describe the relation of Achilles to the tortoise in the famous paradox, where Achilles is unable to overtake the tortoise after the latter's head start: "Trifle as that is, it constitutes a debt against Achilles, which debt *must* be paid" (5: 331). But while that paradox may be resolved and the debt canceled, this is not the case with De Quincey's narrator. Achilles' ability to traverse physical space does not provide a suitable analogue to De Quincey's effort to write across imaginative space, but seems instead to parody it. De Quincey's finish line is his human subject, Sir William Hamilton, and his language aims to overtake that subject, to achieve a satisfactory portrait of the man in language. The essay would then become a reduplication in language of a vivifying human subject. De Quincey's technique undermines any possibility that the linguistic portrait and the external subject can ever coincide, and so raises the question of just what kind of representation language then does offer.

De Quincey is writing in the wake of a revival of idealism and subjectivism in philosophy. Hamilton himself was the champion of a loose, vaguely Kantian philosophy that rested on the subjective premise that "to think is to condition," that any knowledge is qualified by the presence of the knowing subject.[11] So De Quincey, writing on perception in an essay on "Style," notes that "difficulty commences when we have to combine with this outer measurement of the object another corresponding measure of the subjective or inner qualities by which we apply the measure . . . the eye cannot measure itself" (10: 153). Although it cannot measure itself, it can become obsessively aware of its own immeasurable presence, opening the way to a skepticism toward any original, objective truth, a crippling doubt about the possibility of truth as recovery. In the same essay De Quincey employs Greek grammar to describe sentences of inordinate length, ever postponing their own conclusion and demanding "the holding-on of the mind until what is called the *apodosis,* or coming round of the sentence commences" (10: 158). The main clause, which will grant stable meaning, locking the sentence into "self-supporting cohesion," is absent and creates in the reader the suspense (like that of De Quincey's graveside observer) of "holding on." The etymological root of *apodosis* itself means a giving back, a restitution or repayment. Language itself, in the standard terms of De Quincey's grammar, carries an acknowledgment of a perpetual indebtedness, an inability to repay in full the referential meaning that it promises to deliver.

De Quincey locates a certain impotence in the very act of writing, particularly when writing is supposed to represent the reflective, self-observing consciousness. His inability to assert the presence of "power in things earthly and sublunary births" does not propel him into a world of compensatory imagination, but instead acts analogously to his inability to assert a cohesive unity over his own text. De Quincey's climactic phrase to describe the woman in the grave establishes on a general level the occasion of his anxiety: what he sees is a "crazy superannuation incarnated in perfect womanly loveliness." Here incarnation becomes the embodiment of opposing and discontinuous features, the crazy and the perfect, and seems to border on contamination. Concepts are joined that are not merely exclusive, but actively repulsive: they violate the decorum of our perceptions.

This sort of contamination, the persistent presence of an otherness that disrupts the urge to unity, becomes the subject of the essay as it concentrates on Hamilton's contributions to logic.[12] The woman in the grave is a model for a similarly contaminated union of the crazy and the perfect in the domain of language, an incoherent interpenetration of logical

statement and jest. According to De Quincey's view of the historical situation, "Ordinary books of logic had gradually come to trespass more and
more upon the regular province of Joe Miller" (5: 327). One of the most
humorous of authors, De Quincey here treats the jest not simply as an
exercise in wit, but as a kind of negation that persists within the province
ruled over by a homogeneous, logical language. He looks to Hamilton as
the man who will take the "final step to restore [logic's] homogeneous
character to the science, by separating the two incoherent elements" (5:
336). This restoration becomes equivalent to a number of other movements
in the essay, and finally coincides with the major concerns of imaginative
power and potency and, by extension, with the power of animation and
revivification: "It is not a sound logic that is wanted, so much as a potent
and life-giving logic" (5: 341).

A logical language, not only univocal and homogeneous, but able to
guarantee a positive, concrete truth—"something to write . . . that may
occupy the blank" of a merely formal logic (5: 337)—this might well ensure
the restoration of the narrative voice to a position of power over the text.
Recent criticism (recent, at least, insofar as it has been available to English-
speaking readers) offers categories that try to deal with the assertion of
narrative power: Mikhail Bakhtin's *Dostoevsky's Poetics* makes a useful distinction between "monological" and "dialogical" forms of discourse.
Dialogical structures involve a multiplicity of voices or views in conflict,
and the author either declines or fails to discover any unifying reconciliation for them. On the other hand, univocity of meaning is the aim of an
"official *monologism* which claims to possess the ready-made truth."[13] The
"official" nature of the monological voice appears in De Quincey in the
geographical-political functions that different kinds of language exercise:
different discourses are properties or "provinces" presided over by different languages that maintain order, but there is always the threat of "trespass" and violation.

The monological voice implies that there is a truth that exists prior to
any enunciation of that truth: written or spoken speech is such a dependent, referential enunciation. The "ready-made truth" for De Quincey's
narrator would be the implicit wholeness or homogeneity of his own text.
But throughout the essay he writes in a way that parodies this idea. Early
in his essay De Quincey writes as though he is trying to put a limit to his
digressiveness, implying that thereafter the substance of the essay will
begin: "You will see a full stop or period a very few inches farther on,
lurking immediately under the word *earnest* on the off side; and, from and
after that full stop, you are to consider me as having shaken off all
troublesome companions, and as having once for all entered upon business in earnest" (5: 308). Two actions seem to be taking place at once here.
The narrator apparently indicates that the sentence ending in "earnest
period" has already been formulated, somehow thought in the mind and

written out prior to the reader's seeing it. But at the same time, the narrator short-circuits the sentence he has written. He tries to appear independent from the text: it is as if, having completed the sentence, he is able to run back to its beginning and address the reader directly, guiding the reader's path through the sentence.

At another point in the essay, De Quincey directs his readers to another portion of the physical text, and exploits that physicality: "Look below, reader, into the footnote, which will explain it. Whilst you are studying *that*, I'll be moving on slowly overhead; and, when you come up from that mine to the upper air, you'll easily overtake me" (5: 321). By playing upon the physical subordination of the footnote to the text proper, De Quincey appears able to hover. This hovering is both spatial, as if he were in a balloon floating over the footnote, and temporal, as if the reader's return to the point where he left the text were a momentary slowing of the speed of the author's literary creation, designed to allow the reader to absorb the footnote with little or no loss of comprehension of the main text. In both cases, the narrator exploits the physical presence of the written word to create an illusion. The illusion is not only one of temporality, but suggests a narrative "I" with some kind of presence or embodiment outside the text in which this "I" occurs. From this extra-textual vantage point, the narrative figure is able to assert his independence from, and control of, the text. But he is only able to do so when language ceases to strive after a model of logic and homogeneity, when it no longer tries to justify itself in terms of truth or a mimetic representation of an external world—in short, when language operates in the province ruled by jest.

The jest, the conundrum, the riddle are all forms of language that contradict the impulse toward a logical language and a monological domination of discourse. The bafflement caused by riddles or paradoxes, like that caused by the woman in the grave, comes from an apparent incarnation of opposing qualities. The paradox of Achilles, who can never pass the tortoise in a footrace, is a "pure mathematic or ideal case made perplexing by being *incarnated* in a case of physical experience" (5: 331; emphasis added). Once again, the analytical process that distinguishes the ideal from the physical tries to present the distinction itself as a solution to the problem. But, in a long footnote that is one of his best, De Quincey goes on to discuss the failure of such a solution to obviate our discomfort, to create in effect the right vision of the problem at hand.

The occasion of the footnote is a gloss written by the philosopher Leibnitz on the paradox, in which he assures a worried correspondent that such a case can be laid to rest by a geometric investigation. To this De Quincey replies: "But all this only sharpens the sting of the problem. That there should exist for the reason, what to a certainty would *not* exist for the actual experience, exactly this it is which constitutes the difficulty. . . . So far from solving any difficulty, as Leibnitz supposes, St. Vincent's geometrical investigation, on the contrary would have repeated and published the difficulty in a broader shape" (5: 349–50). The conflict of an empirical certainty that exists in the same space as a contradictory certainty of reason is closely analogous to De Quincey's experience in the graveyard, where an attempt to solve the problem appeared instead to be a repetition of the problem in the field of language. He goes on to an even more dramatic expression of the difficulty:

> It is precisely *because* Achilles will in practice go ahead of the tortoise, when, comformably to a known speculative argument, he ought *not* to go ahead—it is precisely this fact so surely to be anticipated from all our experience, when confronted with this principle so peremptorily denying the possibility of such a fact—exactly this antinomy it is, the *will be*, as a physical reality, ranged against the *cannot be*, as apparently a metaphysical law—this downright certainty as matched against this downright impossibility, which in default of the Leibnitzian solution, constitutes our perplexity, or to use a Grecian word still more expressive, which constitutes our *aporia*, that is, our resourcelessness. (5: 350)

In a revaluation of what he has attempted earlier, De Quincey again exploits the effects of antithesis and repetition, but they are no longer in the service of a faith that human reason can adequately resolve "contradictory conceptions." They have been used before to order and to domesticate an uncanny situation, but they ring here with the monotonous repetition of a tolling bell, drowning out human efforts to silence contradiction. This antinomic pairing becomes increasingly plangent as the sentence progresses, refusing to allow the furtherance of any proposition without the immediate expression of its opposite, and threatening the controlling voice of the speaker.

In this aggressive affront to the possibility of a monological control over a univocal truth, De Quincey's rhetorical effects lead to an *"aporia."* Literally the *aporia* is a point that is not "porous," that allows no passage through itself to another point, and so permits no further progress. De Quincey suggests by the "perplexity" that this is somehow a defect in the external world, that it makes an appearance through a folding together of opposites, an "involute," as he describes it elsewhere (1: 39; 5: 334). But the involution of experience is only important and threatening as it signifies a subjective "resourcelessness," a lack on the part of language or perception. The perplexity of reason is not a rich density, but a blank of powerlessness. It is not the "blank power" of Kant to integrate the insights of other philosophers, nor the "carte blanche" of a restored logic that permits further development (5: 314, 337). Instead, it allows nothing positive to be written. It is a kind of *tabula rasa*, canceling out any positive statement by demonstrating its contingency and marrying it to its own negation.

De Quincey extends his footnote by adducing another example of paradox, and in so doing, extends the implication of his argument. The example is that of Zeno, who, according to the story, refuted an argument against the possibility of motion by silently standing up and walking back and forth. The change in the example puts some interpretation of motion and progress even more explicitly at the thematic base of the essay. Almost imperceptibly, we move from a race of one being relative to another, with its implicit acceptance of some kind of motion, to a kind of absolute question, where no geometric solution can even be proposed. And again, De Quincey faults those who would simply affirm one side of the question without attempting to invalidate or negate the other:

> Reason, as then interpreted, said, This thing cannot be. Nature said, But though impossible, it is a fact. Metaphysics denied it as conceivable. Experience affirmed it as actual. There was, therefore, war in the human mind, and the scandal of an irreconcilable schism. Two oracles within the human mind fought against each other. (5: 350)

Up to this point there has been some effort by the narrative voice to assert itself as derived from or modeled upon, or somehow a substitute for, a consciousness that exists above or outside the text. But this claim is suddenly reduced to the point where the human mind is made the locus for some modern version of a psychomachia. Consciousness itself is caught between two "oracles," two modes of discourse, each claiming some kind of privilege for itself. One is the voice of a metaphysically pure reason, the other the voice of pragmatic certainty, but each manages to contradict the other without finally silencing either. No argument that advances itself by positive methods can be finally victorious, since every argument is "strong as the centrifugal force," but "knowing *that*, however, does not enable you to hide yourself from the antagonist argument, or to deny that in power it corresponds to a centripetal force" (5: 351). Instead of the "reciprocal illumination" that the meeting of opposites at the grave was intended to provide, we are faced here with the mutual cancellation of forces that work in opposite directions. The two forces continue to exist, but they create the unity of a stasis, a still point within which the "I" exists. But by reason of its very "punctuality," this point offers no field for the exercise of power.

De Quincey concludes by repeating his insistence that what is at issue here is not the fact that rationalist discourse seems to run shockingly counter to experiential discourse, but that each retains its power in the face of every refutation: "The antinomy it is—the frightful co-existence of the *to be* and the *not to be*—this it is that agitates and distresses you. But how is that antinomy, a secret word of two horns, which we may represent for the moment under the figure of two syllables, lessened or reconciled by repeating one of these syllables, as did Zeno, leaving the secret consciousness to repeat the other?" (5: 351). With a tone of rather ghoulish relish at the predicament he has created, De Quincey leaves the reader in the position of a modern Hamlet, facing not a choice between *"to be"* and *"not to be,"* but a necessity of embracing them both.

Hamlet is at least able to articulate a freedom of choice and action. The narrator in this essay is in a position of necessary inactivity, rendered helpless by the awareness that no positive discourse, however hard it tries to control its opposite, can ever erase that negation or eliminate its own contingency. Language carries that necessary opposition with it as a kind of shadow or double.[14] An act or a language truly expressive of power would, in this context, have to be able to speak both "syllables" of the "secret word," a totemic kind of power that confesses to a duality in its own discourse. But in practice, the process that De Quincey describes here acts out some of the more mechanical and stifling aspects of psychic repression. Each antinomy acts like one of Freud's "primal words," bearing an antithetical sense, but the antithetical sense is not repressed here because of a degraded or degrading content that perverts a publicly approved meaning.[15] Antithesis here is abstract and formal, appearing as an automatic act of denial and negation, an immediate and necessary contradiction of any statement.

This footnote would seem to mark the absolute dead point of the essay, beyond which no further movement is possible. Some awareness of this might be seen in the fact that it is strategically placed at the conclusion of the second part of this tripartite essay, as if the narrator had reached a debilitating extreme of self-awareness. The attempt to create a logical language seems to founder, and with it goes the attempt by "the struggling intellect" to exercise "the free movement of its powers" (5: 341). But if language offers a bifocal perspective upon experience, showing "reason" and "nature" in perpetual conflict, De Quincey's essay does hold out the tentative hope that such a unity may still exist, prior to articulation, in the subjective perceiver. The mere presence of a narrator-figure is inadequate to guarantee the coherence of his discourse. Writing in the *Confessions*, De Quincey claims a strict relation between his early sufferings and later afflictions that goes beyond mere empty identity: "The opium miseries . . . connect themselves with my early hardships in London . . . by natural links of affiliation—that is, the early series of suffering was the parent of the later. Otherwise, these Confessions would break up into two disconnected sections . . . would have no link whatever to connect them, except the slight one of having both happened to the same person" (3: 412). In this essay the narrator, with "this brain, so time-shattered," is a very weak link through which to connect his materials, and he denies the metaphor of affiliation, in which one circumstance is united to another through a parental relation.

An ideal model for the linking power De Quincey describes is Kant, with his "blank power," which has "integrated" scattered clues into a unified philosophy. Hamilton himself is not a figure of such "blank," overriding power, but rather a "polyhistor" whose "combining power" and vast reading make possible an erudite and synthesized philosophy. But De Quincey's narrator, with his "few facts," presents the impoverished reverse side of Hamilton's encyclopaedic knowledge. His doubts about his ability to grant "significancy and value" to the facts at his disposal become most apparent at the end of the first section of the essay, when he finds himself unable to say all that he had planned. It then becomes a question whether he can continue to write beyond the limits of the essay, a problem exacerbated by the fact that this is the last issue in that volume of the journal: "The several monthly divisions of the journal may *inosculate,* but not the several volumes. If any one volume were allowed to throw out great tap-roots into a succeeding *volume,* no section of the journal would ever be finished, or capable of being regarded as a separate and *independent* whole" (5: 316).

From this point, two different routes can be taken, but either involves a violation of the reader's conventional view of the text. De Quincey could acknowledge some kind of continuity that resides in his subject, the identity of Sir William Hamilton the man guaranteeing the identity of "Sir William Hamilton" the text. But to do so would ignore the conventional limits set by the idea of a magazine's "volume," a self-enclosed, autonomous space that is supposedly the receptacle of an independent, autonomous set of ideas. On the other hand, by conforming to the limitations set by the volume, he would appear to abjure any pretension to present more than a fragmentary and discontinuous set of observations in which, in a pictorial term that De Quincey employs in the text, the portrait of the man is reduced to a "silhouette" (5: 316).

In answer to this problem, De Quincey offers not a solution, but a new set of terms that puts a new metaphorical perspective on his activity: "Volume the fifteenth, it is true, cannot *succeed* to property in the fourteenth volume. It cannot receive it as an *inheritance.* But *that* will not prevent it from holding such property as an original endowment of its own. This article, for instance, cannot prolong its life into another volume; but it may rise again—it may receive a separate birth *de novo* in the future volume" (5: 317). De Quincey suggests a model of the continuity of meaning based on the image of inheritance. In a controlled text, the truth that is its property can be handed on without loss from one essay to the next. There is an unspoken implication that De Quincey is the father of his text, that the text is his child, and somehow partakes of a synecdochal relationship, having its own wholeness by being a part of his greater, engendering wholeness. But the image is withdrawn at once. He is not in a paternal position from which he would be able to "endow" or "will" meaning from one volume to the next. Instead he causes the text to "rise again," recalling the earlier image of the phoenix arising as a "memento of power in earthly things." Again this seems to emphasize the problem rather than to resolve it: rather than overcoming the problem of continuity from one volume to the next, a continuity that can be referred back to a controlling subject, the essay acts to question the possibility of continuity from one moment to the next.

De Quincey, recognizing this, begins the second part of the essay with a teasing challenge to the reader:

> Here I am, viz., in vol. xv. Never ruffle your own temper, reader, or mine, by asking *how*, and with what right. I *am* here. . . . As to saying that, though I may be here "de facto," nevertheless "de jure" I am not so; that I have no *locus standi*; that I am an usurper; an intruder; and that any contraband process by which I can have smuggled myself from vol. xiv. to this present vol. xv., is not of a kind that will bear looking into. Too true, I answer: very few things *will* bear looking into. (5: 318)

We are again faced with the insistence of *aporia:* "de facto" presence mocks "de jure" absence. De Quincey suggests that this is a normative situation, to be met with elsewhere in experience, by comparing it to an analogous historical experience, the struggle for royal legitimacy. Such legitimacy must come from a historical genesis and continuity, and so must make the same appeal to a synecdochal relation to the past as does the narrator.

Just as his claim to presence and to power smacks of usurpation, so the Glorious Revolution becomes an *aporia* of aggravating discontinuity in the text of English history:

> The revolution of 1688–9 will not bear looking into with eyes of philosophic purism. The object of the purist is to effect the devolution of the crown through a smooth lubricated channel known and conformable to old constitutional requisitions. . . . As it is, I grieve to say that there is a deadly hiatus in the harness which should connect the pre-revolutionary and post-revolutionary commonwealths of England. It is not merely a screw that is loose, it is a link that is missing. (5: 318)

Not only are the two commonwealths tied together in a knot that becomes an *aporia* when the discontinuity it conceals is revealed; there is as well a "deadly hiatus" between history itself and the "purism" of a historical discourse that must interpret the overthrow of a king into the "lubricated channel" of a narrative of orderly and legitimate succession. Both kinds of discourse, historical and logical, that appear in this essay are caught between claims for a mimetic fidelity to the subject they represent and the internal demands of their own consistency, neither of which is able to make its claims absolute.

This seems to be a paradigmatic situation in De Quincey, a moment of ironic self-awareness that occurs when a subject or a language is forced to acknowledge that its wholeness, and so its authority to speak, come only at the cost of abandoning the idea of an objective and originating truth to which it can return through the invoking of synecdochal relations. De Quincey, at the end of the essay, evokes the kind of projected logic that he would like to see Hamilton undertake, a project that we know was never undertaken because it exceeded the abilities of the man on whom he had laid the burden. But this evocation too is cast in an optative mood, and although it remains as an imaginative telos, it must be deferred indefinitely, not because of an individual's deficiencies, but because of the nature of language as it has been practically demonstrated in the essay.

Even De Quincey's evocation of this logic is expressed in terms that are undercut by the essay's historical scheme. He calls for a "revolution" that will bring about a "potent and life-giving logic . . . that will break down obstructions and impediments such as make even the right road impassable" (5: 341). But this revolution would have to follow exactly the same pattern as the revolution of 1688. It comes on the heels of a restoration, indeed would claim to be a "devolution" from it, but in this case the restoration is Kant's, the restoration of logic to its integrity as a formal science, an integrity that it had only in a fictionally located antiquity. In the essay's terms then, a further revolution in logic would "not bear much looking into." This is not to suggest that such a logic would be wrong (or indeed that De Quincey had anything other than an amateur's apprehension of the nature and use of logic), but only that it could not present its credentials on the basis of its fidelity to the logic of antiquity. Its only true credentials would rest on its ability to effect the forward movement of thought, that is, on its function rather than its genesis. And such a function could never truly be to create movement along the "right road," but only to give us a kind of map, one that describes the road even as we are in the act of creating it.

In the essay Hamilton is praised for a particular athletic ability, his standing leaps: "Sir William Hamilton's prowess did not exhibit itself in [boxing]. Professor Wilson had *thumped* his way to consideration; he had also *walked* and *run* into fame. But standing leaps it was—leaps upward without any advantage of a run—in which Sir. W.'s pre-eminence was illustrated" (5: 325). The ability to leap might well be translated into a positive image of discontinuity—and a prolonged, extended leap might become the narrative effect of floating noted above, a consciously maintained attitude of dissociation from the war of antinomies and a withdrawal into an interior space. The extended leap that becomes an effortless hovering (almost a romantic version of *sprezzattura*) also becomes a defining image for romantic irony in the critique of the European tradition offered by Kierkegaard. Kierkegaard faults irony for its failure to provide a

positive alternative to "historical actuality": "As irony contrives to overcome historical actuality by making it hover, so irony itself has in turn
become hovering. Its actuality is sheer potentiality."[16] The last sentence
recalls De Quincey's praise of Hamilton as a man who "stands in a possible
relation to all things" (5: 326). Kierkegaard sees such "sheer potentiality" as
a refusal of the demands for practical, ethical action. De Quincey instead
stresses that it is evidence of "potentia," of the ability to confront actuality
at each discrete point of time.

In fact, many of the characteristics of irony that Kierkegaard notes in
his subjects, Schlegel and Tieck—its hovering and eternally potential
stance, its will to live "hypothetically, subjunctively," its passivity, its equation of subjectivity and power—many of these are apparent in De Quincey's work. Baudelaire, one of De Quincey's more interesting critics, called
him "un des espirits les plus originaux, les plus vraiment humoristiques de
la vieille Angleterre," but says that De Quincey's talents do not fit our
ordinary conception of a genius necessarily generous, expansive, seeking
sympathy. Rather, he is gifted with "l'espirit envieux et quinteux du critique moral."[17] The word *quinteux* means "crotchety," and we can surely
identify the idiosyncratic features of De Quincey's temperament that
would support such a judgment. But the word also describes the crotch-
etiness of a horse that makes sudden and unexpected stops, rebelling
against the demand for continuous movement and progress. When applied to De Quincey's style rather than his personality, such a description
unites him to Schlegel's definition of irony as a "permanent parabasis," a
constant activity of discontinuity.[18] Each time that the pressure for unity or
continuity makes itself felt in "Sir William Hamilton," De Quincey manages to relieve that pressure by subjecting the idea of unity at issue to an
analysis that destroys it. Each version of unity—historical, logical, linguistic—is exposed as a fiction, freeing De Quincey for the wildly manipulative
use of language and thought that is apparent everywhere in the essay.

The power to be gained by such a distanced and self-conscious stance
is of a special kind, and we can begin to understand its nature by comparing what De Quincey has to say with other relevant visions of power. De
Quincey is famous for the distinction he makes between the "literature of
knowledge" and the "literature of power." He discusses it in two essays,
the *Letters to a Young Man* and *The Poetry of Pope*, and in both, the differences between the two are consistent and clear. The literature of knowledge is discursive, abstract, mechanical, while that of power is immediate,
affecting, organic, appealing to the whole man rather than to a disembodied faculty of reason. Like so much of the imagery in "Sir William
Hamilton," the two literatures are presented as antinomies, concepts
whose premises are irreconcilable.

De Quincey claims to have got the distinction from Wordsworth. But it
is interesting to note that, in the incident of the drowned man,

Wordsworth claims that he is presenting an illustration precisely of how the distinction between knowledge and power is to be overcome. In the passage that forms a transition between the "boy of Winander" and the "drowned man" episodes, Wordsworth imagines the children of the spot who have replaced him. In a voice that sounds like a much-softened version of Gray's "Eton College" ode, he blesses them: "May books and nature be their early joy!/And knowledge, rightly honor'd with that name,/ Knowledge not purchas'd with the loss of power."[19] The episode of the drowned man follows immediately. Wordsworth stands "mute" over the blank grave of the boy of Winander, as if the meaning of the incident has "baffled his best skill," but in the episode of the drowned man, his "inner eye" prefigures, indeed, almost calls forth the abstracted and hallowed vision of the body. The ability to create an image of death becomes an act of both knowledge and power, and seems to be compensation for the absolute silence and absence at the end of the "boy of Winander."

The idealist rhetoric exploited by continental practitioners of irony was not English but Hegelian, and Hegel, too, writes of a relationship between knowledge and power that does not involve a necessary loss in the one area or the other. One of the dialectical movements of his *Phenomenology* is the passage from "Force" to "Understanding" (*die Kraft* and *der Verstand*), terms that sound remarkably like those of De Quincey and Wordsworth. In the *Phenomenology*, Hegel describes how we see the phenomenal world around us alternately as a multiplicity of independent sensations—colors, tastes, textures—and as a unity of these sensations, the grain of salt, say, which "contains" whiteness, saltiness, and granular texture. The movement between these states of unity and diversity is what Hegel calls force, the way in which we attribute a binding power to apparently chaotic sensations. Having adopted this vision of a universe of interacting forces, the mind looks for the forces behind these forces and moves steadily toward a new vision of the world, based on laws and concepts. The ability to conceive the world in terms of "*law*, which is the *stable* image of unstable appearance,"[20] marks an advancing power to abstract and to think conceptually. As with Wordsworth, this is a knowledge not purchased with the loss of power. Rather, knowledge takes over power, or, in Hegel's terminology, "sublates" it, preserving the nature of power while simultaneously moving beyond it.

Hegel's ideas here are based on the physics of his day, which saw the universe as a medium of independent, universal qualities lodging themselves in particular, individual entities. The whiteness of the particular grain of salt, for instance, is only one manifestation of a universal property of whiteness. The fact that a piece of salt can have more than one property, can be simultaneously white *and* salty *and* granular, meant for Hegel that all of these properties "are absolutely porous,"[21] always able to interpenetrate. But this porousness is exactly what De Quincey denies in the idea of *aporia* and in the many instances of his essay that treat interpenetration as contamination and incongruity. By stressing the idea of *aporia*, the difficulty of the passage from experience to the laws of reason, De Quincey's irony in effect writes out a new contract. Knowledge is *necessarily* purchased with the loss of power, or more exactly, it is knowledge *of* the loss of power, of a break between the abstractions of reason and the world of experience.

Notes

1. Thomas De Quincey, *The Collected Writings of Thomas De Quincey*, ed. David Masson, 14 vols. (Edinburgh: Adam and Charles Black, 1889). All parenthetical references are to volume and page number of this edition.
2. Edward Young, *Night Thoughts on Life, Death, and Immortality*, ed. James R. Boyd, 4th ed. (New York: A. S. Barnes, 1856), p. 109.
3. Ibid., p. 79.
4. Ibid., p. 109.
5. William Wordsworth, *The Prelude, or Growth of a Poet's Mind*, ed. Ernest de Selincourt, 2d ed. rev. Helen Darbishire (Oxford: Clarendon Press, 1959), pp. 158–59.
6. Thomas De Quincey, *Recollections of the Lakes and the Lake Poets*, ed. David Wright (Harmondsworth: Penguin, 1970), p. 160.
7. Wordsworth, *The Prelude*, pp. 162–63.
8. Ibid.
9. Ibid.
10. Richard Onorato, *The Character of the Poet: Wordsworth in "The Prelude"* (Princeton, N.J.: Princeton University Press, 1971), pp. 191–95, discusses the two incidents in terms of Wordsworth's understanding of his own death.
11. Sir William Hamilton, "Philosophy of the Unconditioned," in his *Discussions on Philosophy and Literature, Education and University Reform*, 3d. ed. (Edinburgh: W. Blackwood, 1866), p. 14.
12. Background to Hamilton's relation to nineteenth-century philosophy can be found in John Passmore, *A Hundred Years of Philosophy*, 2d ed. (New York: Basic Books, 1966), pp. 122–24. See also Alan Ryan's introduction to John Stuart Mill, *An Examination of Sir William Hamilton's Philosophy and of the Principal Questions Discussed in his Writings* (Toronto: University of Toronto Press, 1979).
13. Mikhail Bakhtin, *Problems of Dostoevsky's Poetics*, trans. R. W. Rotsel (Ann Arbor, Mich.: Ardis, 1973), p. 90.
14. Hamilton, "Philosophy of the Unconditioned," p. 14, compares the conditioning presence of the mind to the "greyhound [who] cannot outstrip his shadow—the eagle [who cannot] outsoar the atmosphere in which he floats."
15. Sigmund Freud, "The Antithetical Sense of Primal Words," in *On Creativity and the Unconscious*, ed. Benjamin Nelson (New York: Harper and Row, 1958), pp. 55–62.
16. Søren Kierkegaard, *The Concept of Irony with Constant Reference to Socrates*, trans. Lee M. Capel (Bloomington: Indiana University Press, 1965), p. 296.
17. Charles Baudelaire, *Les Paradis artificiels* (Paris: Gallimard, 1961), pp. 209–10.
18. The concept is discussed in a treatment of irony by Paul De Man, "The Rhetoric of Temporality," in *Interpretation: Theory and Practice*, ed. Charles Singleton (Baltimore, Md.: Johns Hopkins University Press, 1969), p. 200.
19. Wordsworth, *The Prelude*, p. 158.
20. G. W. F. Hegel, *Phenomenology of Spirit*, trans. A. V. Miller (Oxford: Oxford University Press, 1977), p. 90.
21. Hegel, *Phenomenology*, p. 81. Hegel's original German reads: "Damit ist zugleich auch ihre reine Porosität oder ihr Aufgehobensein gesetzt." Hegel, *Phänomenologie des Geistes* (Frankfurt am Main: Suhrkamp Verlag, 1970), p. 110.

"The True Romance": Philosophy's Copernican Revolution and American Literary Dialectics

Evan Carton

"Life is not dialectics," writes Emerson in "Experience," an essay unsurpassed in the rhetorical energy with which it seeks to reconcile its author's dual commitment to the sensible and the intelligible, the thing and the idea. The tension between life and dialectics that Emerson's sentence contains (and releases) undercuts its ostensible assertion. More generally, it reflects the ambivalent structure of language itself, which is informed by the simultaneous unity and difference of its signs and significations. Finally, this tension suggests the ambivalent status of literary art, an enterprise which at once can only and can never "build . . . [its] own world (1: 76)[1] and one in which "life," a represented image of an absent essence, is necessarily dialectical. The irony of Emerson's sentence reverberates in the punning image that grounds his *descendental* argument in "Experience": the image of the *highway*. ("Everything good," he twice proclaims, "is on the highway"—3:62). Most ironic, perhaps, is the fact that Emerson's position here echoes that of his century's premier dialectician, G. W. F. Hegel, who, at the outset of his *Phenomenology of Spirit*, set philosophy the task of recovering a "solid and substantial" life for Spirit "by running together what thought has put asunder, by suppressing the differentiations of the Notion and restoring the feeling of essential being" (4–5).[2]

For Hegel, both human life and dialectical philosophy embody the principle that every relation—including the oppositions of Notion and substance, thought and feeling, and differentiation and unification that the passage above evokes—at once constitutes a division and a connection, implies antithesis and synthesis. The full realization of this principle by history, and (prospectively) by Hegel, is the phenomenology of Spirit: "in the phenomenology of Spirit," Hegel writes, rhetorically enforcing the relation between the world and his book, "each moment is the difference of knowledge and Truth, and is the movement in which that difference is cancelled" (491). The desire to realize (to recognize and to make real) the convergence of moment and movement, of absence and presence, the desire to sustain the symbiosis of difference and identity without sacrificing their meanings and thereby sacrificing the possibility of meaning itself, lies at the heart of Hegel. The very notion of a "phenomenology of spirit" bespeaks this desire and attempts to answer it. At the heart of Emerson lies the same desire, which, however, he expresses and pursues in terms more intimate to the American literary tradition that he shaped (but did not invent).[3] The final words of "Experience" announce and perform convergences very much like those which concern the *Phenomenology,* while defining the literary enterprise that dominates and long outlives the American Renaissance.

Emerson's essay concludes: "and the true romance which the world exists to realize will be the transformation of genius into practical power" (3:86). Modified by the adjective "true," "romance" here verges on paradoxical identification with the truth, with ultimate reality. Romance, however, remains (perhaps by definition) unrealized, and the phrase "the true romance" admits the skeptical reading "the pure, or ultimate, romance"; in any event, the truth that romance represents is present only through and as representation, as promise, as absence. "The world" itself partakes of the same ambivalence, standing here both as a substantial fact (the goad and bearer of romance's transformational enterprise and thus a separate and prior entity) and as the sign of an unfulfilled purpose (the "true romance" that it "exists to realize" and to which it is at once posterior and merely preliminary). Like Hegel's absolute Spirit, Emerson's "true romance" undergoes and comprises the process of its own realization. But whereas Hegel plainly identifies Spirit as the authentic source and the culminating truth of its odyssey, Emerson's depiction of romance—especially of its basis and its consummation—is equivocal. It must be so, for romance, however aspiring, remains an imaginative and linguistic mode that cannot claim the world as its construct, or even as its evolving form, without abandoning the category of the objectively real (and convicting itself of what Kant termed "dreaming idealism" [49])[4] or relinquishing its autonomy, and, in either case, obviating its critical and creative force. Romance's fulfillment, then, is not the self-recognition as Truth or Absolute Knowing that Hegel's Spirit achieves. Emerson's sentence finally yields no epistemological claim for romance, although it initially appears to be proceeding toward one, nor does it deliver the eschatology that it has certainly heralded. "Genius," in the end, does not unite with essence but is transformed, instead, into "practical power." And power is potency, or potential, which implies transformation while it defers realization. Romance, in Emerson's construction, foretells a potential transformation and harbors a transformative potency. It dwells, that is, in possibility, in dialectical process or self-conscious quest. Its crucial difference from Spirit, a difference whose implications I wish to explore in this essay, is that it dwells, ineluctably, in language.

I have protractedly entertained (some may say, bludgeoned) the conclusion of "Experience" in order to profile the informing issues and to suggest the rhetorical strategies of the literary enterprise, exemplified in (but not limited to) Emerson, Poe, Dickinson, and Hawthorne, that I shall call *romance*. A jointly critical and creative mode that self-consciousness sustains and self-referentiality annihilates, romance may be compared with the philosophical enterprise that helps furnish its context and with the self-reflective critical enterprise that is ours. My hope here is that, in juxtaposition, these three endeavors will prove mutually illuminating. In my use of the term *romance*, I mean to designate a shared kind of imaginative project or linguistic performance rather than a manifold ideology, while acknowledging that this project reflects and responds to the complex of concerns and values often capsulized as *romanticism*. My approach engages traditional formal definitions of *romance* as it recalls and endorses Friedrich Schlegel's sense of *Roman* as a protean modern form that challenged classical generic distinctions, an "inwardly disrupted" form (to borrow Hegel's description of the Unhappy Consciousness). The historical identity of romance as the fiction of speculation, the fiction of wandering or deviation that often turns out to have disguised and enabled a deliberate pursuit of *the* way, *the* home or *the* self, is also pertinent to the mode I take up; beyond this connection, though, my formulation seeks to elucidate and examine the larger recent claim that "romance is the structural core of all fiction."[5] Finally, I characterize the enterprise of these American writers as romance because the term has been so prevalent (but so unrevealing) in both the production and the criticism of American literature, a phenomenon that goes back to William Gilmore Simms and, what is more important, to the interested and subtly disingenuous self-explanations that have proved the most authoritative of Nathaniel Hawthorne's fictions.

A terse poem of Emily Dickinson's playfully but significantly tests the customary notion of American romance as an extravagant or unqualified prose narrative:

> No Romance sold unto
> Could so enthrall a Man
> As the perusal of
> His Individual One -
> 'Tis Fiction's - to dilute to Plausibility
> *Our* Novel - When 'tis small enough
> To Credit - 'Tisn't true!
>
> (669)[6]

Dickinson opposes the escapist literary commodity of the first line to another "Romance," the intimate imaginative formulation or representation of the self ("His Individual One") of line four. This latter romance is aligned, by syntactical implication, with precisely those things from which romance is usually differentiated: the novel and the truth. The intimacy and validity that the poem seems about to grant this romance, however, are caught up in the interlocking tensions of the last three lines. We turn to fiction for plausibility. Our own self-representations, though bent on truth, are too novel to command our belief. Now we feel the force of "enthrall" in its insidious doubleness: our romance captivates and, in its magnitude, paradoxically enslaves us by betraying the boundaries of our faith. That our credibility extends only to the limit of our bank balance ("Credit") precludes the purchase of truth; this suggestion, though, does not indict so much as it flatly recognizes the extent to which the material world—the world in which literature is produced and sold and read—conditions our imagination. Dickinson shows us the self divided against its aspiration to a novel vision, against its pursuit of what she elsewhere calls "Another way—to see" (627). But this division, reflected in the two opposed romances, is not totally unmitigated. " 'Tis Fiction's - to dilute to Plausibility / *Our* Novel," Dickinson writes, and dilution implies relationship, mixture. Through the adulterations and even the parodies of fiction, the essential imaginative truth—though still suspect and presentable only in the form of possibility—is paradoxically preserved. The true romance.

Beyond their reliance on Hawthorne's prefaces, traditional discussions of American romance have canonized a single passage from Henry James's preface to the New York Edition of *The American*.[7] There, James detects romance by "the kind of experience with which it deals—experience liberated, so to speak; experience disengaged, disembroiled, disencumbered, exempt from the conditions that we usually know to attach to it. . . ."[8] In fact, James's main concern in this piece is to disengage, disembroil, disencumber and exempt his own mature sensibility from an early novel that he now considers to be riddled with naivetés, while finding a rubric under which he might still grant the book sufficient merit to justify his continued fondness for it. Two pages earlier, though, ruminating less defensively on other writers, James offers a more interesting and fruitful discrimination that itself implies a failing of the celebrated one:

> The real represents to my perception the things we cannot possibly *not* know, sooner or later, in one way or another; it being but one of the accidents of our hampered state, and one of the incidents of their quality and number, that particular instances have not yet come our way. The romantic stands, on the other hand, for the things that, with all the facilities in the world, all the wealth and all the courage and all the wit and all the adventure, we never *can* directly know; the things that can reach us only through the beautiful circuit and subterfuge of our thought and our desire.[9]

The romantic, as James defines it here, is hardly unencumbered. That it proceeds by "circuit and subterfuge" indicates its constant apprehension of impediments and dangers; James's phrase even imputes a certain sophistical artifice, a self-conscious illegitimacy, to the nonetheless "beautiful" romantic enterprise. Its beauty lies for him, along with its inevitable failure, in the subtle shift from "represents" to "stands . . . for.".

The epistemological distinction that enables James to differentiate the real from the romantic is the foundation of Immanuel Kant's philosophy. James's "real" concerns itself with what Kant, in the *Prolegomena to Any Future Metaphysics*, repeatedly refers to as "possible experience" (46, 67, 72, 73). For Kant, phenomena—the forms that the understanding prescribes to and therefore recognizes in nature—are well characterized as "the things we cannot possibly *not* know, sooner or later," while noumena cannot be known "with all the facilities in the world" precisely because they do not inform those facilities but stand instead for what lies beyond them. Upon this division, this limitation, depends nothing less than the possibility of valid experience itself and a meaningful Beyond. Faced with a confirmative reciprocality between human understanding and external Absolute that, under the pressure of Hume's skeptical enquiries, has come to seem a vicious circle, Kant severs the tie. The transcendent truth that is confirmed or comprised by complexes of sensuous impressions, or by cognitive processes grounded in them, is either an illusion or a mere construction; the material reality that is ratified, in turn, by its correspondence with such a truth is either indeterminable or arbitrarily determined, immaterialized. In abandoning the idea of demonstrable correspondence, Kant salvages the knowability of the physical world and rescues metaphysical investigation from despair. But there lurks, at the heart of Kant's brilliant solution, an irony that Hegel pounced on and Kant himself uneasily circumnavigated: "objective reality" (the reality of objects in the world), although the only knowable reality, is preserved as "a form of our sensuous faculty of representation," as a complex of "mere appearances," as—in some lingering sense—a fiction, while "the field of chimeras" into which the mind stumbles by "wandering inadvertently beyond objects of experience" may be the field of truth (42, 74–75).

The Copernican Revolution in philosophy that Kant declared, then, is not exactly the recentering of the orbital relation of reality and understanding that his analogy implies. Rather, it seems an attempt to sustain a precarious double orbit in which reality (things-as-perceived) revolves around the understanding and this entire solar system itself revolves, remotely and blindly, around the dark source, the thing-in-itself. The delicacy and tension of these dynamics are manifested in Kant's vehement protestation against the charge of idealism, a defense that he considers "so valid and clear as even to seem superfluous, were there not incompetent judges, who . . . never judge of the spirit of philosophic nomenclature, but cling to the letter only" (48). Pronouncing his "transcendental idealism" an antidote to "the empirical idealism of Descartes" and "the mystical and visionary idealism of Berkeley," Kant continues:

> My idealism concerns not the existence of things (the doubting of which, however, constitutes idealism in the ordinary sense), since it never came into my head to doubt it, but it concerns the sensuous representation of things, to which space and time especially belong. Of these [viz., space and time], consequently of all appearances in general, I have only shown, that they are neither things (but mere modes of representation), nor determinations belonging to things in themselves. But the word "transcendental," which with me means a reference of our cognition, i.e., not to things, but only to the cognitive faculty, was meant to obviate this misconception. Yet rather than give further occasion to it by this word, I now retract it, and desire this idealism of mine to be called critical. (48–49)

The difficulties here are not merely terminological; on the contrary, Kant is laboring to make his language preserve a volatile dialectic. He proposes an idealism that does not threaten things in themselves and that consciously leaves room for a realism in relation to which it is the opposite of transcendent. The word *transcendental* strains against the limits within which he has confined it and invites confusion. Finally, Kant offers an alternative denomination for his philosophy, *critical idealism*. It is an appropriately paradoxical substitution and a label that conveys the stress of an idealism that holds something apart from itself to criticize or turns constantly back upon itself to examine its own premises and define its bounds.

Time and again in the *Prolegomena*, Kant admits the presence of "something seductive in our pure concepts of the understanding, which tempts us to a transcendent use,—a use which transcends all possible experience" (76). Under such pressure, "the understanding inadvertently adds for itself to the house of experience a much more extensive wing, which it fills with nothing but creatures of thought, without ever observing that it has transgressed with its otherwise lawful concepts the bounds of their use" (76). The issues of transgression (moral, conceptual, and linguistic) and the definition or construction of a home, linked in this passage, are also crucial and connected in American romance.[10] They will persist in this essay, as they do for Kant, who later acknowledges that "the understanding is forced out of its sphere" by reason's need to complete its own, that the mind *commits itself* to "an unavoidable illusion" (98). Against this bleak necessity, however, Kant once again pits the notion of "boundary," skillfully and suggestively representing it not as a line of defense but as "a narrow belt"[11] of mediation:

> If we connect with the command to avoid all transcendent judgments of pure reason, the command (which apparently conflicts with it) to

proceed to concepts that lie beyond the field of its immanent (empirical) use, we discover that both can subsist together, but only at the boundary of all lawful use of reason. (128)

A boundary, Kant insists, "is something positive, which belongs as well to that which lies within, as to the space that lies without the given complex" (133). It is at once a division and a connection, the locus of relation.

Dickinson defines this boundary in poem after poem. It is the place where transformation seems most imminent and most intensely lacking, where the mind is enthralled by its proximity to truth and by its consciousness of the enormity of their difference:

> My Cocoon tightens - Colors tease -
> I'm feeling for the Air -
> A dim capacity for Wings
> Demeans the Dress I wear -
>
> A power of Butterfly must be -
> The Aptitude to fly
> Meadows of Majesty implies
> And easy Sweeps of Sky -
>
> So I must baffle at the Hint
> And cipher at the Sign
> And make much blunder, if at last
> I take the clue divine -
>
> (1099)

Swelling toward transformation and transcendence, the speaker here experiences her limitations as all the more constrictive. The poem suspends her between mastery of the air and suffocation, but the loss of her present bounded life seems to be more certain than her assumption of a freer one. Her "dim capacity for Wings" debases the trappings of her world, unfits her for them and even empties them of meaning ("Demeans"). Left to mere presumption, she strives to infer a presence from its poignantly felt absence, the reality of power from her capacity for it and her intuition of a similar aptitude in the landscape.[12] The final stanza perpetuates this limbo and leaves the speaker determined to sustain herself on hints and clues and to take her bafflement as a prelude to ultimate realization. Meanwhile, in self-conscious recognition of her quest's difficulty, obscurity, and risk, she urges herself (or admits her compulsion) to "cipher at the Sign"—to labor, through the use of figures, at its comprehension; to employ guarded and mysterious writing toward its revelation; to become as nothing before it.

If the poem just considered affirms, however equivocally, that a capacity for knowledge of the divine may be attained at the boundary of human experience, others satirize such claims and represent the mind's power of transcendence as inadequate and finally illusory:

A transport one cannot contain
May yet a transport be -
Though God forbid it lift the lid -
Unto its Ecstasy!

A Diagram - of Rapture!
A sixpence at a Show -
With Holy Ghosts in Cages!
The *Universe* would go!

(184)

The opening lines of this poem seem affirmative, but their sense is somewhat skewed: would not "transport," taken as "rapture" or "ecstasy," *depend* upon its power to overwhelm containment, restriction? Lines three and four answer this dilemma and force a revision of our probable reading of "contain." God does thwart and restrict the transport that man cannot *accommodate*, cannot embody. The irony with which the poem undercuts its reader's assumption and its own aspiration is sharpened on the double edge of line three: "God forbid" may be a report or an entreaty or both. Depending upon the interpretation of this line, the second stanza either depicts the state of balked transport or describes the capacity that transport could fulfill in the absence of God's (merciful) veto. Whichever is the case, its characterization is a mocking one (as the battery of exclamation points suggests). The understanding or imagination can render only an obviously inadequate diagram of rapture, can approach divine mysteries only by turning them into cheap circus acts. The futility and perversity of such an enterprise are epitomized in the image of encaged Holy Ghosts. Perhaps playing on another meaning of "transport," Dickinson gives us, throughout, not a vision of transcendence and ecstasy but various forms of imprisonment and exile.

Kant's sense of "boundary" as a locus of relation is virtually hypostatized by Hawthorne as the "neutral territory" of romance, the enchanted meeting ground of the actual and the imaginary (1:36).[13] Legitimate artistic power for Hawthorne, imaginative truth, may obtain only in this convergence; the alienation of the two terms or the vanquishment of one by the other renders art a dream, a slave, or a sham. In his prefaces, however, Hawthorne fails to stake out the stable territory he envisions. Rather, like Dickinson in "A transport one cannot contain," he alternately charges his enterprise with impotence and transgression. The preface to *The House of the Seven Gables* claims for the work "a certain latitude" but insists, too, that "it must rigidly subject itself to laws" (2:1). Pursuing the legal metaphor, Hawthorne proposes "to keep undeviatingly within his immunities" and seems concerned to establish the definition of "a literary crime" (2:1)—the phrase itself, permitting a stress on either its adjective or its noun, neatly bespeaks impotence *and* transgression. The preface's concluding paragraph repeatedly denies, in terms no less significant for their playfulness, the narrative's illegal appropriation of or infringement upon existent property and other "realities of the moment" and offers the defense that the seven-gabled house is composed solely "of materials long in use for constructing castles in the air" (2:3). In the next preface, Hawthorne equivocates about the connection between Blithedale and Brook Farm, contending that the historical commune is "altogether incidental" to his artistic purpose and warning against "too close a comparison" of the imaginary and the actual (3:1). He convicts his own art of imposture and illusion, while betraying its balked desire for meaningful relation, when he claims to seek a "Faery Land, so like the real world, that, in a suitable remoteness, one cannot well tell the difference" (3:2). So exploded is the notion of a "neutral territory" by the preface to *The Marble Faun* that the Atlantic Ocean now separates, for Hawthorne, its intended inhabitants, and Italy must afford him his "poetic or fairy precinct, where actualities [are not] so terribly insisted upon as they are, and must needs be, in America" (4:3). The dominant suggestion of this passage—that the weight of American actualities inevitably crushes imaginative enterprise—is countered by the intimation of "must needs be" that Hawthorne perceives the threat to be reciprocal. Accordingly, he punctuates his prefatory confession of impotent exile with the boast that, on his own creative authority, he has exercised "a quite unwarrantable freedom" and "laid felonious hands" on the actual productions of several living American sculptors (4:4).

Jacques Derrida, articulating the problem that romance embodies and cannot afford to solve, identifies "two interpretations of interpretation, of structure, of sign, of freeplay":

> The one seeks to decipher, dreams of deciphering, a truth or an origin which is free from freeplay and from the order of the sign, and lives like an exile the necessity of interpretation. The other, which is no longer turned toward the origin, affirms freeplay and tries to pass beyond man and humanism, the name man being the name of that being who, throughout the history of metaphysics or of ontotheology—in other words, through the history of all of his history—has dreamed of full presence, the reassuring foundation, the origin and the end of the game.[14]

Derrida's first interpretation, living like an exile its own necessity, is already conscious of itself as interpretation, but self-consciousness is precisely self-exile for it because its source of meaning (truth, the unconditioned, the noninterpretational) is that which it cannot be. Interestingly, this description of interpretation bears a close resemblance to Georg Lukács's description of the novel as "an expression of [man's] transcendental homelessness" in the modern world, the product and vehicle "of an age in which the extensive totality of life is no longer directly given, in which the immanence of meaning in life has become a problem, yet which still thinks in terms of totality."[15] The irony of literature in the circumstances that Lukács outlines, the same irony that informs the practice of criticism,[16] lies in its assumption of a quest, its investment in an object, which by identity it cannot realize. Such literature is doubly alienated: self-denied its transcendent object, it can neither give full assent to the free play of its constructive power, for to take this second course—to become the equivalent of Derrida's second interpretation—would be to abandon its fundamental dream of presence and even, as Derrida suggests, to obliterate the concept of self that rests on that foundation. Thus, at the end of *The Marble Faun*, Hawthorne suspends his American artists and narrator between Rome—the lost "central home of the world," now the uninhabitable "home of art" (4:213, 214)—and their native home; the neutral territory that they have gained is clearly a no man's land, the putative locus of relation a doubly empty space.

Hegel fills this void with motion. If consciousness's alienation from both poles of its divided identity can be seen as a centripetal movement toward a higher, depolarized self-consciousness, then apparent loss is becoming gain and self-exile is actually a phase of self-recovery. This insight, this strategy, is revealed early in the *Phenomenology*:

> The disparity which exists in consciousness between the "I" and the substance which is its object is the distinction between them, the *negative* in general. This can be regarded as the *defect* of both, though it is their soul, or that which moves them. That is why some of the ancients conceived the *void* as the principle of motion, for they rightly saw the moving principle as the *negative*, though they did not as yet grasp that the negative is the self. (21)

The life of Spirit, Hegel writes, "wins its truth only when, in utter dismemberment, it finds itself. . . . This tarrying with the negative is the magical power that converts it into being" (19). Suspended in the void between its two homes—the wings of Kant's divided "house of experience," the seemingly antithetical loci of selfhood—the Hegelian consciousness recognizes itself, recognizes its predicament as itself. Tarrying with the negative, it finds itself to be the difference between the projective poles of its identity and thus incorporates that difference, re-members itself. Hegel describes this form of self-consciousness, the form that most suggestively characterizes the American writers and texts that I would affiliate with romance, as "one which *knows* that it is the dual consciousness of itself, as self-liberating, unchangeable, and self-identical, and as self-bewildering and self-perverting, [one which] is the awareness of this self-contradictory nature of itself" (126). The incorporation of difference is still preliminary, for Hegel, to any ultimate eradication; consciousness's initial self-identification as a dual-natured being only internalizes its division:

This *unhappy, inwardly disrupted* consciousness, since its essentially contradictory nature is for it a *single* consciousness, must for ever have present in the one consciousness the other also; and thus it is driven out of each in turn in the very moment when it imagines it has success- fully attained to a peaceful unity with the other. . . . Since it is, to begin with, only the *immediate unity* of the two and so takes them to be, not the same, but opposites, one of them, viz. the simple Unchangeable, it takes to be the *essential* Being; but the other, the protean Changeable, it takes to be the unessential. The two are, for the Unhappy Conscious- ness, alien to one another; and because it is itself the consciousness of this contradiction, it identifies itself with the changeable conscious- ness, and takes itself to be the unessential Being. (126–27)

In view of Hegel's determined pursuit of ultimate unity, his elaborate tracking of Spirit through its myriad polarities to the absolute self-knowing in which it obliterates the Kantian boundary between subject and truth, it is ironic that some of his closest readers distinguish two *Phenomenologies*. Jacob Loewenberg, citing the implicit discrimination in Jean Hyppolite's French translation between the *Phenomenology* of consciousness, self- consciousness, and reason and the one that comprises the second half of Hegel's work and deals directly with Spirit, characterizes the first as "a humanistic" and the second as "a superhumanistic *Phenomenology*."[17] Loewenberg's demur matches a central apprehension of romance, one that is most basic and most evident in the writings of Dickinson and Poe: the apprehension that the moment of fulfillment in the quest for the absolute, the moment of the self's integration with God, is the moment of the self's annihilation and meaning's irredeemable loss. And indeed, Hegel vividly anticipates such a fate for the individual self in accounts sometimes worthy (rhetorically, if not ideologically) of Michel Foucault:

The single individual is incomplete Spirit, a concrete shape in whose whole existence *one* determinateness predominates, the others being present only in blurred outline. In a Spirit that is more advanced than another, the lower concrete existence has been reduced to an incon- spicuous moment; what used to be the important thing is now but a trace; its pattern is shrouded to become a mere shadowy outline. (16)

Although its essence is the universal, individuality nonetheless "maintains itself at the expense of the universal"; the self has meaning only in incom- pletion, in the ongoing dialectical process, for "this dividedness of the differenceless fluid medium is just what establishes individuality" (108). The self's dialectical crossing into the final "beyond" collapses the dialectic, collapses the distinction between "here" and "beyond" or "self" and "other," and thus empties these terms of meaning. A remarkable passage, which occurs in the *Phenomenology* on the verge of Spirit's advancement from self-consciousness to reason, illustrates the collapse of the concepts "life," "actuality," "individuality," and "form" in their completed integration wih their opposites:

> Consciousness, therefore, can only find as a present reality the *grave* of its life. But because this grave is itself an *actual existence* and it is contrary to the nature of what actually exists to afford a lasting possession, the presence of that grave, too, is merely the struggle of an enterprise doomed to failure. But having learned from experience that *the grave* of its *actual* unchangeable Being has *no actuality*, that this *vanished individuality*, because it has vanished, is not the true individuality, consciousness will abandon its quest for the unchangeable individuality as an *actual* existence, or will stop trying to hold on to what has vanished. Only then is it capable of finding individuality in its genuine or universal form. (132)

This is the redemption toward which the *Phenomenology*, championed by Jean Hyppolite as "the science of ordinary experience and of ordinary language," directs its efforts—a redemption that, because it simultaneously presents itself as an annihilation, forces Hyppolite to conclude his discussion by confessing that "there is something which is not redeemable, and I would not follow Hegel to the end; I can't."[18]

No writer in English has imagined the implications of the *Phenomenology* so vividly, and with such force of fascination and horror, as Edgar Allan Poe, whose dialectical representations of man's progress toward the Absolute reveal some fundamental relationships between literary and philosophical modes of romantic enterprise. (The probability that Poe never studied Hegel's text only enhances the significance of these relationships.)[19] Poe's typical narrative, in fact, involves the pursuit of an experience beyond redemption or the desperate attempt to redeem—to rescue, recover, repent, or report—such an experience. His art explores the human desire to transgress ordinary spatial, temporal, moral, conceptual, and even ontological boundaries, but more crucial still is its self-conscious questioning of the nature, the status, and the sheer possibility of any linguistic expression beyond these boundaries. Thus Poe's narrators are balloonists, addicts, hypnotics, future historians, victims of mental or physical disease, murderers of victims intimately associated with themselves, doomed or dead men, and disembodied spirits. Situated on or over the brink of human existence, they seek to win essential selfhood in self-abandonment and to voice ultimate meanings in the collapse of both meaning and voice.

Such abandonment and such collapse necessarily attend the final realization of the Unity that Poe champions in his criticism, strives for in his fiction, and apotheosizes in his metaphysical prose poem *Eureka*. This "Book of Truths," which Poe presents "as a Romance" and dedicates "to those who put faith in dreams as in the only realities" (16:183), almost seems a parodic redaction of the *Phenomenology of Spirit* and is a self-parodic version of the same endeavor—"self-parodic," not because Poe scorns his own enterprise but because he can sustain it only in the mode of self-parody. Like Hegel, Poe demands a historically embodied metaphysics that proceeds from an original to an eventual identity of subject and object through phases of alienation and incomplete union. Spirit, the source and the fulfillment of this identity, informs the material universe through its self-differentiation or, in *Eureka*'s term, its "irradiation." Spirit, then, may be defined as "the ultimate or unparticled matter" (5: 245–46) which, in Poe's religiophysical cosmogony, undergoes a consecrated big bang that generates the material universe by setting in motion the dialectic of attraction and repulsion through which it can exist. For Poe, the phenomenology of Spirit is not only the story of consciousness, or even of human history, but is literally the story of the cosmos as well. And, like his own lower-case imitations, its one structural principle is symmetry or *"reciprocity of adaptation"*: the energy of attraction (the irradiated particles' "spiritual passion . . . for oneness") produced as a consequence of the original act of irradiation equals and eventually exceeds the waning energy of repulsion or diffusion and precipitates a reflective reaction, a *"progressive collapse"* (16: 300) that leads back to the original Unity:

> I have already alluded to that absolute *reciprocity of adaptation* which is the idiosyncracy of the divine Art—stamping it divine. Up to this point of our reflections, we have been regarding the electrical influence as a something by dint of whose repulsion alone Matter is enabled to exist in that state of diffusion demanded for the fulfillment of its purposes:—so far, in a word, we have been considering the influence in question as ordained for Matter's sake—to subserve the objects of matter. With a perfectly legitimate reciprocity, we are now permitted to look at Matter, as created *solely for the sake of this influence*—solely to serve the objects of this spiritual Ether. Through the aid—by the means—through the agency of Matter, and by dint of its heterogeneity—is this Ether manifested—is *Spirit individualized*. It is merely in the development of this Ether, through heterogeneity, that particular masses of Matter become animate—sensitive—and in the ratio of their heterogeneity;—some reaching a degree of sensitiveness involving what we call *Thought* and thus attaining Conscious Intelligence.
>
> In this view, we are enabled to perceive Matter as a Means—not as an End. Its purposes are thus seen to have been comprehended in its diffusion; and with the return into Unity these purposes cease. The absolutely consolidated globe of globes would be *objectless*:—therefore not for a moment could it continue to exist. Matter, created for an end, would unquestionably, on fulfillment of that end, be Matter no longer.

Let us endeavor to understand that it would disappear, and that God
would remain all in all. (16: 308–9)[20]

"The Universe is a plot of God" (16: 292), Poe affirms, allowing the
multiple pun on "plot" to convey his complex and uneasy understanding
of the fact. The Universe, as *Eureka* represents it, is God's design or intention as well as the actual layout, the graphic distribution, of God; finally, it
is the sinister machination by which God at once bestows and withholds
his identity, by which he invites the individual to a divine convergence
whose price is the individual's existence. As an American and a literary
artist, Poe cannot quite relinquish his commitment to the integral and
independent self, and thus his work communicates the devastating irony
along with the Hegelian sublimity of "finding individuality in its genuine
or universal form." Man's inability to realize his spiritual identity, to survive Spirit's transformation, is the underlying joke of Poe's gruesome
comic tales in which individuals are negatively conceived as mere "masses
of Matter" that can impassively endure dismemberment, evisceration, and
suffocation. The violence of these tales is largely self-directed, meant to
lacerate Poe's own metaphysical ideals and pretensions. Even his early
blueprint for *Eureka*, "Mesmeric Revelation," betrays the inconceivability of
its central metaphysical claim, as in this exchange between hypnotic (V)
and hypnotist (P):

V: Divested of corporate investiture, [man] were God. . . .
P: You say that divested of the body man will be God?
V: (after much hesitation) I could not have said this; it is an absur-
    dity. . . . Man thus divested *would be* God—would be unindi-
    vidualized. But he can never be thus divested. (5:249)

Like "unparticled matter," undifferentiated language is self-
annihilating or simply absurd. Nonetheless, Poe sees the poetic principle
as the effort to embody in language "that Loveliness whose very elements,
perhaps, appertain to eternity alone" (14:274). That such loveliness is necessarily nameless is the ironic knowledge with which Poe's tales repeatedly
struggle. His narrators discover the inexpressibility of the most profound
insights and experiences in the moment of their attainment, or else they
and their voices are lost altogether on attainment's brink. The aesthetic
ideal of sensation or "effect" is ultimately incompatible with sense, with
meaning. "Ms. Found in a Bottle," by virtue of its conspicuous display of
this incompatibility, is Poe's prototypical tale—the tale that is named (and
simultaneously rendered nameless) by an alien title that flaunts its
unverifiability and further implies that it is legitimately incommunicable.
Poe's enterprise requires what the experimenting mesmerist in "The Facts
in the Case of M. Valdemar" tries to obtain, a speaker suspended "*in*

articulo mortis," but all that is likely to flow from such a man, as the wry last words of the story reveal, is a "liquid mass of loathsome—of detestable putridity" (6:155, 166). Such fluency is not merely unpalatable but also unreadable, and while Poe values and often courts unreadability (his "Philosophy of Composition" prescribes "a suggestive indefinitiveness of meaning" as the path to spirituality in art, and "The Man of the Crowd" opens and closes with the observation that the deepest text or secret "does not permit itself to be read"—16:28 and 4:134) he knows that his own language, as long as it remains language, will frustrate and mock that goal. In "How to Write a Blackwood Article," a vicious parody of his own literary practice, Poe has his Mr. Blackwood reduce the criterion of "indefinitiveness" to a matter of calligraphy: "In the first place your writer of intensities must have very black ink, and a very big pen, with a very blunt nib. . . . You may take it for granted, that when manuscript can be read it is never worth reading" (2:273). As to subject matter, the editor suggests that one "tumble out of a balloon, or be swallowed up in an earthquake . . . or run over by an omnibus, or bitten by a mad dog, or drowned in a gutter" (2:275) and then simply record one's sensations. The advice reflects Poe's sense of language's futility and of its extraordinary potential.

Absolute Knowing, the goal of the *Phenomenology,* entails Spirit's *"withdrawal into itself* in which it abandons its outer existence and gives its existential shape over to recollection" (492)—actual cosmic re-collection, for Poe. Any lesser satisfaction "remains burdened with the antithesis of a beyond" (478). But this ultimate satisfaction, which marks the end of history and of expression, cannot be won in history or in language, both of which depend upon partiality or distinction and upon the "beyond" that preserves the meaning of "here." Hegel recognizes in the forms of human experience and expression their constitutive dependence upon the particular, but he also sees in art—especially in poetry—a preternaturally acute opposing tendency. The value of art, he suggests in *The Philosophy of Fine Art,* lies in the comparative insubstantiality of its objects; already abstracted from the world of experience, these both exemplify the possibility of breaking through form to discover idea and, as represented and spiritualized objects, are themselves easily and willingly broken.[21] Literature epitomizes art's tendency toward self-negation or self-transcendence, for its medium—being "mere sign without independent significance"[22]—is the most artificial and the least palpable. Locating his ironically enabling absence in the ephemerality of the spoken word, rather than in the orphanhood of writing, Hegel characterizes speech as "a vanishing existence . . . [in which] objectivity remains too much shut up within the self, falls short of attaining a lasting shape and is, like Time, no longer immediately present in the very moment of its being present" (432). Because art—at least its highest type, romantic art, whose truest medium is language—"points beyond itself,"[23] Hegel grants it a penultimate station on the path of Spirit's self-satisfaction. Albert Hofstadter capsulizes its situation:

> [T]he destiny of art lies beyond the fulfillment of any task that art can accomplish by its own means. . . . And the task of romantic art is precisely to express this expressive impossibility, to show sensuously the ultimate inability of the sensuous to satisfy the spirit's true need. . . . Sensible form must be brought to show the negation of its very own self as a possible vehicle of spiritual truth.[24]

For the American writers of romance, art also stands in a preliminary and paradoxical relationship to Truth. As artists rather than philosophers, however, they cannot accept the notion of a wholly disembodied (inexpressible) Absolute or believe in the pure negativity of their enterprise. The indissolubility, for them, of the link between conception and expression prescribes their rejection of Spirit's final Hegelian abandonment of "outer existence." "Cohesive as the Spirit," their linguistic constructs must serve doubly as means and end. And if, as mere construct, art cannot comprise but can only obstruct Truth's realization, it nonetheless does constitute Truth's vehicle and preserver. The significance of its mere signs, Emerson claims, lies in their function "as signs of power" (2:363), tokens of a potential that finds its precarious existence in the tension between man's Kantian and Hegelian alternatives, self-exile and self-subsumption. Romance, then, the art of this potential, must both transgress and sustain the boundary between the sensible and the intelligible, must at once enact and thwart its own ultimate fulfillment. Emerson attempts to capture such dialectical energy—such mediative tension between absence and presence, liberation and limitation—in the concept of transition. "Our strength is transitional, alternating," begins a passage in the essay "Plato," which proceeds to a striking illustration:

> [T]he experience of poetic creativeness . . . is not found in staying at home, nor yet in travelling, but in transitions from one to the other, which must therefore be adroitly managed to present as much transitional surface as possible. (4:55–56)

Emerson's "transitional surface" exists only in and as the self-conscious process of its representation. It is the product and the manifestation of the struggle between emergence (traveling) and reflexivity, between performance and criticism. It is the locus of possibility defined by the interaction of known and unknown, existence and essence, that the imaginative feat of absenting presence (home) while presenting absence (Beyond) affords. Art's relation to reality, writes Northrop Frye, "is neither direct, nor negative, but potential";[25] romance understands this relation, and both actively exploits and self-consciously "thematizes" it. Moreover, the literary mode that is romance tests the capabilities and reflects the enterprise of language itself. For language only functions by presenting what is absent, an office epitomized in the instance that Tzvetan Todorov notes: "language alone enables us to conceive what is always absent: the supernatural."[26] At the same time, language absents what is present or, in Emerson's phrase, "abate[s] somewhat of the angular distinctness of objects" (1:47). It rarefies as it represents the material world. Thus, in *Nature*, Emerson places language between natural and spiritual fact, at once a boundary and a vehicle of transgression or transformation,[27] at once—to borrow the opposing terms of two important critics of American literature—the medium of a self-authorized "world elsewhere" and "the most thoroughly collective and environmental pressure the creative mind knows."[28] Romance is the literary art that sets itself the task of illustrating language's enterprise; insisting (as art) on its own substantial identity while serving (as language) to join experience and imagination, thing and idea, it is aptly characterized as a "transitional surface."

Beyond the fragility of this surface noted by Hegel, the writers of romance recognize the illusiveness that its dependence on adroit management implies. Another of Emerson's images, one that approximates (and virtually glosses) the image of "transitional surface" and occurs in a similar context, more overtly conveys such recognition: "The party-colored wheel," Emerson observes, "must revolve very fast to appear white" (3:57). Synthesis, here, can only be the product and process of the "eternal agility" that Schlegel celebrates in his aphoristic doctrine of romantic irony.[29] Indeed, American romance, informed by a kindred desire to generate and preserve a relation—or the possibility of relation—between the real and the ideal, exemplifies many of Schlegel's principles. Sustained in its "continuous alternation of self-creation and self-destruction," romance answers Schlegel's call for a literature able to "mingle and amalgamate . . . genius and criticism,"[30] and, in so doing, suggests the fundamental likeness of literary and critical enterprise. Each represents an object, whether a world or a text, that it can neither contrive nor afford to present immediately. For each, as for Hegel's "Force," power resides in an expression "which at the same time is nothing else than a supersession" (86) of the thing expressed. Thus literature and criticism stand in ironic relation to both their sources and their aspirations, but also stand as acts of faith. Like faith (Dickinson's "Pierless Bridge" [915]), they depend upon difference and span it, and like faith they require self-conscious examination and continual renewal to keep from attenuating into mere charm or ossifying into mere dogma.

The jointly critical and creative mode I have called romance, an enterprise that exploits language's capacity to preserve dialectical relations from the equally deadly detachment and integration of their terms, informs the diverse literary productions of the American Renaissance. The model in-

stance, perhaps, of this mode is a text that substantively concerns "relation" and recalls the passion of "romance." It is Emerson's "Friendship,"
and I invoke it to illustrate and summarize my discussion.

We are exhilarated and our sense of belonging in a harmonious universe is enhanced, Emerson begins, by "the indulgence of [our] human
affection" (2:191). But the illustration that follows his introductory en-
comium is unsettling. Not a close friend but a "commended stranger"
comes on the scene:

> He stands to us for humanity. He is what we wish. Having imagined
> and invested him, we ask how we should stand related in conversa-
> tion and action with such a man, and are uneasy with fear. The same
> idea exalts conversation with him. We talk better than we are
> wont. . . . But as soon as the stranger begins to intrude his partialities,
> his definitions, his defects into the conversation, it is all over. He has
> heard the first, the last and best he will ever hear from us. He is no
> stranger now. Vulgarity, ignorance, misapprehension are old ac-
> quaintances. (2:192–93)

The exhilarating relation here is our relation to our imaginative projection,
the stranger whom we have "invested" with broad, symbolic significance.
Inevitably, the prospective wholeness of our intercourse is broken up by
the first intrusion of his "partialities," which, in turn, uncover ours. There
is a wry self-awareness—indicative of the kind of double consciousness
that pervades "Friendship" and that finally is crucial to the enterprise of
romance—in the last two sentences I cite above. When the statement "He
is no stranger now" signals the death rather than the birth of satisfying
relation, a circumstance that the characterization of vulgarity, ignorance,
and misapprehension as "old acquaintances" immediately reiterates,
Emerson risks—and knows he risks—making a mockery of the very idea of
friendship.

Emerson's peculiar approach to his topic leads him, in the next paragraph, to offer a description of the effects of friendship which, by its
painstaking hyperbole, nearly confesses friendship to be a delusion breed-
ing further delusions. "The moment we indulge our affections, the earth is
metamorphosed; there is no winter and no night; all tragedies, all ennuis
vanish,—all duties even; nothing fills the proceeding eternity but the forms
all radiant of beloved persons" (2: 193). The echo, in this context, of the
earlier phrase about indulging human affection invites us to reconsider the
activity and, perhaps, to discover self-indulgence rather than the bestowal
of affection to be its essential ingredient. But, if Emerson here implicitly
allows that friendship may prove mere delusion and self-indulgence, he
simultaneously demonstrates what extraordinary criteria one may possibly
set for it and invest it with the potential to meet. That he recognizes both
what he stands to lose, or already has lost, and what he stands to gain by

enforcing such criteria is indicated in the very next sentence: "Let the soul be assured that somewhere in the universe it should rejoin its friend, and it would be content and cheerful alone for a thousand years" (2: 193).

As the essay continues, Emerson more openly acknowledges his awareness that he is conceiving friendship as the projection of an individual imagination; correspondingly, the issue of the projection's substantiation by another, to the extent that it ever was immediate, becomes more remote:

> [T]hus we weave social threads of our own, a new web of relations; and, as many thoughts in succession substantiate themselves, we shall by and by stand in a new world of our own creation, and no longer strangers and pilgrims in a traditionary globe. (2: 194)

Thoughts substantiate themselves as imaginative activity gains momentum, but, since we never exclusively inhabit the world we create, we cannot sustain our belief in its "new web of relations." "I have often had fine fancies about persons which have given me delicious hours; but the joy ends in the day; it yields no fruit" (2: 195). Neither the "world of our own creation" (in which real relation is annihilated by our thought's production of our friend) nor the daily world (in which the relation we conceive is attenuated in quality to the point of dissolution) will suffice; only the interaction of the two, managed through the perpetual alternation of one's focus, can sustain the possibility of friendship. This is the revelation or confession on which "Friendship" pivots and which, starting with the following critical passage, Emerson seeks to honor in its remaining pages:

> Friendship, like the immortality of the soul, is too good to be believed. The lover, beholding his maiden, half knows that she is not verily that which he worships; and in the golden hour of friendship we are surprised with shades of suspicion and unbelief. We doubt that we bestow on our hero the virtues in which he shines, and afterwards worship the form to which we have ascribed this divine inhabitation. In strictness, the soul does not respect men as it respects itself. In strict science all persons underlie the same condition of an infinite remoteness. Shall we fear to cool our love by mining for the metaphysical foundation of this Elysian temple? Shall I not be as real as the things I see? If I am, I shall not fear to know them for what they are. . . . I must hazard the production of the bald fact amidst these pleasing reveries, though it should prove an Egyptian skull at our banquet. (2: 196–97)

The "bald fact"—both the fact of the actual friend and the fact that he does not incarnate the ideal shape that we envision—*must* be introduced into the essay at this point to prevent its consumption of friendship amidst its "pleasing reveries" and to keep Emerson himself (and, consequently, the things he sees as well) "real." But the introduction of the fact no more invalidates the reverie than the reverie does the fact. On the contrary, the two stand by virtue of their dialectic. The lover "half knows" that his beloved is not what he worships because he recognizes that his worship transforms her into something she is not and that its true object, therefore, is its own power of transformation. Yet she both provides the occasion for this worship and, by her continued, untransformed existence, resists its voracity, thus sustaining its engagement with the world it has not made, retaining her claim to be its object (the other half, perhaps, of the lover's knowledge) and preventing it from achieving the complete self-referentiality that would mark the metamorphosis of power into power-lessness. Similarly, our actual friend both stimulates the act of imagination by which we contrive to lessen the "infinite remoteness" that "in strict science all persons underlie," and, failing to enact with us quite the union we imagine, protects the distance between person and person, or between mind and world, which allows for relation. "Pleasing reveries" and "bald fact," then, may be taken to be mutually creative and mutually critical. By so taking them, and by interweaving them successfully ("The law of nature is alternation for evermore" [2: 197]), Emerson is able to accommodate paradox, to preserve his vision as he discredits it, to exercise his power through self-parody.

The discussion of friendship proceeds from this point by paradox and by juxtaposition of faithful affirmation and subtle mockery. "A friend," Emerson asserts, "is a person with whom I may be sincere":

> Before him I may think aloud. I am arrived at last in the presence of a man so real and equal that I may drop even those undermost garments of dissimulation, courtesy, and second thought, *which men never put off*. (2:202; emphasis added)

The inconsistency that, perhaps, seems incidental here is reinforced a few sentences later. "Every man alone is sincere. At the entrance of a second person, hypocrisy begins" (2: 202). If one wished to complete a syllogism that would render these propositions consistent, one would have to con-clude that "With his friend a man is alone" or that "A friend is the self's own reflection." Such, in fact, is the implication with which Emerson's paragraph closes:

> A friend therefore is a sort of paradox in nature. I who alone am, I who see nothing in nature whose existence I can affirm with equal evidence to my own, behold now the semblance of my being, in all its height, variety and curiosity, reiterated in a foreign form; so that a friend may well be reckoned the masterpiece of nature. (2: 204)

Or is he, rather, the masterpiece of art, of "semblance"? This is the suspicion that attends the too-close imaginative identification with one's friend and that prompts the counterargument in support of retaining one's actual remoteness.

Emerson begins his retreat from the danger of identification with the seemingly moderate assertion that friendship requires a "rare mean between likeness and unlikeness" (2: 208). It quickly becomes evident, however, that such a mean is no fixed point that may be settled upon but is, rather, the sustained state of dialectical tension:

> I am equally balked by antagonism and by compliance. Let him not cease an instant to be himself. The only joy I have in his being mine, is that the *not mine* is *mine*. (2: 208)

As Emerson has exacted the most extreme formulations of the likeness and convergence on which friendship depends, his formulations of its correspondingly essential unlikeness and divergence must also be extreme. They become increasingly so:

> Better be a nettle in the side of your friend than his echo. The condition which high friendship demands is the ability to do without it. . . . Treat your friend as a spectacle. Of course he has merits that are not yours, and that you cannot honor if you must needs hold him close to your person. . . . To a great heart he will be a stranger in a thousand particulars, that he may come near in the holiest ground. (2: 208–9)

And finally:

> Why should we desecrate noble and beautiful souls by intruding on them? Why insist on rash personal relations with your friend? . . . Let him be to thee for ever a sort of beautiful enemy, untamable, devoutly revered, and not a trivial conveniency to be soon outgrown and cast aside. (2: 210)

If the remoteness proposed here almost hopelessly attenuates the relation, it also revives the possibility of imaginative identification between friends; distance invites imagination to span it despite the risk, perhaps even the certainty, that it may thus be spanned by illusion.

The concluding pages of "Friendship" eloquently join the most naked admissions of illusion and failure with the most extravagant claims to truth and triumph. The knowledge that has been implicit from the start is made explicit now: "The higher the style we demand of friendship, of course the less easy to establish it with flesh and blood. We walk alone in the world. Friends such as we desire are dreams and fables" (2: 213). Out of flesh-

and-blood companions we weave our dreams and fables; in one sense, they are sacrificed to the possibility of these fictions, but in another, Emerson insists, they are invested with that possibility. The intimate union of sacrifice and investment, both for Emerson and for the friend he would have, reaches its climax in the penultimate paragraph:

> It would indeed give me a certain household joy to quit this lofty seeking, this spiritual astronomy or search of stars, and come down to warm sympathies with you; but then I know well I shall mourn always the vanishing of my mighty gods. It is true next week I shall have languid moods, when I can well afford to occupy myself with foreign objects; then I shall regret the lost literature of your mind, and wish you were by my side again. But if you come, perhaps you will fill my mind only with new visions; and I shall not be able any more than now to converse with you. So I will owe to my friends this evanescent intercourse. I will receive from them not what they have but what they are. They shall give me that which properly they cannot give, but which emanates from them. But they shall not hold me by any relations less subtile and pure. We will meet as though we met not, and part as though we parted not. (2: 215–16)

Emerson's resolution to receive from his friends "not what they have but what they are" hints of violation and even of a sort of cannibalism. But "what they are" only is revealed in their "lustres" or in "that . . . which emanates from them" when they are taken into the light of imaginative vision. By making our friends give us "that which properly they cannot give," Emerson proposes, we may give them themselves. In return, they may use us to ends as "subtile and pure." This "mutuality of adaptation," to borrow Poe's phrase, between imagination and actuality constitutes friendship for Emerson and is heralded in the final sentence of the above passage. In the sustenance of the state of *transition* between meeting and not meeting, parting and not parting, "is" and "as though," relation is sustained.

"Friendship" establishes such a state in words, but it remains, despite its frequent direct addresses to Emerson's reader and prospective friend, an individual production. The possibility of friendship has been evidenced, if at all, by its performance alone. Emerson seems to note this fact at the outset of the last paragraph. His sentence both logically culminates and insidiously subverts the small epiphany achieved in the preceding ones: "It has seemed to me lately more possible than I knew, to carry a friendship greatly, on one side, without due correspondence on the other" (2:216). This is a claim and a confession; if it renews the imputation of illusoriness to Emerson's sense of friendship, it also articulates his sense of power—which he proceeds to display—to meet that imputation head-on:

It never troubles the sun that some of his rays fall wide and vain into ungrateful space, and only a small part on the reflecting planet. Let your greatness educate the crude and cold companion. If he is unequal, he will presently pass away; but thou art enlarged by thy own shining, and no longer a mate for frogs and worms, dost soar and burn with the gods of the empyrean. It is thought a disgrace to love unrequited. But the great will see that true love cannot be unrequited. True love transcends the unworthy object and dwells and broods on the eternal, and when the poor interposed mask crumbles, it is not sad, but feels rid of so much earth and feels its independency the surer. Yet these things may hardly be said without a sort of treachery to the relation. (2:216–17)

That the objects of Emerson's affection are characterized in the end as "frogs and worms," as "so much earth," and as mere stepping-stones to a higher "independency," bluntly exposes the manipulativeness and the violation that have informed his sense of friendship all along. We take our friends, Emerson has suggested, for raw materials to be worked up by our imagination; friends "underlie" the acts of imagination by which we seek to enlarge ourselves and to approach the eternal. In fact, given its repeated metaphorical association with literary forms, friendship seems ultimately and only to inhere in individual acts of imagination. (Emerson likens it to "poetry" that we quickly "translate . . . into stale prose" [2:199], terms it a "masterpiece" [2:204], and demands of it so high a "style" that it must take the form of "dreams and fables" [2:213], claims to "do . . . with my friends as I do with my books" [2:214] and regrets "the lost literature" [2:215] of his friend's mind.)

If these individual performances are acts of violation and indulgences of illusion, they are also acts of faith: faith in our friend's real capacity to be worked up and to show us ours in return; faith in his potential to meet our imaginative projection with one of his own, thus genuinely establishing the bridge between us and actualizing our illusion. We seek "correspondence" and preserve its possibility by upholding our end of it, even if, as in Dickinson's poem 441, the world never writes back. Appropriately, the ideal friendship for Emerson takes the form of an exchange of letters:

To my friend I write a letter and from him I receive a letter. That seems to you a little. It suffices me. . . . In these warm lines the heart will trust itself, as it will not to the tongue, and pour out the prophecy of a godlier existence than all the annals of heroism have yet made good. (2:211)

The reader of "Friendship" may recognize "these warm lines" as the lines of Emerson's essay. For this essay, which contains a sample letter to "each new candidate for [one's] love" that closes with the words, "Thine ever, or never" (2:198), is itself a sort of letter and concludes with a similar challenge. After addressing his friend in the second person in an intimate plea for understanding, Emerson discovers that he can—and that he has just proved it—"carry a friendship greatly, on one side, without due correspondence on the other." His confession, several sentences later, that this enterprise involves "a sort of treachery to the relation" points again to the self-referentiality and self-worship with which the imagination flirts and acknowledges the necessity of correspondence to the full realization of friendship. Still, the essay will not countenance despair or compromisingly "provide for infirmity" (2:217). In the continued abeyance of the "godlier existence" that it prophesies, "Friendship" resolutely continues to practice the dialectical self-responsiveness that enacts relation and saves it. As romance, it embraces a possibility that lives by and in "this consent of language / This loved Philology."

Notes

1. All quotations from Emerson refer to *The Complete Works of Ralph Waldo Emerson*, 12 vols., ed. E. W. Emerson (Boston and New York: Houghton, Mifflin, and Company, 1903–1904). Volume and page numbers appear between parentheses in the text.

2. G. W. F. Hegel, *Phenomenology of Spirit*, trans. A. V. Miller (Oxford: Oxford University Press, 1977). Page numbers of quotations from the *Phenomenology* appear between parentheses in the text and refer to this edition.

3. As scholars such as Perry Miller and Sacvan Bercovitch have shown, the Puritans' ambivalent efforts to realize God's truth through faculties (conceptual and expressive) and in a life that, by definition, could not accommodate it largely comprise the origins of American literature and "the American Self." For these colonial Americans, the complete identification and the complete severance of physical and spiritual reality (Antinomianism and Arminianism, for instance) posed equally grave dangers, and the attempt to mediate between them— often a matter of imaginative and linguistic enterprise, particularly of metaphor—took on prodigious significance. The dialectical and metaphorical habits of mind that they cultivated and bequeathed to the literary tradition that developed earliest in New England rendered that tradition especially receptive to the issues and influence of romantic philosophy and aesthetics.

4. All quotations from Kant refer to *Prolegomena to Any Future Metaphysics*, trans. and ed. Paul Carus (Chicago: The Open Court Publishing Co., 1902). Page numbers appear between parentheses in the text.

5. Northrop Frye, *The Secular Scripture: A Study of the Structure of Romance* (Cambridge, Mass.: Harvard University Press, 1976), p. 15. A recent study of Ariosto, Spenser, Milton, and Keats that relies on the notion of "romance" and shares my interest in it as "a form which simultaneously quests for and postpones a particular end, objective or object" (p. 4) is Patricia A. Parker's *Inescapable Romance: Studies in the Poetics of a Mode* (Princeton, N. J.: Princeton University Press, 1979).

6. All quotations from Dickinson's poetry refer to *The Complete Poems of Emily Dickinson*, ed. Thomas H. Johnson (Boston: Little, Brown, and Co., 1960). Quotations are identified by Johnson's poem number, which appears between parentheses in the text. Reprinted by permission of the publishers and the Trustees of Amherst College from *The Poems of Emily Dickinson*, edited by Thomas H. Johnson, Cambridge, Mass.: the Belknap Press of Harvard University Press, Copyright 1951, © 1955, 1979 by the President and Fellows of Harvard College.

7. James's definition of romance in this passage underlies Lionel Trilling's distinctions in "Manners, Morals, and the Novel," in *The Liberal Imagination* (New York: Anchor Books, 1950)

and is quoted by both Richard Chase in *The American Novel and Its Tradition* (New York: Anchor Books, 1957) and Joel Porte in *The Romance in America* (Middletown, Conn.: Wesleyan University Press, 1969).

8. Henry James, *The Art of the Novel* (New York: Scribners, 1962), p. 33.

9. Ibid., pp. 31–32.

10 Eric J. Sundquist masterfully explores their interrelations, applying Freud's "family romance" scenario to four representative American texts, in his recent book, *Home as Found: Authority and Genealogy in Nineteenth-Century American Literature* (Baltimore, Md.: Johns Hopkins University Press, 1979).

11. The phrase is Emerson's, from "Experience": "We may climb into the thin and cold realm of pure geometry and lifeless science, or sink into that of sensation. Between these extremes is the equator of life, of thought, of spirit, of poetry,—a narrow belt" (3:62).

12. In this effort Dickinson's speaker resembles the Kant who writes: "The sensuous world is nothing but a chain of appearances connected according to universal laws; it has therefore no subsistence by itself; it is not the thing in itself *and consequently must point* to that which contains the basis of this experience, to beings which cannot be cognised merely as phenomena, but as things in themselves. In the cognition of them alone reason can hope to satisfy its desire of completeness in proceeding from the conditioned to its conditions" (124; emphasis added).

13. All quotations from Hawthorne refer to *The Centenary Edition of the Works of Nathaniel Hawthorne*, ed. Roy Harvey Pearce, et al. (Columbus, Ohio: Ohio State University Press, 1962–1977).

14. Jacques Derrida, "Structure, Sign, and Play in the Discourse of the Human Sciences," in *The Structuralist Controversy: The Languages of Criticism and the Sciences of Man*, ed. Richard Macksey and Eugenio Donato (Baltimore, Md.: Johns Hopkins University Press, 1972), pp. 264–65.

15. Georg Lukács, *The Theory of the Novel*, trans. Anna Bostock (Cambridge, Mass.: MIT Press, 1973), pp. 41, 56. Many of Lukács's observations on the novel are especially pertinent to romance, a mode to which the sorts of irony and self-consciousness that Lukács examines are, I think, more intrinsic than they are to the novel form in general.

16. Louis Mackey brilliantly demonstrates how this irony informs the critical practice of Northrop Frye ("Anatomical Curiosities: Northrop Frye's Theory of Criticism," *Texas Studies in Literature and Language* 23 [Fall 1981]: 442–69). Classifying *Anatomy of Criticism* as "anatomy," according to Frye's definition of the term ("satire . . . characterized by a great variety of subject-matter and a strong interest in ideas"), Mackey notes that "the relation between criticism and literature is, on [Frye's] own showing, ironic" (449). "The center of criticism," he continues, "is the center of literature—is literature itself in its immediacy. From this center criticism is excluded. It is therefore alienated from its subject-matter and from itself at the same time" (450). An implication of Mackey's argument is that criticism functions in relation to literature much as literature does in relation to experience: "At once bound to the service of literature and released to its own autonomy, criticism is—shiftily—both truth-telling science and fictive artifice" (460).

17. Loewenberg's remarks are included in the discussion that follows Jean Hyppolite's "The Structure of Philosophic Language According to the 'Preface' to Hegel's *Phenomenology of the Mind*," in Macksey and Donato, eds., *The Structuralist Controversy*, pp. 171–72.

18. Ibid., pp. 165, 185.

19. The only reference to Hegel in Poe's work occurs in *Marginalia* and is characteristically double-edged: " 'Philosophy,' says Hegel, 'is utterly useless and fruitless, and, *for this very reason*, is the sublimest of all pursuits, the most deserving attention, and the most worthy of our zeal.' " The quotation is certainly spurious, derived or concocted by Poe, perhaps, from his general readings in German literature and philosophy. Poe's familiarity with German writers, however, particularly with Hoffman, Tieck, the Schlegels, and other theorists and practitioners of Romantic irony who, like Hegel, were responding to philosophical issues that Kant had raised, helps account for the sometimes uncanny resemblance of his metaphysics to Hegel's. For documentation of this familiarity and a stimulating reading of Poe that, in some respects, anticipates mine, see G. R. Thompson's *Poe's Fiction: Romantic Irony in the Gothic Tales* (Madison, Wis.: University of Wisconsin Press, 1973). The above quotation from Poe refers to *The Complete Works of Edgar Allan Poe*, 17 vols., ed. James A. Harrison (New York: T. Y.

Crowell and Co., 1902), 16:164. Volume and page numbers of future quotations from Poe will also refer to this edition and will appear between parentheses in the text.

20. Compare to Poe's account Hegel's consideration of "Force," the manifestation of Spirit in the world, which is actual only in its state of supersession and is lost in its realization: "Force, as *actual*, exists simply and solely in its *expression*, which at the same time is nothing else than a supersession of itself. This *actual* Force, when thought of as free from its expression and as being for itself, is Force driven back into itself; but in fact this determinateness, as we have found, is itself only a moment of Force's expression. Thus the truth of Force remains only the *thought* of it; the moments of its actuality, their substances and their movement, collapse unresistingly into an undifferentiated unity, a unity which is not Force driven back into itself (for this is itself only such a moment), but is its *Notion qua Notion*. Thus, the realization of Force is at the same time the loss of reality; in that realization it has really become something quite different, viz. this *universality . . .*" (86).

21. G. W. F. Hegel, *The Philosophy of Fine Art*, 3 vols., trans. F. P. B. Osmaston (London: G. Bell and Sons, 1920), 1:11.

22. Ibid., 1:119.

23. Ibid., 1:11.

24. Albert Hofstadter, "Art: Death and Transfiguration: A Study in Hegel's Theory of Romanticism," in *Review of National Literatures* 1 (1970):154.

25. Northrop Frye, *Anatomy of Criticism* (Princeton, N.J.: Princeton University Press, 1971), p. 93.

26. Tzvetan Todorov, *The Fantastic: A Structural Approach to a Literary Genre*, trans. Richard Howard (Ithaca, N.Y.: Cornell University Press, 1975), p. 82.

27. Joseph Riddel makes the similar observation that language, for Emerson, can only originate in the difference between nature and spirit. He also supports the case for the mingled power and onus that language assumes in Emerson—and that, I would add, it assumes as a central condition of romance in general—when he points out that "nowhere in his writing can Nature, or God, or Unity, appear outside of a linguistic chain." "Decentering the Image: The 'Project' of 'American' Poetics?," in *Textual Strategies: Perspectives in Post-Structuralist Criticism*, ed. Josué V. Harari (Ithaca, N.Y.: Cornell University Press, 1979), pp. 338, 335.

28. See Richard Poirier, *A World Elsewhere: The Place of Style in American Literature* (New York: Oxford University Press, 1966) and Warner Berthoff's review of it, "Ambitious Scheme," *Commentary* 44 (1967): 114.

29. Friedrich Schlegel, *Dialogue on Poetry and Literary Aphorisms*, trans. Ernst Behler and Roman Struc (University Park, Pa.: Pennsylvania State University Press, 1968), p. 155.

30. Ibid., pp. 136, 144.

Signing Off: Dickens and Thackeray, Woolf and Beckett

Garrett Stewart

> There exists an old rule—so old and trite that I
> blush to mention it. Let me twist it into a
> jingle—to stylize the staleness:
>
>> The I of the book
>> Cannot die in the book.
>
> —Vladimir Nabokov, *Look at the Harlequins!*

> The Author, when believed in, is always con-
> ceived of as the past of his own book: book and
> author stand automatically on a single line di-
> vided into a *before* and an *after*.
>
> —Roland Barthes, "The Death of the Author"

Literature may be the handmaiden of philosophy, particularly of linguistic
philosophy, but it is also the harbinger. This essay will explore the philosophy of literary discourse implicit in the way certain novels choose to desist
from inscription. For all the defiantly revisionist speculation in current
poststructuralist circles about the paradoxes of speech, the elusive and
vertiginous nature of all signification, many of our great novelists seem to
have been there first—and in many cases to have got there first with their
last words. So that in "THE END" is our beginning, the very word *end*
boasting a teleological as well as a terminal sense that may disclose purpose even as it closes down plot.

When a given literary discourse has run its appointed course, fictional
closure can well become the touchstone of any theory designed to explain
the status of the preceding act of linguistic invention. The binary pressure
at the roots of modern linguistics, the differentiating tension between written or spoken language and the absence or silence against which it is

117

defined, is seldom more readily available to scrutiny than at the point where an act of discourse wills its own cessation, cedes itself back to blankness, and particularly so when that discourse is a scriptive fiction imagining itself as a first-person speech act. The I of the book must always at least say goodbye in the book. Fiction is raised upon the vacancy it scribbles over and fills in, to be razed again by absence when all is said. Closure thus opens us directly to all questions of literary signification, as Dickens knew before Derrida, Thackeray before Barthes. The present discussion will bring those two Victorian masters alongside the experimental fiction of Virginia Woolf and Samuel Beckett to demonstrate a deep compulsion of the novel for rounding off by turning round on its finished form in order to assess the logic and ontology of its composition—what comprises it, that is, as well as who can be thought to have composed it. No few novelists rest their case on the end in intend. With surprising frequency in any period, fictional leave-taking becomes an investigation of the very authorizing impulse that gives a fiction leave to begin in the first place.

It should be instructive to start with the first and last final sentences Dickens as novelist ever wrote, the close of *Pickwick Papers* (1836) and of the postscript to *Our Mutual Friend* (1864–65):

> Every year, he [Pickwick] repairs to a large family merry-making at Mr. Wardle's; on this, as on all occasions, he is invariably attended by the faithful Sam, between whom and his master there exists a steady and reciprocal attachment which nothing but death will terminate.
> THE END

> I remember with devout thankfulness that I can never be much near parting company with my readers for ever, than I was then, until there shall be written against my life, the two words with which I have this day closed this book:—THE END.
> *September 2nd, 1865.*

After the wedding breakfast that ends the main body of *Pickwick,* a white hiatus conveys us to a coda in which the editorial masquerade of the preceding chronicle is replaced at long last by the omniscient author's admission of pure fictionality. This candid valedictory voice compares the personal losses attendant on the "course of nature" (a given lifeline) to those incurred in the "course of art" (the plotline of any fictional discourse), wistfully saluting his own creations as they take up their places in that enclosed memorial rather than unfolding drama that the novel, ended, comes to be. In that future-looking but still elegiac last sentence about Sam and Pickwick, the tacit echo of the matrimonial liturgy ("till death do us part") lends its vocabulary to a nonsexual attachment guaranteed in the wake of a real marriage, though secured between men who are now unabashedly present to us as mere characters in a book. The historical preterite of the main novel, shifted to a perpetual present tense for the coda, veers off into a mortal future for that last subordinate clause. Yet the death that must come, presumably first to Mr. Pickwick, is not only postponed but supplanted by the fictional terminus of "THE END." In this "steady and reciprocal attachment which nothing but death will terminate," even the adjective of expected duration and continuance ("steady" for "uninterrupted") seems redefined as a spatial rather than temporal modifier (for "balanced," "stable") as putative biography yields to confessed invention, history to fiction, scriptive sequence to the roundedness of spatial form. For men who are only characters, "THE END" is the sole finality that applies, preemptive but at the same time redemptive, calling a halt that exalts to permanence, immobilizing but also immortalizing.

Though the specter of death at the end of *Pickwick* is raised only to be aesthetically disarmed, the novel's coda nevertheless gives us an instance of fictional closure seen under the aspect of human mortality. The process seems reversed for that postscript to *Our Mutual Friend*, where, in a more modern and potentially disturbing manner, human life itself and its mortality are viewed under the aspect of textual closure, life more a volume than an event. Writers have of course frequently amused themselves with this conceit, Keats notably in Dickens's own century; just before his death the poet asked that this punning message be delivered to his publisher: "Tell Taylor I shall soon be in a second Edition—in sheets—and cold press."[1] Dickens at the end of *Our Mutual Friend*, however, by making death a mutual and equivalent threat to himself and his scripted people, achieves something more than this reflexive textual metaphor. Explaining his close call with death, Dickens writes that "Mr. and Mrs. Boffin (in their manuscript dress of receiving Mr. and Mrs. Lammle at breakfast) were on the South Eastern Railway with me in a terribly destructive accident." After tending to the injured victims among the human participants in the disaster, Dickens "climbed back into my carriage . . . to extricate the worthy couple. They were much soiled, but otherwise unhurt." Which is of course because, being only words on paper, they had no other vulnerability. This charming conceit of characters as fellow travelers with their author soon backfires in the metaphysical surprise that Dickens's own life can justly be analogized to a text awaiting its final caesura. Closure ("until there shall be written against my life . . . THE END") becomes a gesture of some higher omniscience that matches both life's and literature's originating fiat with a countering finality: so let it be written, so let it be done in the sense now of "over." What is most intriguing here is that this idea of life as a script under the peremptory pen of some overseeing power emerges reciprocally with the elevation from textual to existential presence of Dickens's own characters. In some mysterious creative economy, the extent to which fictional lives wax authentic is the extent to which authorial presence (when put forward as an "I") becomes part of the fiction. In a dizzying relativism of scriptive incarnation, Mr. and Mrs. Boffin are only as real, and no less real, than Dickens himself would be if he were a divine artificer's own invention, which, for all the otherwise agnostic Dickens is willing to suggest or question here, he may well be. As if it were a postscript to the whole Victorian novel, Dickens verges in this last ending he lived to complete on a model of selfhood that will become predominant in Virginia Woolf and Samuel Beckett, an understanding of identity psychologically as well as linguistically deconstructive. Selfhood comes to be suspected as perhaps only the soliloquies of psychic speech by which it must be made equivocally present to itself from moment to moment, as dubious and tentative a mode of being as that of any character on any page, soiled or otherwise, who is only and always mere words. Woolf and Beckett will thus imply that we are only the narratives we tell ourselves—and by which we tell ourselves from others—until our ends.

E. M. Forster writes in *Aspects of the Novel* that " 'The king died and then the queen died' is a story. 'The king died, and then the queen died of grief' is a plot."[2] Subsequent questioning of language and narrative insinuates the thought that "Once upon a time the king and queen lived happily ever after" is a kind of death, whether as story, as plot, or even as sentence, a death inherent in narration line by line, word by word. This Thackeray in *The Newcomes* (1854–55) has already begun to hint. Unnamed narrators in *Pickwick Papers* and *Our Mutual Friend* evaporate into the authorial "I," still a character by being still within the confines of the fictional structure, still an unnamed character at that, and yet obviously Dickens himself. In a similarly self-conscious nesting of narratives, Thackeray introduces the recording voice of his novel as a dramatized character named Arthur Pendennis, named and situated within the plot, but then arranges the closural mechanism so that not only Arthur's "I" drops away to "he" but it does so just before the supervening authorial voice surrenders its own first person to a fictionalized distance from the scene of reading. Thackeray further complicates (so as to explicate more fully) the relation of closure to finality, to any deathlike removal from presence, by tightly binding his coda to latecoming death scenes embedded in the main plot of *The Newcomes*. These are deaths that precede and prepare for the novel's conclusion as the "demise" of immanent authority—in the archaic sense of a "transmission" or "passing on."

In the novel's last chapter the internal "editor" and narrator of *The Newcomes*, Pendennis, carries news about the death of the hero's wife to *The Times*, where it is converted to the evanescence of newsprint; he then declaims: "So, one day, shall the names of all of us be written there; to be deplored by how many?—to be remembered how long?—to occasion what tears, praises, sympathy, censure?—yet for a day or two, while the busy world has time to recollect us who have passed beyond it." Following this travesty of public commiseration, we turn to the genuine impact of the girl's death on the ailing Colonel Newcome, whose grief is compounded by a sense that he is being punished by this added familial tragedy for his own sins of materialism and revenge. The Colonel seems gradually to sense the profoundly literary or aesthetic possiblities of dying as an exchange of duration for shape; to salvage meaning, even beauty, from the end of his days he must bring them to a resonant halt, must substitute certainty for flux, past for present, death for life. His death scene is an artfully contrived network of revery, irony, and symbol, with these his last moments: "And just as the last bell struck, a peculiar sweet smile shone over his face, and he lifted up his head a little, and quickly said, 'Adsum!' and fell back. It was the word we used at school, when names were called; and lo, he, whose heart was as that of a little child, had answered to his name, and stood in the presence of The Master." This raising to exponential power and a capital letter in death of one of life's earlier rites of passage, God becoming the Great Tutor, also epitomizes, in conjunction with the bibilical overtones of "as . . . a child," the innocent heart of this man who fancies himself more sinned against by the world than sinning. Further, that Latin verb for "I am present" sets up curious resonance when the question at issue is in fact mortal absence. It is a foreign idiom, a dead language, that draws its meaning entirely from a separate sphere of reference, where far past and near future converge in eternity. Colonel Newcome's last words in this world are thus hinged by ambiguity into another world. This real death, with its sundering of reference, seems immediately to precipitate a double displacement from presence, a double death of sorts, in the pivotal shift from inner to outer narrative.

Upon the death of the Colonel, Pendennis too dies away from narrative authority across a white blank and a dividing line setting off the supposedly edited narrative from the confession of pure fabulation by the author. "As I write the last line with a rather sad heart, Pendennis and Laura, and Ethel and Clive, fade away into Fable-land. . . . And have we parted with them here on a sudden, and without so much as a shake of the hand?" So the author at last comes forward to conjecture, but which "last line" does he mean? Of the main plot? Of the coda, as each new sentence fades away to become the last one? Or does he mean "line" in the geometric rather than scriptive sense? "Is yonder line (_____) which I drew with my own pen, a barrier between me and Hades as it were, across which I can see those figures retreating and only dimly glimmering?" The line he points to "yonder" by reduplicating interposes itself as follows the first time around, just after the Colonel's last words:

. . . had answered to his name, and stood in the presence of The Master.

> Two years ago, walking with my children in some pleasant fields . . . .

As at the end of *Pickwick Papers,* to pass from text to its externalization and dismissal as fiction is a crossing of the bar fully as extreme as that which succeeds by negation to "Adsum." It is only provocatively anachronistic, not inappropriate I trust, to think here of the Saussurean bar (S/s) between signifier (narrative act or consciousness) and signified (narrated scene) in this fictional re-signation of the author's Fable-land to its own effacement. Even the putative editor-narrator, Pendennis, has retired "to the shades" without answering the "sentimental question" upon which novels so often choose to end: whom did Clive marry after Rosey's death? The answer will have to be invented, and Ethel is the logical and sentimentally satisfying choice. But nothing in this belated appliqué of marital closure can erase that aura of mortality, metaphoric and otherwise, that consigns the shadows of the cast to the shades beyond.

Pendennis "has disappeared," says the valedictory authorial voice, "as irrevocably as Eurydice," who dies, we are to recall, in the very instant of being looked back upon, dies when a perceiving self tried to recapture, to reread, her image. Not to have stepped in with his intrusive fabrication of admittedly arbitrary futures for his cast would have left an aura of fictional permanence hovering about Thackeray's invented creatures. Honesty demands that a voice come forward to admit that all writing, all narrative, is merely a ghostly trace that vanishes before our gaze line by line, whether the line be more of the same or the final linear bar between artifice and reality. "Ah, happy, harmless Fable-land, where these things are!" the author nears the close by singing, with the verb of being both placement and predication: they are there, not here; there only, not here, they *are.* But the question of receding presence is, as the authorial voice seems to know, a matter of infinite and concentric regression. If Pendennis's narrative, and he its speaking voice, are now passed over and away beyond the bar of signifying presence into signified trace, so too will the encompassing narrator, call him author or invented authorial voice, be evaporated after the final subscript, "Paris, 28 June, 1855," a real space in real time that turns fictive and vaporous, just like his own "I," under Thackeray's pen. By way of suggesting this, there is a shift in pronoun from first to third person toward the close that is the metanarrative equivalent of that neutering within less metaphoric death scenes of he's and she's to it's or of Pendennis's "I" faded to last name: "Friendly reader! may you and the author meet there [in Fableland] on some future day! He hopes so; as he yet keeps a lingering hold of your hand, and bids you fare well with a kind heart." So did the dying Colonel hold out his hand to those near him. This is in an important sense, then, the deathbed valediction of a narrative voice that has already regretted the lack of a chance for "the shake of a hand" with his fading creations. This voice's wished-for return in later works by Thackeray will be dependent upon our revived attendance as readers. The *de te fabula* of incorporated reader consciousness has narrowed to a vanishing point at which our own imagination is the last presence on the scriptive scene, the narrative "I" receding past "he" into the Hades of completion. To activate the satire, we have always had to see ourselves in the reported and anatomized follies of the characters; now that consciousness of ourselves addressed by the text is all the text has left.

What Thackeray executes at the end of *The Newcomes* is a destructuring of the very architecture of narration. The Orphic vision of the fictional artist yields place, unnervingly enough, to the Eurydicean. Not only do characters fade away, transgress the "line" of signification, but so does the author who has set them in motion, whether or not he comes forward (only then to recede) with a confessional I. Thackeray is really more intuitively radical than Barthes in our epigraph, for the single line that textual self-consciousness must straddle in *The Newcomes* rescinds distinctions between before and after in the logic of a continual absenting, both the inventor and his invented scribe evanescing with the other characters from immediacy into memorial. An operable pun in all this is "finish," both as the sheen of aesthetic achievement and as finality. In this demythologizing of the authorial voice according to the Eurydicean archetype, structural closure is merely the truth writ large, and last, that any finished line is looked back on, rendered readable, only as it dies away to fixity and extinction—every syllable a crypt and every chiseled sentence a cenotaph, just as every plot is a graveplot, every tome a tomb.

Thackeray's dyptich of death and closure, the dovetailed ends of Colonel Newcome as a man and Arthur Pendennis as a narrator, lingers on in the mind as an allegory of inscription's primal duality. Every author who sets pen to paper, and who in so doing thinks he is declaring himself (even if by fictional deflection from his own person or name or gender), who in other words thinks that he is saying "Adsum" (or in other words yet "Scribo ergo sum"), is in fact absenting himself from any pertinent here and now as completely as is the Colonel at the instant of his own answered summons to the realm of the atemporal, compacted as it is in his mind of the past and the hereafter. With a death scene that posits heaven precipitating a coda about a referential Hades, Thackeray seems clairvoyantly in tune with the contemporary linguistic thought that would have us believe, in effect, that every bringing to "utterance" is in the obsolete and root sense of the phrase a putting to death.[3] Closure may be understood as the form of finality bestowed by the finality of form. Death stands therefore to story as the image of a natural frame, bordering narration as it borders individual life, ordering it from the outside in. Long the mother of beauty, the must of philosophy, the father of tragedy, the nonidentical twin of closure, death has more recently been unmasked as the firstborn bastard child of all discourse. Like a skeleton disarticulated into the rattling bones of its own anatomy, literary articulation has been deconstructed of late into a double suicide, the belated and fading ghost of the referred world on the one hand and of the wording mind on the other. Dickens himself gets at this grammatological irony not only in the biographical valediction to *Our Mutual Friend* but in an earlier conjunction of physical and scriptural passing that suggests writing's always paradoxical relation to death, prose both extirpating and preserving at once. In the first chapter of *Little Dorrit* (1855–57) Dickens alludes briefly to the death scenes of the world's heartless governors, "the said great personages dying in bed, making exemplary ends and sounding speeches; and polite history, more servile than their instruments, embalming them!" When Thackeray in *The Newcomes* brings into immediate conjunction a fully rendered death scene with a dramatization of the virtual death that is any fabulation as scripted story, he comes even more directly at the paradox of prose incarnation as a simultaneous embalming, or in his terms a consignment to Hades. When further, in his closing invocation of the reader, Thackeray includes his own persona in the deathward recessional from "I" to "the author," he is involving his text in a more searching recognition yet—of a deeper pack between fiction and death that has to do with the nature of reception as well as of inscription.

It has to do with why we go to novels in the first place, with those interiorized death scenes we could never otherwise experience and in which, inscribed or not, secondary or not, we deeply believe. "In the realm of fiction," writes Freud, "we find the plurality of lives which we need. We die with the hero with whom we have identified ourselves; yet we survive him, and are ready to die again just as safely with another hero."[4] Ionesco frames the same thought with Shakespearean example: "When Richard dies, it is really the death of all I hold most dear that I am watching; it is I who die with Richard II."[5] Walter Benjamin, building on Hegel and Freud, would put forward yet more about the relation of death and narration, beyond the partnership of thanatos and catharsis. He would say that death is the virtual author of all our knowing in narrative. The literary deathbed is thus the narrative microcosm and paradigm, the structural synecdoche, for the revelatory relationship of any textual content to its own closure. Not only a person's "knowledge or wisdom," according to Benjamin, "but above all his real life—and this is the stuff stories are made of—first assumes transmissible form at the moment of his death."[6] He might as well be talking about Colonel Newcome's declaration of identity and presence in "Adsum." Benjamin wants us to see that the "authority" so imparted and transmitted is "at the very source of the story" as finished artifact, filled to expectation with definitive and conveyable import. Completion is what sanctions the power of both death and story. More recent linguistic theory would add that so is all discourse sanctioned, not just completed narratives but the phrases and clauses that comprise them. The very words of a discourse become transmissible only by being dismissed from temporal reality into their "real life" as signifiers, passing over from immediacy into medium at a distance comparable to death's remove from life.

George Bataille, in his rethinking of Hegel, echoes Benjamin closely when he writes: "For man to be finally revealed to himself he would have to die, but he would have to do so while living—while watching himself cease to be."[7] Man would have to become the narrator of his own death scene, as the heroes of Woolf and Beckett become, or as Hamlet seems trying to do when he moves into a paradoxical present tense for "I am dead" (5.ii.339), overseeing the providential logic of his own decease. Bataille goes on: "Thus it is necessary, at any cost, for man to live at the moment when he truly dies, or it is necessary for him to live with the impression of truly dying. This difficulty foreshadows the necessity of *spectacle*, or generally of representation, without the repetition of which we could remain foreign to and ignorant of death. . . ."[8] We need, as Freud and Ionesco also demonstrate, the spectacle of death to teach us our own death in the body of another. What Richard II does for Ionesco, art does for the king himself in advance of the end, when he knows by intuition to sit on the ground and "tell sad stories of the death of kings" (3.ii.156). Bataille's redaction of Hegel is of considerable use to Jacques Derrida, who quotes it extensively, mainly as it implies the familiar corollary and converse at the basis of deconstruction: the claim that the negative drama of mortal absence is made present to us not only in the representation of death in tragedy and fiction but in the death that representation itself amounts to. Derrida's central concerns might be thus taken to derive from another quotation from Bataille besides his rendering of Hegel: "The survival of that which is written is the survival of the mummy."[9] Every time, for instant to instant, that our psychic speech—Woolf will call it our stream of consciousness—wells up into utterance, we are being vouchsafed that revelation of self to itself which resembles what Woolf calls in a different context "the sweetness of death in effigy."[10]

I would like to suspect at this point that the reason the poststructuralist critique of signification has found such a ready hearing among literary critics is in large part simply that a certain kind of literature has been paving the way for it over the decades, by self-consciously pulling the rug out from under its own ontology as a scriptive construct, calling itself to closural account by way of sentimental allusion in *Our Mutual Friend*, gently satiric subversion in *The Newcomes*, full-scale psycholinguistic allegory in Woolf's *The Waves*, black comic apocalypse of all chronicle in *Malone Dies*, and so on. Yet what these novels give us, each in its own way, is a theory of character as well as of linguistic characters and signs, each still in touch with the ruling humanism of Western literature and psychology. Woolf and Beckett take the confessional valediction of the authorial I in Dickens and Thackeray and thread it back into the question of death and identity that provides the narrative line of their stories as plots. To do this they introduce first-person heroes who must submit to their own exit from their lives as admitted subjective fictions rather than giving themselves up to the keep of some outer narrator. Woolf and Beckett do this to their characters not to tell us self-servingly about narrative strategy so much as to reinvestigate time-worn notions of the self in the light of articulate discourse and formal closure rather than in the shadow of unexamined duration and mere mortality.

Woolf's *The Waves* (1931) is divided between italicized interchapters of omniscient description, in which the plot's main characters are never mentioned, and the assorted soliloquies that comprise the main body of the novel, the polyphonic speeches (not dialogue) of three men and three women never pointed to by narration except for such unvaried filler as "said Rhoda," "said Neville." Psychic speech, as Derrida would call it, or stream of consciousness, is not only these characters' medium of transmission to us but their whole being as far as we are concerned. Character *is* inner voice, Woolf implies, identity its own articulation to itself—which is to say its own internalized narrator. Accordingly, one of the six characters emerges as the quintessence of the rest, the novelist Bernard, who assimilates other lives to himself as tales rather than presences. Remarks Neville the poet: "Bernard says there is always a story. I am a story. Louis is a story" (200). Two of these stories have ended in death scenes, the accidental fall from a horse of Percival and the suicidal leap of Rhoda, both of which Bernard studiously reimagines, takes unto himself as vicarious effacement, but by the internalization of which he manages to shore up his own identity until the very end of the book. There, as if he were illustrating Walter Benjamin's claims for the parallel between deathbed self-discovery and the closure and portability of fictional form, the aging Bernard begins his confrontation with death by saying: "Now to sum up. . . . Now to explain to you the meaning of my life" (341). Yet meaning and being are at odds, the former a surrender of the latter to form itself. Every *sum* (I am) can be tallied as a narrative sum only at the transit from ongoing to foregone experience, from presence to expression, and this traumatic realization on Bernard's part, agonized over and investigated, is the climactic drama of this last section.

Dickens could describe his own life as a story, awaiting its version of "THE END." Characters within novels, too, appropriate such a textual metaphor for identity. The concept of marital closure for Jane Eyre is seen in scriptive terms as a point of demarcation in the book of her life; she insists to Rochester on the outward vesture of her former self until the day of the wedding, wearing "my old Lowood frocks to the end of the chapter" (24). Or Will Brangwen in Lawrence's *The Rainbow* can be heard thinking how he "did not care about himself as a human being. . . . That was just merely the margin to the text" (6). But in neither Brontë nor Lawrence do these allusions subscribe, as they do in Woolf, to an entire logocentric allegory. When Bernard remarks that he is "perpetually making notes in the margin of my mind for some final statement" (307), he is modeling his identity on textual borders and limits in a profoundly felt way.

Bernard begins his role in *The Waves* as an optimist of speech and inscription, a punster able to pry open in language a functional breathing space where his better presence can roost and be nurtured. Indeed, his own wordplay to this effect—"I shall enter my phrases" (199)—is matched by the poet Neville's sense of him—"Here is Bernard. . . . He is composed" (195)—with that past participle doubling for language and for life, for a passive mood both of the verb and of the mind. When tragedies accumulate later in the novel, Bernard can also give them "composition" in his own speech: "Here on my brow is the blow I got when Percival fell. I . . . feel the rush of the wind of her flight when she [Rhoda] leapt" (377). Phrase does not so much embalm here as reembody the deaths, perpetuating the mortal moment as the inscribed vessel of its only knowing. The sonic bond between "brow" and "blow" evokes in a reverse temporal sequence of cause and effect the personalization of the Other's previous fatality; the play on "flight" as both a psychic fleeing and a downward flying caps perfectly the prepositional cadence of Rhoda's fall, that push and rush of the doubled "of." If Percival and Rhoda are yielded up by their last instant to a purely phrasal incarnation by the sinuous and slippery nature of Bernard's phrases, so will the phrase-maker himself have to submit to oblivion at the end of the novel, a death self-consciously overseen even as it is undergone. After memorializing his friends in the formulated moment of their deaths, Bernard, nearing the end, takes a retrospective vantage on his own life, converting it to that final concentration of mortal import which story shares with death. "Thus when I come to shape here at the table between my hands"—we hear the clause as a grammatical and ontological sufficiency for this self-made man as self-transcribed voice, at least until its completion (or supplementation) by—"the story of my life and set it before you as a complete thing" (377). Satisfied with the intransitive grammar of his coming into "shape" or verbal presence, we can only equate it, not entirely recast it, with the additional sense of his proceeding to shape up his story. The noun of his being cannot be distinguished, that is, from the predicating verb of his autobiography. This is the gap between word and deed, utterance and identity, closed so often by Woolf in this most self-commenting of her texts—but closed so as to call each into question.

Earlier in this final soliloquy Bernard has announced that "once I had a biographer, dead long since" (356), a superintending consciousness formerly responsible for his phrases and now disappeared somewhere behind them. When Bernard later amplifies the point—"All this little affair of 'being' is over" (376)—we recognize that it is over precisely because, once it has quotation marks around it, its continuous breathing has been given up (shaped up) as the spoken breath not of life but of the voiced definition of life. The second draft of *The Waves* is more explicit on this score, yet when Bernard remarks that " 'I' had died"[11] it is again because the quotation of self is the swathing of it as a finished thing. Roland Barthes' summary of deconstruction in "The Death of the Author" provides an apt gloss on Bernard's sense of having outlived his own autobiographer, of speaking on posthumously about a defunct (or suddenly fictitious) first person. As Barthes sees it, "linguistics has recently provided the destruction of the Author with a valuable analytic tool by showing that the whole of the enunciation is an empty process, functioning perfectly without there being any need for it to be filled with the person of the interlocutors. Linguistically, the author is never more than the instance writing, just as *I* is nothing other than the instance saying *I:* language knows a 'subject', not a 'person'. "[12]

Bernard has only words, among them some favorite and trusted metaphors, with which to voice the loss of all self but such words, and he is losing faith even in their vitality: "No fin breaks the waste of this immeasurable sea. . . . No echo comes when I speak, no varied words. This is more truly death than the death of friends, than the death of youth" (374). That "fin" we have come to know as Bernard's private figure for the mark articulation leaves on the sea of eternal otherness, for human declaration slicing by means of voice through waves of tidal indifference. There may be speech still, but it has no "echo," no resonance against a personal reality apart from, outside of, or containing it. The obsessive biographical mutter must proceed without the biographer, who is no longer its premise or even a presumption from it. This is a fate worse than death, the death of others or one's own past, because it is the continual annihilation of the present as defined by one's own presence in it. Bernard as articulate agent, articulate animal, has become "A man without a self. . . . A heavy body leaning on a gate. A dead man" (374). Woolf's stream of consciousness may have tapped more directly than ever before in fiction that stratum of psychic speech which lets us know ourselves, but she refuses to rest easy in the achievement, testing it by a crisis of selfhood wherein no "ergo sum" may be taken on trust to follow from the inner voice of the "cogito." It is no sterile deconstructive exercise but a genuine trial by ab-negation: the voiding of person from voiced subject. In the humanist paradox of Woolf's grammatology, Bernard has a chance to pass this test only in passing on, to recuperate identity even in losing it, to find in "THE END" an entelechy of achieved and freeing self-consciousness.

Bernard summarizes the dilemma to himself this way, knowing that his victory will have to come through the very words that seem to have eviscerated him: "But how describe the world seen without a self?" (376). In any but the autobiographical mode, this is of course the very license of omniscient narrative, however much the authorial self may insist on slipping in through the back door of character. It is a novelistic enterprise that Woolf has carried to its extreme in the interchapters of *The Waves*, where there are human selves occasionally but no personalized consciousness as filter of the vision—just words summoned miraculously to evoke a visible but un*seen* universe. Bernard, in other words, is moving as soliloquizing novelist toward a style that would match Woolf's in these interludes, pure saying without conscious seeing or focal consciousness.

Another way to put this is that the deathless impersonality of the interchapters encroaches upon and is then incorporated by him. "And in me too the wave rises," Bernard says in his last paragraph alive, the surge of self-assertion imaged in terms of the inanimate world that might otherwise rise not within but against him. Harkening back to Percival's death, he then reimagines—reimages—this existential energy as that of a charging beast, with a pun on bounding "mane" for "main" that Woolf dropped in revision.[13] Wordplay or not, it is no less a verbal gambit on the phrasemaker's part. Combining both the fatal accident on horseback of Percival and the rushing flight of Rhoda, knowing his own end in terms he has learned from others (the way Thackeray's I saw formal closure as complement to a deathbed scene), pitting himself against eternity in a spirit of acceptance somewhere between fatalism and suicide, Bernard spins out the conceit of his heroic gallop against negation. It is as if he must mortally depart this world in order to answer his vexing question about the description of that world seen without self. His heroic charge against oblivion in the last sentence is followed by a blank space, and in turn by one last six-word section of italics, an idea that occurred to Woolf far along in the process of redrafting:

> I strike spurs into my horse. Against you will I fling myself, unvanquished and unyielding, O Death!
>
> *The waves broke on the shore.*

If "I" is a fiction whose very declaration is a distancing of self from the inscription that would feebly embody it, then so is the equally conjectural personification in the apostrophe "O Death!"—every naming of death being in the same space, and for the same space of time, the secured deferral of its real advent.

This reciprocal eviction from the instant of voiced defiance both of the "myself" flung against Death and of the fatal adversary Himself justifies also the syntactic detachment that looses to ambiguity the compound phrase of undefeated force, "unvanquished and unyielding," which must now be taken to describe in the moment of their mutual exclusion both I and my Death, both self and the principle of its sure effacement. All that is left is for the sounds of the waves—italicized: self-consciously scriptive—to wash across that gulf of white silence into which story trails off, sounds evoked by words seemingly unauthored, uttered by the world beyond voice in a landscape seen without a self. In *The World Viewed*, Stanley Cavell writes about a kind of phenomenological afterlife whose conditions bear on the end of *The Waves:* "A world complete without me which is present to me is the world of my immortality. . . . That is essential to what I want of immortality: nature's survival of me. It will mean that the present judgment upon me is not yet the last."[14] And of Bernard we are still reading, still forming judgments, in a world where waves still meet the shore.

If every saying is a kind of slaying, death loses its sting in the very teeth of signification. Woolf thus anticipates and detoxifies the mortuary undertone of the entire deconstructive critique, while at the same time adding the last redemptive sentence as if it were an italicized translation not from another discourse but from the mystery of the world's own recurrence as spatial and temporal form. Where we might expect "END" we get instead, in a greater text, the first syllable of an awesome, nonhuman endurance, the world huge and perpetual beyond the self. Death as closure is suddenly discovered to be nothing more or less or worse than the world suddenly without self, voiced in those omniscient italics into which the novelist's own phrases—Bernard's, Virginia's—seem to have been merged, subsumed, sublated. The world "seen without a self" is now recognized not only as the deathless reality of a universe recorded without percipient source in any personal consciousness, but, in the other sense of "without," the seen world that lies inalienably outside the self, vast and forever.

Being over is, in fiction, not only a signing off but a passing over, a transgression of the Thackerayan line between the here and now of imagined presence and the mimetic dismissal to the otherworld of replica, fable, artifice. Woolf inherits such a closural rule and humanizes it to heroism, Beckett to a moving futility. Bernard the novelist in Woolf internalizes the idea of this closural point of no return as a veritable identity crisis by the end of his summing-up, while Beckett's hero in *Malone Dies* (1956) seems to know by morose instinct right from the start that he is nothing more than a subject without a self, not so much a man as a denatured *manus* making its way across the blank pages of its life with a pencil where a crutch should be. Beckett's Malone dwells from the first in the Hades to which Thackeray's characters and narrators are consigned only at the end—and for Malone it *is* hell, the excruciation of a man without self taking down in longhand the drone of his own soliloquies turning to obsequies.

A man closeted off somewhere in a squalid space as claustrophobic as the interior of his own brain, a man maimed but seedily gallant, crippled but never bitter, takes notes all day and all night, not that he knows the difference, on the random humiliations and discomforts of his bedridden misery, all duly in view of the death his limbs give promise of, what there is left of them. This is Malone. This is the solo groan of the self as its own elegiac scribe. It is also in embryo and in parody the modern "scriptor," the demythologized or dead author portrayed by Barthes as "born simultaneously with the text," who "is in no way equipped with a being preceding or exceeding the writing, is not the subject with the book as predicate; there is no other time than that of the enunciation and every text is eternally written *here and now*."[15] *Malone* is preceded in Beckett's trilogy by *Molloy*, whose title figure wonders early on how to speak of what he takes the liberty of calling his life when there is no sign of it, no trace, but the wording of his own virtually posthumous pain: "My life, my life, now I speak of it as of something over, now as of a joke which still goes on, and it is neither, for at the same time it is over and it goes on, and is there any tense for that?" (36)[16] The imperfect? The past progressive? Barthes again serves us, suggesting that the modern scriptor, indistinguishable from his text, exemplifies in the act of writing "exactly what linguists, referring to Oxford philosophy, call a performative, a rare verbal form (exclusively given in the first person and in the present tense) in which the enunciation has no other content (contains no other proposition) than the act by which it is uttered—something like the *I declare* of kings or the *I sing* of very ancient poets."[17] Malone, dying, has found a somewhat different answer to Molloy's question about tense, illustrated by example in a coinage (italics added) to which at least one critic has taken objection,[18] without noting the temporal implications of its perpetual entrapment between past and future: "But let us leave these morbid matters and get on with that of my demise . . . unless it goes on beyond the grave. But sufficient unto the day, let us first *defunge*, then we'll see" (236). It is a tedious "day" that he takes perverse delight elsewhere in calling "the livelong day" (220), with an idiomatic hint of its lifelong deadly ferocity. But far more startlingly, in that etymological dovetailing of *"defunge,"* we have the novel's central paradox locked into a single baroque invention. The portmanteau collapse of "defunct," in all its past-participial finality, upon the transitive echo of "expunge," made passive of course by the drained vitality of context, does necessary violence to the language in order to name the terrible innovation of Beckett's plot, stretching as it does the instant of demise to an interminable torpor. It is a tedium alleviated only by the kind of verbal play that here designates it, all speech in *Malone Dies* being a bereavement over the very void it tries to fill.

Dead metaphors like "livelong day," revived out of desperation in the face of a real death that is really no more than a verbal effacement for a self no more than words—this is the elusive closed circle of Malone's world. Life is found out by death not only in closure but along the way, fortified by its own inevitable default, by the death it is founded on in some sense in the first place. Yet this is by no means to take facile comfort from some existential certainty about death as inherent, abiding, encased in us as the seed of our eventuation. Rather, Beckett's work is a rigorously witty recoil from such philosophical relaxation into death. First-person novels have become not so much the representation or rendering or modeling of a life as a model for it. Their questionable ontology is the embodiment of a never-better-than-conjectural I, their fictive but finished structure the most sustained formal metaphor one could devise for existence seen under the aspect of its limits. *Malone Dies* struggles to be a genuine bipartite title, about dying but also about a man named Malone borne toward identity on the trail of (t)his death—with "trail of" offered here in the sense both of retrospective trace and prospective chase.

Not just a premise to rest on but a feat to achieve, the personalized death in Beckett is an even more heroic endeavor than some branches of existentialism would suggest. If death begins by being partly *out there,* partly other and still coming, then the new heroism in Beckett may rightly be defined as the effort to *make* death mine by force of phrase, to render the expression *my death* with both an objective and a subjective genitive. To do this Malone has only style to work with. The black and rankling jokes of Malone's wordplay serve this metaphysical turn not only by never letting death's metaphors die peacefully, but by tinging all language with hues of the tomb. Demise of course permeates being as it does meaning, waiting both here in space, inside me, as well as there in time, somewhere, sooner or later, patient, ineluctable. More than this, though, we come to recognize that even beyond its local stylization the whole act of novelizing the encounter with death is itself an architectonic allegory of the novel's own attitude toward that dying. The paradox of death for Beckett, at once inner and outer, here and coming, inherent and unarrived, is at last and at large the paradox of narrative art as spatialized temporality. Story, a shape as well as a duration, is present to us as a defined whole even as it moves, or we through it, toward the completion of itself as form. A book is all there before us at once even when taken a sentence at a time, just as death may be no more ours when it is over with than when it is on its way. For it comes from within. Like death, narrative structure is both a frame and an inner mechanism of development. Fictional form is latent in its entirety, even as it is hammered out anew with each reading, a determined shape as well as a labor toward it. The myth that the I of *Malone Dies* is writing out his last hours and minutes before our eyes, bringing his death to light at last, is always qualified by the logic of organic form, which knows and acknowledges that any book is not only a procedure of discovery but an artifact wrought and rounded off. Death too, like art, is an inward impulse at the same time that it is an ordering principle of limit; indeed, art as an imposition upon the amorphousness of reality may seem as antithetical to natural flux as death is to change and growth. But death stands to life not only as a contrary fact, but also as an unfolding and an integral finishing. Such, then, is the formal equivalent for *Malone Dies*, as a novel, of that manifold view of death articulated within it. Beckett more than any British novelist before him espouses the intimate bond between prose and corpse, for art is to its raw materials as death to life, variously and at once a presence, a process, and a product.

But closure, formal or existential, does not in Beckett, in the final throes of his narrator's doubt, grant or guarantee the previous being of that which seems to have ceased. The moribundity of demise can seep through and erode an entire life. "The truth is," confesses Malone, "if I did not feel myself dying, I could well believe myself dead" (183). His unnamable successor in the third part of the trilogy puts it even more clearly: "I was grievously mistaken in supposing that death in itself could be regarded as evidence, or even a strong presumption, in support of a preliminary life" (342). The last adjective cuts with just the right edge, for it is the liminal, the closural, which rules the I without assuring it or its duration. Bernard told himself the "stories" of other preliminary lives and their mortal impasse, especially the stories of Percival's and Rhoda's violent closures in death, so as to approach his own end with an already assimilated understanding. As Hegel, Freud, Benjamin, and Bataille would all agree, (p)representation of a death scene is a psychic strategy borrowed from art to illuminate life. Malone carries it one step farther than Bernard by not simply converting credited separate identities to private psychic allegories, but by inventing characters in his vacuum of real community only so as to kill them off for his own edification, his own benefit, his own deflected fatality.

Malone's envisioned victims in this delegation of death are the surrogate selves whom he slaughters in his imagination at the end, the cryptically labeled doubles, Sapo and Macmann. Widely recognized as a derogatory verbal condensation of "homo sapiens" and a familial code for "son of man" respectively—wordplay substituting for, or generating, character as well as plot—these necrological nicknames also reflect back on their author, Malone, whose name emerges, one may speculate, as a contraction of "I'm alone" in which the "I" has been squeezed out along with the verb of being under the numbing pressure of demise. "On the threshold of being no more I succeed in being another" (194), Malone congratulates himself, with the pun on a willed succession as well as a success. His "threshold" reminds us of the linear bar of Thackeray's recession from his own I on back through the previous avatars of his narration. Malone does not create the bloodthirsty Lemuel as a suicidal deputy to kill off his own narrative alter egos just to see how they die, to see how it might be to die. Rather, by making something (someone) entirely external the agent of a death entirely other, and by acting this out at a desperate pitch of butchery, Malone appears to exorcise that paranoia, justified or not, which haunts him from the start. The terror of death as an enemy closing in on him from outside may thus be supplanted, if only for a last instant of peace before cessation, by a personalized dying that can be felt instead as an inventive giving out from within. Malone forges other selves so as to become the author, not just the victim, of his own effacement. If he can utter it, maybe he can suffer it without inordinate pain. Yet there is another subjunctive hankering that runs counter here to everything the narrative implies about wanting to get it over with. Perhaps if Malone is able to write about his own death so near at hand, he will miraculously have outlived that death.

"My story ended I'll be living yet. Promising lag" (283). Since he too, as only scriptive presence in his exercise book, has the same ontological status for the reader as do Sapo and Macmann, merely a grammatical I to their he's, the end of his text is effectually the end of him for us, after which some sponsoring authorial self (arbitrarily named "Samuel Beckett") may linger momentarily in the text in order to experience the rare joy of having finished something, and thus linger deathlessly as creator. To reverse the emphasis of Thackeray's valediction, there is always an implied I on the near side of the Hades of representation. By a related sleight of identity in *The Waves*, Bernard loses his voiced storytelling self just in time to face death with unmediated clarity, that "world without a self" achievable only in the split-second "lag" between uttered text and the italicized termination of yet another voice, if only the world's noise. But this "promising lag" seems betrayed by the end of *Malone Dies*, which trails off in grammarless and dangling shards, as if not only the named narrator, but also the book named for his death, are expiring as his pencil slows to a halt. Lemuel seems about to slaughter Macmann with his hatchet when the violence of this invention fails Malone, his own continuity as narrative voice itself hacked to fragments; Lemuel is ordered, or at least declared, to do no more violence, no more hitting

> with it or with his hammer or with his stick or with his fist or in thought in dream I mean never he will never
>
> or with his pencil or with his stick or
>
> or light light I mean
>
> never there he will never
>
> never anything
>
> there
>
> any more   (288)

Pointless locatives and severed negatives win out over the very grammar of being in this "defunging" of copulative predication itself. The weapon,

fixated upon with those hatchetlike iterations, includes among its alternatives the same pencil by which this violence has been textually brought off
and is now forever suspended in a final negation of everything: never will
he or anything be there any more. It is a prophetic fact so final that the very
verb of being seems redundant and, to Malone's fading mind, unrecover-
able, in any of the blurted clauses it might serve to complete. Beckett once
said that by the end of his trilogy "there's complete disintegration. No 'I,'
no 'have,' no 'being.' "[19] At one point in the second volume, Malone's
dozing off predicts not only this final disintegration but also the deathly
loss of consciousness imparted by the syntactic fracturings and evacuated
predications in the last pages of his novel, simple sleep being described as
a fainting away from presence when "subject falls far from the verb and the
object lands somewhere in the void" (234). The dwindling voice's "never
anything [there] any more" at the end is just such a falling away of all verbs
and a complete voiding of their possible objects. Among the corpses of
those alter egos who have lent Malone surrogate presence, there never will
be anything there that has "being" any more, or that stands in need of its
locutions.

It should by now be growing apparent how the "promise" of Malone's
"lag" between story and nonexistence may easily confuse the issue, even
by analogy with Bernard's yielding to third-person report at the end of *The
Waves*. Better to think of the term *lag* in some spatial rather than temporal
sense, gap more than lapse. Instead of a split-second's reprieve from void
it becomes an ontological distance between voiced self and its conversion
to trace on the one hand, and on the other between any such trace and its
subsequent reanimation in the act of reading. It is best, in other words, to
sense the probable etymological source of *lag* in *lack*, become that interval
of absence which is the very space of inscription, then of reading, in any representation of the self's own life or death.

The autobiographic paradox of a first-person death scene running
(down) to the instant of closure is opened up as a narrative possibility deep
within that genitive pun in "my story ended I'll be living yet": the storytelling that requires me as signifying subject or the story that takes me as
signified object; the story by me or of me. Malone discoursing on the
deaths of himselves, so to speak, in Sapo and Macmann is this dichotomy
returned to simultaneity. His novel is not a book *about* Malone's death, but
a text that *is*, that constitutes, both by title and content, the proposition
Malone Dies. As single phrase and as plot-length paranoid phantasmagoria,
it is an utterance in the present perpetual tense of art and the fatal performative of the reduced scriptive self, declaring itself over and over again as
out there, other, over. The very text of *Malone Dies*, dropping off, seems to
drop dead as we read, without such an italicized and ontologically independent sentence as *"The waves broke on the shore."* At the end of *Malone
Dies*, in a universe of absence, there are never any waves any more either.

For any study of death in the British novel, this closure in Beckett would be a critical moment. It is the unprecedented death *of* a novel.

It is certainly easy to construe it also as an act of deconstruction, or rather an enactment of deconstruction as a dramatized battle in which the tabula rasa wins out by razing and then, in effect, erasing the personal self and the scriptive "I" who and which, respectively, would defy and defile it. The same could be said about Bernard's tossing of his words, and of the self they name, into the imminence of death at the end of the *Waves*. Yet by naming death, as Malone has no intent or time to do, Bernard rescues himself from deconstruction long enough to deny death's immanence, to make the canceled presence incident to all discourse no less than internecine for both parties to the demise at hand. Denied even the sureties of closure, however, the decided pleasures of signing off, still Malone has not surrendered entirely to the nihilistic drift of deconstruction, as we can discover upon additional reflection.

Moving beyond Thackeray's double conceit of concentric narrators fading over into their own Fable-land, Woolf funnels her whole novel down to a demythologized fictional self, a character as novelist, who is asked to narrate his own lapsing into death as if it were merely the acknowledgment of the world without a wording I. Identity itself has become part of the fable, but one no less worth offering up to other fictions who are content to know themselves as I. However constituted, there is still in Woolf's world community and continuance. Beckett, in apparent contrast, winds up his prose by winding it down to a point where the I who dies in the book is a Woolfian man without a self who must, certainly no less heroically than Bernard, do his seeing without a world, banished to the vacuum of his own fading voice. How describe a universe without even its own credible presence? Malone is the scribbling autobiographer of a never-more-than-fabulated relation between psyche and cosmos, yet, because he lives in an already viciously deconstructed world, his writing, once taken up, takes him out the other side of the closed logocentric circle. Numbing redundancy becomes deliverance. Knowing enough to know there is no verifiable world to address or describe, he goes ahead and makes one, makes one up, and by keeping it going despite his griefs, makes or signs or inscribes a dubious truce with his destiny.

"To begin my life with the beginning of my life, I record that I was born," writes the authorial surrogate and autobiographical figment named I at the beginning of Dickens's *David Copperfield* (1849–50), with a shuttling double pun on the interchangeable connotations of lived "life" and "literary life," a pun devious without being entirely subversive. At the other end of Woolf's and Beckett's novels, the "autobiographer . . . dead long since" could only explain his belated exit as follows: To finish my lifeline with the finish line of my scribbled life, I note that I was born only to record—and thus finally to be interred by my terminal words. Such an autobiographical consciousness may be buried but is also preserved as a vitality that is always there whenever we are there as readers. Bernard from a state of suspended selfhood outside the real world, and Malone without a deconstructed world, both broach fiction's most ennobling paradox: that while literature may seem all epitaph it is at the same time all embodiment, less a charnel mark than it is for the reader an incarnation. Bernard ends with the naming of Death, *verba* deferring *res* as it must always do. Malone ends with the naming of a more utter negation, but cancellation and chaos, denominated and faced down, may also fend off by filling up a void. We have the unforgettable Malone even as we lose him, even as he has never been able to claim or even confidently name himself. Gripped by story, we grow to feel that fiction must be informed in more than the evanescent verbal sense by *figures* seeking to be *composed*, that by its celebration of language as presence, hedged round by all the evidence to the contrary, it is a brave and profoundly humanizing gesture flung against nullity: creative, originating.

One of the most remarkable of Beckett's death scenes, and one that clarifies the itch for narrative projection at identity's last surrender of self, comes with the drowning suicide at the end of the short story "La Fin." Instead of reliving his life as he drowns, the hero remembers a story he once *could have told* about that life, such as it was: "The memory came faint and cold of the story I might have told, a story in the likeness of my life, I mean without the courage to end or the strength to go on."[20] What surprises in this phrasing of narrative prompting is not that the dying mind suddenly recalls to its disappointment that it might have told a story to lighten the burden of living and dying, as Malone or the Unnamable tell theirs, but that the mind seems to have nothing to remember but the untold story itself. It is the absence of the secondhand presence of narrative. The Beckett hero in extreme form, no more than a textual presence, has only narrative memories to replay, and here only the memories of a hypothetical and undelivered narrative.

Yet if all suffered life were storied life, all ends no worse than the penning of a death, Beckett's translation of his own prose from French into English could offer a fanciful prototype for the rescue and redemption of "la fin." Drowning would be no more than a sinking signature across the surface of flux, dying just one more enciphering of the I. We recall Bernard's mysterious "fin" that knifes through the infinite universe of waters, like a stylus scoring a receptive medium—inscribing a linear doodle, as it were, at the outer verge of his interior monologue. Bernard's phrasemanship in this regard asserts itself by syllabic play when he pauses to "note under F. . . . 'Fin in a waste of waters.' I who am perpetually making notes in the margin of my mind for some final statement, make this mark" (307). Under F., that is, we may locate the finlike, final statement that might well appease Bernard's sense that life "had been imperfect, an unfinished phrase" (283). Under F., too, we should therefore not be surprised to find, cross-indexed, some "words of one syllable" that can answer that earlier question of Bernard's: "By what name are we to call death?" If in his own resignation to such death he manages a resolute assertion of self, the identifying fling of a personalized signing off, this willed fate only confirms our sense that his terminal enterprise stands for that of all novelists.

Immediately on the heels of Bernard's "O Death" and the italicized *waves* that follow comes Woolf's own implied fin-al and fin-ishing syllable (there is no requirement that it comprise an English word) which at the end of any novel (or essay) is a way of naming the death latent in all closure as well as the permanence bestowed by termination. Woolf's is that incisive word retrieved at last from the repository of Bernard's phrase book, a word we sense at the end of any text, with or without a subscribed locale and date of completion, and even when recorded only tacitly, as if in disappearing ink. Woolf's text is not placed and dated, as with *The Newcomes'* departing memorial, "Paris, 28 June, 1855," or, say, Joyce's dates of gestation for *Ulysses* as if they traced an entire lifeline, "Trieste—Zürich—Paris, 1914–1921." Such familiar subscripts may well recall temporal inscriptions carved upon a tombstone, the text getting born and then dead so as to be read by us. Whether these subscripts appear or not, however, the decisive final syllable evoked by any closure, slicing off all narrative as its ultimate epitaph, is that fine, swift, irreversible, often invisible

FIN

Notes

Epigraphs: Vladimir Nabokov, *Look at the Harlequins!* (New York: McGraw-Hill, 1974), p. 239; Roland Barthes, *Image—Music—Text*, trans. Stephen Heath (New York: Hill and Wang, 1977), p. 145.

1. Robert Gittings, *John Keats* (Boston: Little, Brown, 1968), p. 425.

2. E. M. Forster, *Aspects of the Novel* (New York: Harcourt, Brace, and World, 1927), p. 86.

3. *OED* subst.[2] 2b.

4. Sigmund Freud, "Our Attitude Towards Death," in "Thoughts for the Times on War and Death" (1915), *Complete Psychological Works of Sigmund Freud*, Standard ed., vol. 14, trans. and ed. James Strachey (London: Hogarth Press, 1955), p. 289.

5. Eugene Ionesco, "Experience of the Theater," *Notes and Counter Notes* (New York: Grove Press, 1964), p. 136.

6. Walter Benjamin, "The Storyteller: Reflections on the Works of Nikolai Leskov," *Illuminations*, ed. Hannah Arendt, trans. Harry Zohn (New York: Schocken Books, 1969), pp. 93–94.

7. Georges Bataille, *Hegel, la mort et le sacrifice* (1955), pp. 32–33, quoted by Jacques Derrida, *Writing and Difference*, trans. Alan Bass (Chicago: University of Chicago Press, 1978), p. 257.

8. Bataille, quoted in Derrida, *Writing and Difference*, p. 258.

9. Bataille (from *Le Coupable*), quoted in Derrida, *Writing and Difference*, p. 266.

10. Virginia Woolf, *Jacob's Room* & *The Waves: Two Complete Novels* (New York: Harcourt, Brace, & World, 1923, 1931), p. 68. Subsequent references to *The Waves* are also to this Harvest paperback edition.

11. J. W. Graham, ed., *The Waves: The Two Holograph Drafts* (Toronto: University of

Toronto Press, 1976), a transcription of holographs in the Berg Collection, New York Public Library, p. 723. Beckett's Malone will put it this way: "I shall say I no more" (*Malone Dies*, p. 282).

12. Barthes, *Image—Music—Text*, p. 145. Hugh Kenner, in his memorial essay, "Decoding Roland Barthes," *Harper's* (August 1980), returns this insight upon Barthes' own posthumous reputation as a generous irony: "Roland Barthes (1915–80), PROLIFIC AND ECLECTIC WRITER WHO WAS ONE OF MOST CELEBRATED FRENCH INTELLECTUALS," was a semiotician (meaning meaning-specialist) and would not have missed the semiotic import of his own *New York Times* obituary, where, as in all obits, Life is reduced to Text. . . . What's entered our heads is a verbal construct called 'Barthes' " (p. 68).

13. Graham, ed., *The Waves*: "The wave in me once more rises . . . something swelling proud as the mane of a horse" (p. 742).

14. Stanley Cavell, *The World Viewed: Reflections on the Ontology of Film* (New York: Viking Press, 1971), p. 160.

15. Barthes, *Image—Music—Text*, p. 145.

16. All page references to the trilogy are to the combined edition, *Three Novels by Samuel Beckett: Molloy, Malone Dies, The Unnamable* (New York: Grove Press, 1965).

17. Barthes, *Image—Music—Text*, pp. 145–46.

18. John Fletcher, *The Novels of Samuel Beckett* (London: Chatto and Windus, 1964), in whose view Beckett "tends to indulge in neologisms that are not always very successful, such as *defunger* for 'to die' (concocted from *defunt*)" (p. 164).

19. An interview with Beckett by Israel Shenker, under the title "Moody Man of Letters," *New York Times*, 6 May 1956, sec. 2, pp. 1, 3.

20. Samuel Beckett, *Stories & Texts for Nothing* (New York: Grove Press, 1967), p. 66. In the same vein Malone thinks of his avatar Macmann as all story, an existence of auto-narration waiting patiently for closure: "This is the kind of story he has been telling himself all his life, saying, this cannot possibly last much longer" (239).

Touching Earth: Virginia Woolf and the Prose of the World

Alan Wilde

I

Near the end of "A Summing Up," the paradigmatic story that brings *A Haunted House* to its appropriately irresolute close, Sasha Latham discovers (for the moment at least) an answer to the dilemma that has surprised her into quizzical reflection.[1] "But what answer?" she asks herself. "Well that the soul . . . is by nature unmated, a widow bird; a bird perched aloof on that tree" (p. 140). Uprooted by imagination from its place in Mrs. Dalloway's garden, the tree becomes, in the last of its transformations, "a field tree—the only one in a marsh" (p. 140); and it hardly requires an allegorical turn of mind to recognize in Sasha's fancy an image of the phenomenal world denied its substantiality and density and made conformable to the subjectivizing, idealistic appropriations of the soul or (the words are used almost interchangeably by Woolf) the self: the solitary bird hovering out of reach of life's dangers and disappointments, free, like Pynchon's Oedipa Maas, to *"project a world."*[2]

Or rather to stabilize it, for Sasha's dilemma derives precisely from the rapid sequence of mental acts whereby she first manages to generate and then fails to sustain a sense of the world's intense significance—its static and ecstatic transcendent unity. So at one moment "the branch of some tree in front of her became soaked and steeped in her admiration for the people of the house; dripped gold; or stood sentinel erect" (p. 139). But at the next, she "could no longer spray over the world that cloud of gold. . . . She looked at the dry, thick Queen Anne House . . . but it seemed to her a logical affair of drains and carpenters" (p. 140). What explains the change, the abrupt descent "into prosaic daylight" (p. 140)? Easiest to invoke Sasha's glimpse over the garden wall of "London again; the vast inattentive impersonal world" (p. 139). But that is *too* easy. London's power to undo her miraculous transfiguration of house, tree, and even a nonde-

140

script barrel is directly proportional to the source of her fragile power, namely, herself—better, her own constituting imagination, which reveals itself in the story's central words: *"she endowed"* (p. 139; emphasis added).

In short, "A Summing Up" testifies to the recurrent extremity of the idealist tendency in Woolf's stories—and, additionally, in the novels from *Jacob's Room* through *The Waves*. Since the world (at best impersonal and inattentive but as often as not hostile and threatening) is there to be acted upon, to be transformed and tamed by the ultimate subjectivity that *is* the self, all its value and meaning derive, must derive, from what the self, consciously or not, does to it through its own metamorphic effort and activity. For so long, at any rate (and that, as Sasha's predicament reveals, is not after all very long), as it can hold at bay the always latent intrusions of life's "Monday or Tuesday," the dailiness that so often presents itself to Woolf's characters as an amalgam of eroding time, fear, habit, other people, and, not least, the debilitating awareness that turns consciousness back upon itself and destroys its power to erase, in its movement toward transparency, the stubborn facticity of the world. But for Sasha and, so it seems, for Woolf at this point the problem poses itself differently, resonating as it does from within the vibrating core of a vulnerable, agitated sensibility. Jolted, by way of London's indifference, from her luminous vision of a "gallant and carousing company" (p. 139) to the dispiritingly ordinary perception of "this party—nothing but people in evening dress" (p. 140), Sasha, mindful of her fall but unwilling or unable to accept its consequences, hypostatizes into a formula of symmetrical interrogation the dynamic and ragged succession of her experience: "Then she asked herself, which view is the true one?" (p. 140).

With that question, and its attendant perception of "the bucket and the house half lit up, half unlit" (p. 140), Sasha inadvertently articulates the paradox that underlies and expresses both the characteristic structure of Woolf's middle novels and the typical form of the modernist crisis: the poised and irrefrangible balance of equal and opposed possibilities that paralyzes choice and substitutes tension for activity.[3] Born of her temperamental belief that she is "unable to join," that she is excluded from "the society of humanity" (p. 139), her question ratifies what it purports to overcome (the division that separates her from the world) and eventuates, as we saw earlier, in a movement that definitively abandons the phenomenal as well as the problematic. Indeed, converting problem into solution, Sasha's metaphoric flight situates her as spectator of the dilemma she is better able to devise than to solve. Her "answer," then, is no answer at all but an evasion. And a precarious one at that. For in the story's final paragraph the world, resisting its coercion by consciousness, asserting its anonymous but vivid presence, emits "the usual terrible sexless, inarticulate voice . . . a shriek, a cry"; at which point "the widow bird, startled, flew away, describing wider and wider circles until it became . . . remote as

a crow which has been startled up into the air by a stone thrown at it"
(pp. 140–41).

Which is to say that in order to maintain the tenuous integrity of her
subjective being Sasha must ascend increasingly and impossibly ever
higher, becoming in the fact of her distance and the virtuality of her control
the very image of the modernist artist. For "A Summing Up," even as it
dramatizes the perplexity of its protagonist's relation to reality, reenacts it
in its form, which offers the reader not, as it seems, resolution but (in its
aesthetic strategies: the patterns of cadence, assonance, repetition, and
rhyme with which the story ends) closure. In this sense, "A Summing Up,"
brief though it is, may be seen as emblematic of much of Woolf's fiction in
the twenties and early thirties. Marked by a sense of personal division
(most notably perhaps in "The New Dress," where Mabel Waring undergoes the tortures of feeling "separate, quite disconnected" [AHH, p. 54]; in
"Moments of Being," with its recurrent image of "the pane of glass which
separated them [the Crayes] from other people" [AHH, p. 102]; and, of
course, in the portraits of Septimus in Mrs. Dalloway and Rhoda in The
Waves), and distinguished too by a more general awareness of life's fragmentation, the stories and especially the novels of this period exercise a
progressively more constraining authority over the fluid, meditative visions of disruption and disorder they enclose. Consequently, if flight re-
currently and variously symbolizes the way characters cope with life's
disconnections (retreating,   sinking   down,   or—the   final   fracture—
committing suicide), it comes even more emphatically to represent Woolf's
own reaction to her world, until, in The Waves, the gesture of abandonment
is unmistakable and complete. Leaving behind altogether—its ostensible
concern with sensation and perception notwithstanding—the phenomenal
for the reified and rarefied perfection of art and establishing between them
an all but unbridgeable gap, that novel makes clear beyond question what
Sasha's widow bird implies: the inevitable impasse of subjectivism and
idealism, which is the dead end of modernism as well.

II

Beginning with The Years, however, Woolf's fiction radically and increasingly restructures the relations of her world, including, of course, the
dynamics of the self. Often neglected and, until recently, generally de-
valued and misunderstood,[4] the book is neither "the 'factual' novel"
Leonard Woolf believed it to be[5] nor yet another effort on Virginia Woolf's
part to "insubstantise" reality,[6] to hollow it out in the service of a more
pressing need for order and control. Seeking instead to give reality its due,
The Years does something more, or more effective, in exploring the possibility of an accommodation between consciousness and (in the phrase once
intended as the novel's title) the "here and now" that consciousness ac-

knowledges, even while moving outward toward the world in order to realize its own potential.

Nevertheless, to speak of a new direction in Woolf's career is not to deny what appear to be adumbrations in the earlier work of what is to come. The opening episodes of *Mrs. Dalloway*; Lily Briscoe's desire "to be on a level with ordinary experience, to feel simply that's a chair, that's a table, and yet at the same time, It's a miracle, it's an ecstasy";[7] Bernard's attraction to "the copious, shapeless, warm, not so very clever, but extremely easy and rather coarse aspect of things" and his praise of life's Monday and Tuesday, now seen, approvingly, as "the mere process of life"[8]—all reveal, or at least seem to imply, Woolf's ability to render the phenomenal world as very substantial indeed. But the most striking prefiguration is probably to be found in the mysterious, suggestive section of *Mrs. Dalloway* that describes Peter Walsh's dream,[9] an episode that will help us to ascertain how authentically and to what degree these tributes to ordinary experience, that is, to the world's autonomous existence and value, in fact determine the overall shape and tendency of the novels in which they intermittently appear.

"Down, down he sank," the scene begins,[10] recalling both Mrs. Ramsay's "wedge-shaped core of darkness" (*TTL*, p. 99) and the desire of the narrator in "The Mark on the Wall" "to sink deeper and deeper, away from the surface, with its hard separate facts" (*AHH*, p. 42); and as Peter abandons in sleep the variousness of the London day that envelops him, he becomes "the solitary traveller" (p. 63), exploring a realm of multiple oppositions that express as much the narrator's as his own intuition of unity and disconnection. "The actual thing" and "visions which ceaselessly float up"; "the sense of the earth" and "a general peace"; "this fever of living" and "simplicity itself"; "myriads of things" and those things "merged in one thing" (p. 64)—in brief, the fallen world and imagination's recreation of it: such are the antitheses that structure Peter's dream. Its motive force—"a desire for solace, for relief, for something outside these miserable pigmies, these feeble, these ugly, these craven men and women" (pp. 63–64)—is clear enough; what matters is its direction. And that, as Peter successively encounters first "the giant figure" from whose "magnificent hands [shower down] compassion, comprehension, absolution" and "who will, with a toss of her head, mount me on her streamers and let me blow to nothingness with the rest"; next, "an elderly woman [earth, surely] who seems . . . to seek, over the desert, a lost son"; and, finally, "the landlady . . . an adorable emblem which only the recollection of cold human contacts forbids us to embrace" (pp. 63–65): that direction appears to describe, roughly but unmistakably, an oneiric passage from the visionary or transhuman (one of those "moments," which all of Woolf's characters experience, "of extraordinary exaltation") back—by way of a reluctant encounter with "the actual thing," a world of expectation and loss and of an impending "august fate"—back to an acceptance, a *near* acceptance, of "ordinary things" (pp. 63–65).

The circle, then, is virtually complete: drifting away from the phenomenal, Peter returns to it at the last. Or—to register again a typical Woolfian reservation—so it seems. For when, just before his awakening, Peter is made to ask: "But to whom does the solitary traveller make reply?" (p. 65), the answer is not the landlady, who has just addressed him, and still less either of the other personified figures. It is, in fact, *himself*, since, believing as he does, as the narrator apparently does, that "nothing exists outside us except a state of mind" (p. 63), Peter is the one who, like Sasha, "endows" (p. 64) with oneiric reality first "the giant figure" ("if he can conceive of her, then in some sort she exists" [p. 64]) and then the other dream-women who succeed her. In sum, if the inner logic of Peter's dream endorses a return to reality, the dream itself (or the dream process) reveals a more fundamental and urgent strategy of the book: the habit, already noted apropos of "A Summing Up," of rendering the phenomenal world— for all its diversity, variety, and discontinuity—somehow transparent, unsubstantial through the constant, even obsessive use of metaphor and other forms of analogy and (to say what is perhaps the same thing) through the attention that this tropological frame of mind calls to itself. Thus, in creating, by way of an insistently (if covertly) directive consciousness, a morphological correspondence between the actual and the visionary (compare Lily's attempt to make ordinary experience simultaneously a miracle, an ecstasy), Woolf presents us, even as she praises reality, with its idealized form: the world purified of its obstructions, disappointments, and impediments—as Peter and Woolf would wish it to be—and too, if even more inadvertently, with the source of that form, the artist as solitary traveler.

Furthermore, as Peter leads us back ultimately not to "things" but to himself, the initiator or creator of things, so Woolf in her own way belies the apparent openness of *Mrs. Dalloway* (as she too facilely denies the persisting irresolutions of the two novels that succeed it) by transforming its ending into an implicit affirmation of art. Repeating in a more fluid and complex way the movement of Peter's dream, the climax of the book returns Clarissa to her party and to process. But Peter's (and the book's) concluding words, "For there she was" (p. 213), are too emphatic, too absolute for what has gone before: an assertion, in a novel that has worked to present the self at its best as creating and exploring, of *being* as now somehow finished and complete. How to respond to this vision of stasis? Something less than convinced that Clarissa has achieved an integration of her problematical identity or that, thanks to her response to the suicide of Septimus Smith, a lasting change in her character has come about, the reader can only look askance at the invitation to participate, along with

Peter, in the tidy but delusive spectacle of frozen perfection, which is, in its air of finality, the seductive and too orderly shaping of the novel's pattern as well. Like "A Summing Up," then, *Mrs. Dalloway* contains but does not resolve the problems it raises; and we are left to contemplate, in despite of its still dialectical nature, the *formal* unity of the book: the triumph of the aesthetic order that allows or, rather, forces us to praise, as Peter praises Clarissa, the artist in her art.

So there is, after all, something misleading about the notion of mining *Mrs. Dalloway* and the novels that are formally akin to it for signs of later developments. Quite simply, the need and desire for control that these books translate into ever stricter, more shapely aesthetic heterocosms take precedence over whatever attraction heteroclite reality offers to Woolf's imagination. There is surely no need at this date to insist on the centrality of the aesthetic to writers of the twenties or to recognize that what is at issue is not a barren reflexivity—whether parading as a doctrinaire pursuit of art for art's sake or as an absolute disbelief in the referential power of words—but a convergence of various literary, personal, and, in the broadest sense, moral ideas and ideals that discover in Yeats's "superhuman / Mirror-resembling dream" a pledge of order, the *possibility* of order, in the human sphere as well: "little vantage grounds," as E. M. Forster calls them, "in the changing chaos."[11] My point is that, even if one grants the overarching integrity of a writer's (any writer's) career, still there is no need to assume a strict developmental continuity in which every swerve and veer of consciousness pays servile tribute to some single, determinative source. The potential for even fundamental change remains and, in Woolf's case, realizes itself in her final novels.

The distance between *The Years* and the major fictions that precede it is evident in an episode of the book's "1907" section. Lying in bed awaiting her family's return, Sara Pargiter muses on a sentence in a book she has been reading, which, although there is no reason to believe that it was intended to do so, adroitly summons up memories of Sasha Latham and Peter Walsh: " 'And he says,' she murmured, 'the world's nothing but. . . .' She paused. What did he say? Nothing but thought, was it? she asked herself as if she had already forgotten. Well, since it was impossible to read and impossible to sleep, she would let herself *be* thought." But as she begins to verify the statement in the only way she can, by becoming something (a leafy tree as it happens), the world comically blocks her effort and refutes its inspiration: " '—the sun shines through the leaves,' she said, waggling her finger. She opened her eyes in order to verify the sun on the leaves and saw *the actual tree* standing out there in the garden. Far from being dappled with sunlight, it had no leaves at all."[12] (So much for the gold-dripping tree of Sasha's idealizing imagination!) A few pages on, when her sister enters the room, Sara poses the problem to her; and Maggie's response, more serious but no less deflating of the original philosophical proposition, brings the reader to the heart of the novel's orientation:

> "Then what about trees and colours?" she said, turning round.
> "Trees and colours?" Sara repeated.
> "Would there be trees if we didn't see them?" said Maggie.
> "What's 'I'? . . . 'I' . . ." She stopped. She did not know what she meant. (p. 150)

The final question, which, taken by itself, would not be out of place in the earlier novels, in fact carries a different freight of significance now, for its context, the context of the book as a whole, makes clear that its motive, as well as its answer, is neither epistemological nor metaphysical (not, that is, of the order of Lily Briscoe's ceaseless interrogations of the universe) but *ethical*; and, further, suggests that the solution to Maggie's doubts and difficulties (she "had been thinking, Am I that, or am I this? Are we one, or are we separate" [p. 150]) lies in the self's dependence upon and interdependence with the world around it.

It follows that the most suggestive of the book's symbols—"a dot with strokes raying out round it" (p. 96)—repeatedly describes a centrifugal movement (so different from the self-centering impulses of Clarissa Dalloway, "collecting the whole of her at one point" [*MD*, p. 42]), which, responsive to Maggie's question, defines the "I" not as some *thing*, independent and self-authenticating, but as one term of a dynamic relationship. So, later in the book, in a conversation whose resonance is explicitly ethical (the question of how "to live differently—differently" [p. 456] permeates the book), Eleanor Pargiter's friend Nicholas answers her broken questions—" 'But how . . .' she began, '. . . how can we improve ourselves . . . live more naturally . . . better . . . How can we?' "—by putting into words what is implied by the relational symbol I am proposing as the novel's hub: " 'The soul—the whole being,' he explained. He hollowed his hands as if to enclose a circle. 'It wishes to expand; to adventure; to form—new combinations?' " (p. 319). And still later, North Pargiter gives the idea what is probably its definitive expression: "To keep the emblems and tokens of North Pargiter . . . but at the same time spread out, make a new ripple in human consciousness, be the bubble and the stream, the stream and the bubble—*myself and the world together* (pp. 442–43; emphasis added).

In short, *The Years* suggests, equally, a rejection of what may be described as the instrumental attitude toward the phenomenal, the attitude, so prevalent in the earlier novels, that takes things as a means, an avenue to vision; and, at the same time, a repudiation of the other, hitherto pervasive notion of losing identity in the nonself. If meaning is attainable, and the book suggests it is, it is meaning made, not preexistent; emergent, not fixed; temporal, not spatial. Recurrence, no longer "the eternal renewal" of *The Waves* (pp. 210–11), is now human, the result of lives lived, well or ill. Not surprisingly, then, as Eleanor wakes from her sleep during the party that dominates the book's final section, she is left, unlike Peter Walsh, "with nothing but a feeling; a feeling, not a dream" (p. 411) and with the sense of "the future before them. Nothing was fixed; nothing was known; life was open and free before them" (p. 412). And when she is challenged for announcing, hesitantly again: "I feel . . . as if I'd been in another world!" (p. 417), she replies—it is the novel's axial perception—"But I meant this world! . . . I meant, happy in this world—happy with living people" (p. 418). Connected somehow (but, in terms of the book, centrally) with "facts" (p. 412), with "something solid" (p. 413), the assertion is authentically of the here and now; and though various of the characters take exception to the assertion, the book itself ratifies it—if too clearly in its final lines, with their symbols of dawn and the rising sun and the closural effects that recall earlier novels, then more satisfyingly and appropriately in the repeated question of the penultimate paragraph: "And now?" (p. 469).

But to say all this is not to explain, or to explain sufficiently, the exhilarating effect of the novel: to make clear not only why its effect on the reader is so different from that of *The Waves* in particular but also how it overcomes its own insistent and copious vision of time, illness, death, sordidness, and decay. There is ample reason to read the book, as many critics have, as a dispiriting record of tediousness, oppression, and gloom, of failed and wasted lives; and it would be untenable to make so much of Eleanor's " 'I' . . . a centre . . . from which spokes radiated" (p. 395), if the novel itself did not sustain, through its structure and, still more, its texture, the thematic emphases I have tried to trace. But *The Years* does precisely that, thereby revealing what is likely most original and significant about it. The point can be made most economically by contrasting the prologues that initiate each section of *The Years* with the interludes that obtrusively punctuate and bind together the various episodes of *The Waves*. Obviously, there is an enormous difference between the concentration on symbolic time (the progression of the day, of life) and the focus offered by the later novel on actual seasons and weather. But there is more to it than that. The temporal progression of *The Waves* is linear, inexorable, even, if one may use the words in a secular context, eschatological and apocalyptic. In *The Years*, by contrast, there is a much greater sense of randomness (season doesn't follow season in regular alternation; the years don't march by at regularly spaced and measured intervals). And if it verges on overstatement to speak of arbitrariness, if there *is* some sort of pattern, it is, as I have suggested, one composed of effort and accident, a pattern in which human repetitions and nonhuman recurrences join to intimate a wholeness the characters are, understandably, never quite able to grasp because it is, precisely, of their own making.

Little wonder, then, that, set beside the interludes, with their carefully calculated symbolic details, the preludes reveal themselves as more tonally varied, more empirically rooted, and, ultimately, as richer, denser in actual detail: acknowledgments not of an ineluctable universal process imaged in the mandarin intensity of poetic prose but of human effort translated into what is after all the more substantive and sustaining prose of the world. No doubt, the effect of multitudinousness and multiplicity that *The Years* conveys derives in part simply from the number of characters, events, and situations that make up the book, but, more important, its source is in the attention the novel pays to the stochastic data of daily life, its stuff, the contingent existence of noises, objects, things, and indeed people—all of which lends to the book a new weight and solidity, while at the same time qualifying its relentless temporal movement with a tension created by the contrapuntal pressure of a world that is, for the reader and obviously for Woolf, *present, felt* as an insistent and finally a stimulating energy. Grounded, as I have argued, in the here and now, the novel is less intimate and shapely but also less constricting and claustrophobic than its predecessors; and in the randomness and heft of its texture it offers a sign, an initial sign, of a new attitude on Woolf's part: the acceptance, with all its complexity, its terrors and disappointments as well as its potential, of a world freed at last (and as a direct consequence of that acceptance) from the manipulative imperialism of self-consciousness and, on another level, from the compensatory domination of art.

III

The process of revision (and re-vision) initiated by *The Years* comes to its fulfillment in *Between the Acts,* though not, perhaps, quite so simply as my organic formula suggests. Like all of Woolf's novels, her final one exhibits its own distinctive form, its special strategies and techniques and thus its own way of seizing and registering the world. There is, consequently, no sense in which the book can be read merely as a more successful version of what she had already done in *The Years.* Moreover, Woolf's way of imagining not only the world but the self and the relation between them in the earlier of the two novels clarifies and expands by the time of *Between the Acts* to the point where it seems reasonable to describe her vision, approximately but properly, as phenomenological.

Given the objections that such a claim are likely to call forth, it is probably wise to insist at this point that my intention is not to turn Woolf into a philosopher *malgré elle;* and even less is it to replace Bergson or G. E. Moore with some still more apodictic figure who will henceforth be seen as presiding over the genealogy of her thought and work. My approach, in other words, is not genetic (there is, to repeat, no question of influence) but comparative; and it is based on the recognition—or the belief—that in phenomenology's rejection of Cartesian dualism one discovers (for in ruling out influence, one needn't gainsay the age's common concerns) an analogue to Woolf's more intuitive but no less effective repudiation of the idealistic tendency manifest in her own earlier work and, as has been suggested, implicit in the entire modernist enterprise as well.[13]

But before attempting to legitimate the analogy, it needs also to be said that, like most such "schools," phenomenology encompasses a good many different and, at times, even divergent assumptions and approaches, not all of them, even in terms of the deliberately nonrestrictve correspondence I am proposing, equally relevant to an understanding of Woolf's thought at the end of her life. I intend therefore, because of its special pertinence, to take as my point of reference the philosophy of Maurice Merleau-Ponty, concentrating in particular on the posthumously published *The Prose of the World* and on the major essay derived from it, "Indirect Language and the Voices of Silence."[14] My choice of texts has to do partly with the centrality and accessibility of these works but most of all with the fact that the essay's major concerns—"perception, history, expression" (*IL*, p. 75)—are, it seems to me, also those of Woolf's final novel. That being the case, it will be most useful and, if I am correct in my assumption, most illuminating to approach *Between the Acts* by way of Merleau-Ponty's three categories, taking them, in roughly sequential order, as so many clues (flexible frames, as it were) to the complex and intricate responses the novel proposes to the mysteries and ambiguities of experience.

"Perception, which is an event," Merleau-Ponty writes, "opens onto the thing perceived, which appeared to be prior to perception and to be true before it. And if perception always reaffirms the preexistence of the world, it is precisely *because it* is an event, because the subject who perceives is already at grips with being through the *perceptual fields,* the 'senses'" (*PW*, p. 123). Two major presuppositions underlie Merleau-Ponty's definition, first, that the objects of perception possess an independence, an autonomy, that is anterior to any perception of them and, second, that perception presumes *activity*. I shall return later on to the question of the world's autonomic existence. What concerns me now is the notion of perception as event, activity, a gripping of being, for if perceptual exploration does in fact constitute one central focus of *Between the Acts*, then the ability of the novel's characters to respond with a sort of unmediated openness to what surrounds them defines their place in the hierarchy of the book's meaning and value structure. Who, then, exactly, is meant to claim the reader's principal interest and attention and to provide the clues needed to make sense of Woolf's most difficult and perplexing novel? According to Roger Poole, eager as always, in his stimulating but wrongheaded study, to discover everywhere in Woolf's work images of the struggle between the rational, overbearing Leonard and the vulnerable, intuitive Virginia, *Between the Acts* centers on the opposition of Lucy Swithin and her brother Bartholomew Oliver.[15] But to make these two pivotal (whatever their importance to the book's overall effect) seems to me not merely questionable but demonstrably wrong. Lucy, for example, her warmth, her charm, and her sympathetic nature notwithstanding, betrays immediately and throughout—and no less than her brother—the fact that her approach to life is fundamentally and thoroughly *conceptual:* that she is someone for whom all the world's data are subordinate to an overarching and predetermined sense of their significance. ("The immediate data of perception," Merleau-Ponty notes, "signify well beyond their own content, finding an inordinate echo in the perceiving subject" [*PW*, p. 123], which is precisely what they fail to do for Lucy.)

"For she belonged to the unifiers," Bartholomew thinks to himself about his sister, "he to the separatists."[16] And indeed, Lucy and Bart represent in every way opposite views (Poole is right about that) that are not only fixed and static but, like Sasha's, equally true—and one must add, in the context that *Between the Acts* provides, equally false; or—and this may well be the most accurate way of describing them—equally irrelevant.[17] Like the annual ritual conversation that precedes the pageant ("Every year they said, would it be wet or fine; and every year it was—one or the other" [p. 29]), brother and sister between them dramatize an attitude that Woolf no longer accepts as either helpful or valid, the modernist attitude that, with its attendant aesthetic formalism, subjects to the ordering imagination the threatening and disorienting economy "of a world of teeming, exclusive things which [can] be taken in only by means of a temporal cycle in which each gain [is] at the same time a loss" (*IL*, p. 50). In short, *Between the Acts* both alludes to and rejects the modernist paradox that allows Mrs. Latham to endow her world with the significance she longs to find in it but that also, when she fails to maintain her illuminated vision, impels her to flee that world's refractory, ominous indifference.

Between the Acts is no summing up. Still less is it an attempt to resolve neatly and symmetrically the problems it evokes. Consequently, one must expect to locate in the book no more than a series of attitudes or, at most, a direction. But to specify even these it is necessary to turn away from the novel's abstracters, from Lucy and her "one-making" especially (p. 204), and to agree that if Merleau-Ponty's notion of perception is correct, then pride of place belongs, in a progression of slightly eccentric circles, to Isa Oliver, Miss La Trobe, and the novel's narrator or (a distinction I'll return to) its voice. To begin with Isa, relatively speaking the least dynamic of the three: compared with Bart, Lucy, and that other seamless character, Mrs. Manresa, the "wild child of nature" (p. 52), she is, it seems safe to say, relentlessly indeterminate; and her incessant poetry-making (in a book filled with verbal activity that signifies less the created than the creating) bespeaks, in however confused and puzzled a way, a greater openness to the world than we have so far seen. To be sure, Isa is also the novel's most dichotomous character. Thus her tendency to think in terms of "love; and hate" (p. 109); her double reaction to her husband; and, most interestingly, her fascination on the one hand with a newspaper account of a brutal and extravagant rape and, on the other, with a recurrent, unspecified somewhere where "one sun would shine and all, without a doubt, would be clear" (p. 76). But Isa's dichotomies are fluid, unstable, not the stuff of genuine paradox; and her longing for escape (flight is, in one form or another, her most obsessive metaphor: "What do I ask? to fly away, from night and day, and issue where—no partings are" [p. 101]) is tempered by an awareness of "the future disturbing our present" (pp. 100–101).

In addition, Isa predicts from time to time the novel's emergent configuration of experience, as she does when her usual meditation on that realm where "change is not" produces the afterthought: "nor the mutable and lovable" (p. 181). More to the point, her subsequent and familiar plaint—"How am I burdened with . . . memories; possessions. This is the burden that the past laid on me, last little donkey in the long caravanserai crossing the desert" (p. 182)—terminates for once not in another flight but in an acceptance of the actual, the existent, that is reminiscent, but only superficially so, of Peter's dream: "On little donkey, patiently stumble. . . . Hear rather the shepherd, coughing by the farmyard wall; . . . the brawl in the barrack room when they stripped her naked; or the cry which in London when I thrust the window open someone cries . . ." (p. 183). Progressing from an emblem of reality (the coughing shepherd) to a mediated image of it (the newspaper story of the rape) to, at last, a fragment of her own perceptual experience (the cry that startles Sasha, here made part of the ordinary and daily), Isa demonstrates the possibility at least of the self pursuing, consciously and deliberately, its completion in what Merleau-Ponty refers to as an "already constituted" world (*PW*, p. 124). But only, it must be granted, the possibility. Like her husband, Giles, Isa, as critics repeatedly assert,[18] is, for the most part and to use her own word, "abortive" (p. 21)—at any rate until the novel's final scene; and for a more complex dramatization of Woolf's position one needs to consider the last of her artist-figures, the redoubtable Miss La Trobe.

Confronting La Trobe raises for the reader the knottiest problem of *Between the Acts:* the significance or—since even at the last it signifies differently for each of the characters—the meaning of the pageant. But to find that meaning one must avoid the almost irresistible temptation to view La Trobe as Woolf's *porte-parole* and so to find in the pageant yet another of our century's *mises en abyme,* which, according to this reading, intimates in its inner logic, as Lily Briscoe's painting does, the larger structure it pre-

sumably reduplicates and mirrors. In fact, searching the pageant for clues
to Woolf's own sense of past and present leads inevitably to an interpretation of the work (to take for granted other, intermediate accounts) as a
record either of historical decline or of transhistorical advance. So Alex
Zwerdling and Maria DiBattista, in what are probably the two most illuminating and persuasive recent commentaries on the book, describe the
pageant, in Zwerdling's case as an attempt, born out of nostalgia, diminished hope, and an awareness of "the gradual but persistent decay of the
sense of community," "to trace the pervasive sense of fragmentation and
isolation in the modern world to its historical roots";[19] and, in DiBattista's,
as an effort—facilitated "by denying to historical process any teleological or
rational principle except the love and hate by which it, like Nature, is
goaded and impelled to manifest itself"—to reveal "the triumph of time
the preserver and continuer over time the destroyer."[20]

But to infer from the pageant alone an attitude of affirmation *or* negation on Woolf's part is, I believe, to overconceptualize that curious, erratic
drama, to see it, as it were, from the outside. Such readings, in other
words, contrive to decontextualize the pageant and thus evade the task of
understanding it specifically as La Trobe's work—the representation of her
personality—and, more generally, as her highly equivocal response to the
situation that occasions it. The evasion is understandable enough, not only
because La Trobe, like the rest of the book's characters, invites a less
analytic approach than earlier, more psychologically developed figures,
but because of the difficulty one experiences, even when accustomed to
Woolf's new method of characterization, in specifying La Trobe's intentions and her attendant attitudes to herself, her work, and her audience.

To begin with, though so much more volatile and abrasive than Lily
Briscoe, La Trobe unexpectedly reveals herself through most of the performance as very much the typical artist of the twenties. Which is to say
that, the necessarily episodic nature of the pageant notwithstanding, her
concerns are with illusion and continuity and that, in her most striking act
of self-definition, she becomes "one who seethes wandering bodies and
floating voices in a cauldron, and makes rise up from its amorphous mass a
recreated world" (p. 180); becomes, in short, the artist as magician, producing heterocosms, visions of unity that transcend the partial and fragmented worlds that are their ostensible subject. Longing "to write a play
without an audience—*the* play" (p. 210), she is at the same time intensely
concerned to keep the spectators from "slipp[ing] the noose" of her aesthetic sorcery (p. 145). It follows that at this point La Trobe's enemy is, in a
manner of speaking, the view that so absorbs the audience and that is for
the reader the symbolic representation of both time and space: the flow of
history, which becomes less La Trobe's subject than the instrumentality of
her more imperious vision, and the diversity of the world, which, ironically (and predicting Woolf's final position), constantly but *at its own will*

rescues her from the hated interruptions, the failure of illusion she defines as death.

Curiously, however, as the pageant continues, La Trobe's attitude appears to change: " 'After Vic.,' she had written, 'try ten mins. of present time.' . . . She wanted to expose them, as it were, to douche them, with present-time reality" (p. 209). And though the experiment threatens to founder, until nature again intervenes, La Trobe proceeds in a yet more dramatic reversal of her aesthetic position (as she holds up to the audience its reflections) to confuse and blur boundaries and divisions ("the reticence of nature was undone" [p. 215]) and so to destroy the heretofore cherished autonomy of art. Is what we witness in this process a transformation of La Trobe's attitude not only to her art and her audience but toward the phe-nomenal and, since it occurs as we move into the present, toward history? Perhaps to a degree; and I shall return shortly to that possibility. But I think it comes closer to the truth to see in her various strategies an affective continuity that expresses, equally and more or less consecutively, her re-sentment of the play's subject ("this skimble-skamble stuff" [p. 113]) and her possibly unacknowledged defiance of its spectators. An outsider her-self, "a slave to her audience" (p. 113), forced to restrict herself to the limited, provincial story of England and, worse, to cut and gash her play so as to make it suitable for a fund-raising entertainment, La Trobe betrays throughout and in a variety of ways the repeated frustration of her will to order the world into unity or her audience into an acknowledgment of her artistic power over its sensibility.

No doubt, taken in and of itself, the pageant demonstrates a decline of sorts (how could it not, since decline is what its premise—England as *"A child new born"* [p. 95]—entails?); but what is at issue, to repeat, is not Woolf's but La Trobe's perspective on *"our island history"* (p. 94). Obliged by convention, one imagines, to celebrate England pastoral and Elizabethan ("What made her," Cobbet of Cobbs Corner, another outsider, asks with some reason, "indue the antique with this glamour—this sham lure. . . ?" [p. 116]), La Trobe modulates thereafter from the ironic to the sarcastic and then, in the dangerous freedom of "Present time. Ourselves" (p. 206), from ambiguity to the paradox with which, to no one's satisfac-tion, the pageant ends. In a sense, then, what changes is not the pageant's theme, which is on one level less England than its author's state of exclu-sion (imposed and self-imposed), but its tone: the increasingly embittered response to that state of isolation which everything seems to force upon her.

On the other hand, the play does convey *a* view of history, though (and this strikes me as Woolf's position) in its bitterness, its defiance, and its attempt to appropriate the world (England, the audience, nature itself) to its author's needs and will, it twists the roots of its endeavor into what Merleau-Ponty calls "false" or "cruel history":

There are . . . two historicities. One is ironic or even derisory, and made of misinterpretations, for each age struggles against the others as against aliens by imposing its concerns and perspectives upon them. This history is forgetfulness rather than memory; it is dismemberment, ignorance, externality. But the other history, without which the first would be impossible, is constituted and reconstituted step by step by the *interest* which bears us toward that which is not us and by that life which the past, in a continuous exchange, brings to us and finds in us, and which it continues to lead in each painter [or writer] who revives, recaptures, and renews the entire undertaking of painting in each new work. (*IL,* p. 60)

It would be easiest to fasten on the word "dismemberment" and thereby to invoke a comparison with the *"orts, scraps and fragments"* (p. 219) of the play's final speech. But the point is not that La Trobe is *objectively* wrong or right in her gloomy view of history and the present, which is anyhow contradicted by another voice that brings "from chaos and cacophony measure" (p. 220) and leads the spectators to ask: "Was that voice ourselves? Scraps, orts and fragments, are we, also, that?" (p. 221). The point is, rather, that in "imposing [her] concerns," La Trobe misinterprets, simplifies, and, in an ultimate sense, falsifies, reifies, both past and present; denies them their situation and their horizon in the service of her more pressing subjective needs. The captive and her audience, she is also, or consequently, its antagonist, expressing *and* distorting, mocking, contesting its values and beliefs; challenging but not, after all, completely overturning its spirit; leading it and herself, as I have suggested, through ambiguity to a conclusive, paralyzing paradox that is the final cruelty of a movement whose end is (paradoxically) stasis: "The gramophone gurgled *Unity—Dispersity*. It gurgled *Un . . . dis . . .* And ceased" (p. 235). For it *is* an end, the death La Trobe has feared all along, and a recall, though on a larger scale, of Sasha Latham's equally valid polarities. (How else, except by recognizing that state of equal poise, to account for the persuasiveness of both Zwerdling's and DiBattista's arguments?) In sum, what the pageant lacks is the *"interest"* of Merleau-Ponty's "other history," which accords to past and future a vitality, a dynamism, and an independence that are at the same time an acknowledgment of "that which is not us": the world's facticity.

The resolution or transcendence of paradox lies precisely in that acknowledgment, and if there are hints of it in the pageant, they are to be located in the fact that its injunctions to unite are less triumphant than Mr. Streatfield's, less mechanical than their translation into the journalistic predictions of Mr. Page and the *Times*. But also in the fact that its ambiguities to some degree (and thanks to La Trobe's aesthetic spirit: "she was always all agog to get things up" [p. 71]) resist, equally, the warring claims of unity and chaos and the gramophone's neat summation of their uneasy truce. In any case, the pageant is not coterminous with the novel; nor is it the last of La Trobe, whose briefer but arguably more significant dramatic work—the to-be-written play with which *Between the Acts* ends—turns opposition into qualification, as "cruel history" gives way, through a more authentic (because more disinterested) attempt at expression, to what Merleau-Ponty (borrowing from Paul Ricoeur) calls "advent": "a promise of events" (*IL*, p. 70).

That second play originates in the most symbolically dense and central episode of the novel. Reviewing in her mind the effect of the pageant, imagining for a moment its success, La Trobe ends, in her recognition of the limitations and evanescence of art, by pronouncing the work, bitterly, miserably, "a failure" (p. 244). But something odd and unexpected happens at that point: "Then suddenly the starlings attacked the tree behind which she had hidden. . . . The whole tree hummed with the whizz they made, as if each bird plucked a wire. A whizz, a buzz rose from the bird-buzzing, bird-vibrant, bird-blackened tree. The tree became a rhapsody, a quivering cacophony, a whizz and vibrant rapture, branches, leaves, birds syllabling discordantly life, life, life, without measure, without stop devouring the tree" (pp. 244–45). There is no way, as one reads this pulsating description of untamed energy, to avoid the memory of Sasha as widow bird in a solitary tree or to resist the awareness of how differently, indeed oppositely, Woolf's symbols function in *Between the Acts*, where the tree surely signifies that La Trobe is not just abstract or abstracting consciousness but consciousness embodied and situated in the world ("the subject of perception," Merleau-Ponty writes, "is a body made to explore the world" [*PW*, p. 123]), and where the birds represent the world imposing itself on her, initiating through perception the process of what will in time become expression. To quote Merleau-Ponty again (the passage is basic and essential): "In one and the same movement knowledge roots itself in perception and distinguishes itself from perception. . . . Perception opens us to a world already constituted and can only reconstitute it. This reduplication signifies both that the world offers itself as prior to perception and that *we do not limit ourselves to registering the world but would like to engender it.* . . . However firm my perceptive grasp of the world may be, it is entirely dependent upon a centrifugal movement which throws me toward the world" (*PW*, pp. 124–25; emphasis added).

The scene, in other words, must be read as an affirmation of Husserl's *Lebenswelt* and, as Merleau-Ponty makes clear, of the intricate relations between perception and expression (as well as, by extension, between them and history, which is "not an external idol . . . [but] ourselves with our roots, our growth, and, as we say, the fruits of our toil" [*IL*, p. 75]). The roots of La Trobe's second historical work are in her symbolic encounter, its growth in what follows—the creativity that, despite the interruption of death (Mrs. Chalmers on her way to and from her husband's grave), despite the disappointments of her life, continues nonetheless, imaged in words that express uncannily Merleau-Ponty's sense of human beings "caught up in the push and shove of being":[21] "From the earth green waters seemed to rise over her. . . . Words of one syllable sank down into the mud. She drowsed. She nodded. The mud became fertile. Words rose above the intolerably laden dumb oxen plodding through the mud. Words without meaning—wonderful words" (pp. 246–48). Woolf's conception is itself wonderfully of a piece; and it is altogether fitting that the completion of the process occurs not like Lily Briscoe's on the grassy lawn of a summer house but in a pub, amid acrid smells, smoke, and resentment; that there, surrounded by the things and inhabitants of the world ("She no longer saw them, yet they upheld her" [p. 248]), her vision rooted in and arising out of her situation in that world, she brings "meaning into existence" (*PW*, p. 141), incarnates *it* in art: "Suddenly the tree was pelted with starlings. She set down her glass. She heard the first words" (p. 248).[22]

The "fruits of [her] toil" are made more visible and concrete still in the novel's final episode, in its ending especially, where the lives of the major characters become indistinguishable from those of La Trobe's new play. But at this point we as readers become aware that the relation La Trobe's characters bear to her and to the inhabitants of Pointz Hall she and they bear to Woolf—or to what I earlier and deliberately referred to as its voice. Voice rather than narrator since that apparently (more or less) traditional figure is, paradoxically, so much less definable, locatable than her supposedly transparent predecessors in the novels from *Mrs. Dalloway* through *The Waves*. Woolf provides the clue to what we are dealing with in one of her diary entries (April 26, 1938): "Why not Poyntzet Hall [that is, *Between the Acts*]: a centre: all literature discussed in connection with real little incongruous living humour: and anything that comes into my head; but 'I' rejected: 'We' substituted . . . 'We' . . . the composed of many different things. . . ."[23] In light of the obsessive interwar concern with the self, the notion of substituting "We" for "I" is in itself momentous, since, whatever else the passage intends, it seems safe to say that "We" suggests a less subjectivist approach and the "many different things" a less monolithic sense of truth or reality than one finds in the earlier novels; or, to put the matter differently, that "We," being by definition an assumption of relationship, entails a denial of idealistic and also of dualistic modes of thought and, in pointing to a more comprehensive vision, offers (like phenomenology) a way out of what Christopher Caudwell referred to as the epistemological crisis of modernism.[24] Finally, if the "centre" carries the force of the rayed-around dot in *The Years*, it becomes evident that the narrator is, so to speak, incarnated in the novel and that what is at issue is not, as in the earlier books, the concealing of perspective but its diffusion:

its expression through the variousness of the novel's techniques and, most of all, through the density and heterogeneity of its texture.

So much richer in this respect than even *The Years, Between the Acts* acknowledges and pays tribute to the absolute dailiness of life; bespeaks the "coexistence of perceived things as rivals in [one's] field of vision" (*IL*, p. 49). The rivalry is central. Nature, people, things, all fill the world with their presence—and with the noise that announces that presence—giving to the book a plenitude, vibrancy, and thickness that counterbalance and perhaps prevail over the struggles and frustrations the characters repeatedly undergo. Again as in *The Years* and again still more determinedly, things exist in their own right and not as so many agents of a transcendent symbolic design. "Glazed in their self-centered world, fish swam" (p. 55); animals pass, as they like, in and out of the barn; a cow coughs, birds chuckle, "swallows darting . . . dancing . . . [move] to the unheard rhythm of their own wild hearts" (p. 80); everywhere there are "minute nibblings and rustlings" (p. 120); Streatfield is "ignored by the cows, condemned by the clouds which continued their majestic rearrangement of the celestial landscape" (p. 222). Examples could be multiplied indefinitely, but the point is clear: if for the reader the book's effect is most immediately the result of an involvement with the disjunctions of its human level, it is still more emphatically the outcome of a less conscious and calculated response to the experience—mediated by the book's texture, by the representation of the natural world's refusal to be appropriated and objectified—of *touching earth.*

Introduced, ironically enough, by Lucy Swithin, herself "up in the clouds, like an air ball" (p. 139), the phrase carries with it a reference to Antaeus ("Antaeus, didn't he touch earth?" [p. 32]), the most appropriate emblem of Woolf's later vision—the sign of her rapprochement with a world now recognized, willy-nilly, as her horizon and her ground, the source of her being and of her art. Given the substantiality, the jostling fullness of that world and, as I have been insisting, the rendering of it through what is for Woolf a new, apparently more casual deployment of detail, it is hardly surprising that the form of *Between the Acts* should seem so much more open, inclusive, and, in Merleau-Ponty's sense of the word, unfinished. In fact, if the novel embodies, in La Trobe's pageant and play, Merleau-Ponty's two historicities, it reveals as well two structures: the first (whose final irrelevance I have asserted) of opposition, which assumes or presumes the possibility of "thoughts without words" (p. 68); the second, of qualification or modification, which accepts, at least as the preliminary stage of an ongoing process, "words without meaning" (p. 248): structures based, in short, on the oppositive force of *or* and on the moderating deliberativeness of *but* and *yet*.

The structure of opposition (Lucy and Bart; unifiers and separatists;

unity and dispersity) is unquestionably the more visible in the book, since the modifications and qualifications are, by comparison, relatively covert or, rather, microcosmic—functions primarily not of clashes on the level of character, action, and plot but of syntactic adjustment and rhetorical nuance. What matters, of course, is the cumulative effect of these qualifications, which is such that even apparent oppositions ("It was a shock to find . . . how much she felt . . . of love; and of hate" [p. 60]) resolve themselves into less absolute states of conflict: "Blunt arrows bruised her; of love, then of hate. Through other people's bodies she felt neither love nor hate distinctly" (p. 82). But not always so neatly as in these two correlative examples. My point is intended to be less obvious and more far-reaching, namely, that under the pressure of the novel's language even its most intransigent antitheses (Isa's "Yes, No" is one [p. 251]) gradually give way (for the reader) to a sense of impulses and feelings that complicate each other instead of canceling one another out. All of which is to say that the state of paradox that opposition figures and that has as its symbol and result the desire for some place out of time inevitably becomes in the more earthbound *Between the Acts* a state of ambiguity whose images are "a mellay; a medley; an entrancing spectacle . . . of dappled light and shade" (p. 112).

The effects and consequences I am describing naturally enough derive from something more, and more substantial, than merely the repeated use of *or* or *but* as coordinating conjunctions (important though those repetitions are). What is at stake is, in fact, Woolf's general attitude to language in the book, of which the following passage gives a reasonably typical impression:

> Across the hall a door opened. One voice, another voice, a third voice came wimpling and warbling: gruff—Bart's voice; quaveringly—Lucy's voice; middle-toned—Isa's voice. Their voices impetuously, impatiently, protestingly came across the hall saying: "Keep it hot"; saying: "We won't, no Candish, we won't wait."
> Coming out from the library the voices stopped in the hall. They encountered an obstacle evidently; a rock. Utterly impossible was it, even in the heart of the country, to be alone? That was the shock. After that, the rock was raced round, embraced. (p. 47)

Filled with alliteration, assonance, repetition, and rhyme, these lines are yet extraordinarily different, both in intention and result, from the poetic prose of the earlier novels, which so often aims at a transcendence or penetration of the phenomenal and the achievement of some more enduring reality. Working in her last novel not to create and sustain but to subvert illusion, Woolf uses language in such a way—incessantly mocking, playing, teasing—as to call into question, it would seem, not only its representational and mimetic force but even its power to signify. Nevertheless, however reflexive its linguistic strategies, *Between the Acts* patently refuses the lure of the hermetic and the self-referential (as firmly as it does that of the transhuman); and, far from rushing into the prison-house of language, opens itself to the task of expressing the world.

How exactly it does that is the problem at issue; and once more Merleau-Ponty comes to hand to clarify the matter. Writing of language very much as he does of knowledge, he both roots his theory of expression in and distinguishes it from its source, which is in this case the work of Ferdinand de Saussure. Thus, to begin with the inevitable gesture of distinction, he maintains that "try as each word may (as Saussure explains) to extract its meaning from all the others, the fact remains that at the moment it occurs the task of expressing is no longer differentiated and referred to other words—it is accomplished, and we understand something" (*IL*, p. 81). Further, what we understand and "*mean* is not before us, outside all speech, as sheer signification [that is, as preexisting meaning]. It is only the excess of what we live over what has already been said" (*IL*, p. 83). Expression, in other words, is creative, generative, ongoing, the bringing of meaning into being, as La Trobe does in the second of her plays. On the other hand, although, given his belief in the reciprocal relations of consciousness and the world, Merleau-Ponty rejects the semiotics of enclosure, he retains in a fundamental sense the Saussurean idea of language as diacritical: "Meaning appears only at the intersection of and as it were in the interval between words" (*IL*, p. 42). Now, *Between the Acts* clearly exceeds the normally diacritical nature of language, makes capital, in its verbal texture as in its deployment of details or in its highly discontinuous, if minimal, plot, of "intervals" (and indeed of "excess") as the very basis of its semantic thrust. The massive use of semicolons (Woolf's preferred form of punctuation, to be sure, but here both pandemic and eccentric: would anyone else have written "love; and hate"?); the repeated embeddings of phrases and clauses within the distended frame of her sentences; the consequent interruption and suspension of syntactic order; the reflexiveness of the books' rhetoric; and, of course, the ubiquitous modifications of thought and feeling (the *buts* and *yets* to which I have already called attention)—all contribute to the novel's structure of qualification, which demands to be seen in turn (for what else are qualifications?) as the configuration of a series of significative and generative gaps: "a *determinate gap* to be filled by words."[25]

Thematically, the presence of these determinate gaps in *Between the Acts* is articulated through the constant allusions to silence, with which the book is as filled as it is with noise. And understandably so: "The idea of *complete* expression is nonsensical . . . all language is indirect or allusive— that is, if you wish, silence" (*IL*, p. 43). Silence is, then, the counterpart of language, in a sense its source; and its paradoxical presence has some resemblance to that of Pointz Hall, the novel's *mise en scène*, which, situated at the heart of everything (time, space, "this remote village in the very heart of England" [p. 22]), is also the *point* from which everything radiates: "Empty, empty, empty; silent, silent, silent. The room was a shell, singing of what was before time was; a vase stood in the heart of the house, alabaster, smooth, cold, holding the still, distilled essence of emptiness, silence" (p. 47).[26] Several things need to be noted about the description: first, that the room, though (or because) empty and silent, *sings* ("We must consider speech before it is spoken, the background of silence which does not cease to surround it and without which it would say nothing" [*IL*, p. 46]); second, that its song is "of what was before time was"; and, last, that the imagery of the passage looks forward to the novel's final scene, in which the same room again becomes a "shell" (pp. 250 and 252) and in which the inhabitants of Pointz Hall, thinking still of the pageant, gradually evolve (or Giles and Isa do) into the characters of La Trobe's next play. We move, that is (leaving far behind the England of the pageant), back even before recorded history: "It was night before roads were made, or houses. It was the night that dwellers in caves had watched from some high place among rocks" (p. 256). But back too, surely, in validation of the episode of starlings and tree (and by way of metaphorical transference) to consciousness at its most primordial and elemental. The book, in short, enacts a movement from the conceptual (the structure of opposition) to the perceptual (the structure of qualification: "Alone, enmity was bared; *also* love" [p. 255; emphasis added]), revealing perception not as superior but anterior: the ground of history, conception, and creation.

Thus the novel's thematic silences *are* its linguistic gaps; and as they work together to uncover the structures of history and consciousness, they demonstrate as well an attitude on Woolf's part that, as noted earlier, begins to emerge only with *The Years:* an *acceptance* of those discontinuities (heretofore, for Woolf and for the modernists in general, the source of horror and the impetus for transformation and escape) that now become the potential for further and continued activity. In fact, the "acts" of the novel's title are viewed as directly dependent on what is between them. Or, to reverse the proposition: the gaps are the mud out of which La Trobe's inspiration effloresces; the daily, unspoken antagonisms as a result of which Giles's and Isa's final confrontation emerges; the dreary pageant of history from which the future must grow; and the silences between which new words arise. To say this is certainly to controvert the unremitting gloom of Zwerdling's interpretation; but it is hardly to see hope sweeping before it everything the novel makes problematical. "There was a fecklessness," runs a description early in the book, "a lack of symmetry and order in the clouds, as they thinned and thickened. Was it their own law, or no law, they obeyed?" (p. 30). The question goes unanswered— unless it is by the later allusion to "a criss-cross of lines making no pattern"

(p. 136); but, and this is the point, the answer no longer matters as it once did to Woolf. Accepting the contingent and unresolved in a way we now recognize as postmodern, the novel does not stop there but affirms nonetheless—or, more accurately, *as well*—the possibility of engendering from the diversity, facticity, and openness of experience new modes both of expressing and of being in the world. The chief sign of Woolf's new and complex response, the view toward a fluid and shifting horizon, is of course in the book's last words—"Then the curtain rose. They spoke" (p. 256)—the deliberately unresolved and open ending, which, resisting the artfully orchestrated effects that generally close her novels and bend them back upon themselves, points instead to the unfinished, the never-completed obligation to create: to achieve, against the persisting, intransigent, and acknowledged background of disappointment and failure, modest and limited affirmations of what lies available to consciousness in the gaps and silences of the already constituted world.

Early in the novel, standing in her room and looking at the scene outside (once again the separating pane of glass appears, symbol of embattled subjectivity), Isa surveys the effectively distanced garden landscape and (she too) endows it with meaning: "Isolated on a green island, hedged about with snowdrops, laid with a counterpane of puckered silk, *the innocent island* floated under her window" (p. 20; emphasis added). Both the act of transformation and its resultant image are ubiquitous in the novel: in Isa's dreams of changeless perfection, in Lucy's "one-making," in La Trobe's conception of England as *"A child new born,"* and perhaps even in Mrs. Manresa's repeated definition of herself as "a wild child of nature." In brief, most of the characters cherish, in one form or another, the peace and stability of an ideal realm removed from the actualities of time and space. In a real sense, then, the supersession of the innocent island by Antaeus, the prose of the world, describes the development of *Between the Acts* and the movement of its leading characters from the seductive charms of enchantment ("Islands of security" [p. 239]) to the more complex reality of "the battle in the mud" (p. 237). But the progression from the hypostatic to the existential, from idealism to phenomenology, does something more: it recapitulates the shape and direction of Woolf's career as a whole.[27] Divided by only some fifteen years, "A Summing Up" and *Between the Acts* describe a curve that wrenches the assumptions and imperatives of modernism away from the need to order and transcend a broken world toward the recognition of the phenomenal, whatever its gaps and fissures, as the locus and source of experience. Seen in these terms, the distance between the two works figures nothing less than a revolution in the nature of twentieth-century thought, as Sasha's impulse to flee the stubborn, inattentive presence of all that surrounds her gives way to the willingness—Isa's, La Trobe's, and finally Woolf's—to accept contingency: to shatter the window that separates consciousness from the world and so, at last, to touch earth.

Notes

1. The position of "A Summing Up" in the collection obviously relates most directly to Leonard Woolf's decision to group together his wife's previously unpublished stories at the end of *A Haunted House*. Whether it appears as the last of these out of deference to its title or because Leonard recognized in it a central statement of his wife's concerns, it is impossible to say. In any case, the story is by no means (as its placement in *A Haunted House* might suggest) a product of Virginia Woolf's final years. In the "Short Story Sequence" she has entitled *Mrs. Dalloway's Party* (London: Hogarth Press, 1973), Stella McNichol assigns the stories that concern her, including "A Summing Up," "to the period between *Jacob's Room* (1922) and *To the Lighthouse* (1927)" (p. 10) and conjectures that they were written "probably not later than May 1925" (p. 14). The story is, then, a summary not of Woolf's entire career but of the work of her middle period, which, I want to argue, ends with *The Waves*.

My references to "A Summing Up" and to Woolf's other short fictions are to *A Haunted House and Other Short Stories*, new ed. (London: Hogarth Press, 1953). Subsequent references to this book (hereafter abbreviated as *AHH*) and to all other works quoted in this essay will be given, after their first citation, parenthetically in the text.

2. Thomas Pynchon, *The Crying of Lot 49* (New York: Bantam Books, 1967), p. 59.

3. I have dealt briefly with this aspect of the story in "Modern/Modernist," *Contemporary Literature* 20 (Summer 1979):369–70. For a more extended discussion of modernist paradox, see my book *Horizons of Assent: Modernism, Postmodernism, and the Ironic Imagination* (Baltimore and London: The Johns Hopkins University Press, 1981), chap. 1.

4. The "Virginia Woolf Issue" of the *Bulletin of the New York Public Library* 80 (Winter 1977) indicates a significant change in attitudes toward the novel, which has frequently been ignored in recent critical studies of Woolf. Among older books, James Hafley's *The Glass Roof: Virginia Woolf as Novelist* (1954; reprint ed. New York: Russell & Russell, 1963) is a notable exception to the generally negative evaluations of the novel. For Hafley, *The Years* is "Virginia Woolf's best novel" (p. 145).

5. Leonard Woolf, *The Journey Not the Arrival Matters: An Autobiography of the Years 1939–1969* (London: Hogarth Press, 1969), p. 42.

6. In a diary entry (dated Tuesday, June 19, 1923), Woolf wrote: "I daresay it's true, however, that I haven't that 'reality' gift. I insubstantise, willfully to some extent, distrusting reality—its cheapness." See *A Writer's Diary*, ed. Leonard Woolf (New York: Harcourt, Brace and Co., 1954), p. 56.

7. Virginia Woolf, *To the Lighthouse*, new ed. (London: Hogarth Press, 1930), pp. 309–10. The novel will be referred to hereafter as *TTL*.

8. Virginia Woolf, *The Waves*, new ed. (London: Hogarth Press, 1943), pp. 174 and 185.

9. For another reading of this episode, see Julia Carlson, "The Solitary Traveller in *Mrs. Dalloway*," in *Virginia Woolf: A Collection of Criticism*, ed. Thomas S. W. Lewis (New York: McGraw Hill, 1975), pp. 56–62.

10. Virginia Woolf, *Mrs. Dalloway*, new ed. (London: Hogarth Press, 1947), p. 63. The book will be referred to hereafter as *MD*.

11. Yeats's phrase is from "The Tower," in *The Collected Poems of W. B. Yeats* (New York: Macmillan Co., 1951), p. 197. Forster's appears in "Art for Art's Sake," in *Two Cheers for Democracy* (New York: Harcourt, Brace and Co., 1951), p. 94. On the question of the aesthetic, see my book *Art and Order: A Study of E. M. Forster* (New York: New York University Press, 1964), chap. 5.

12. Virginia Woolf, *The Years* (London: Hogarth Press, 1937), p. 142. The italics in the second quotation are mine.

13. I want to make clear that my aim in this essay is not to provide a phenomenological reading of *Between the Acts* but to read the novel *in terms of* phenomenology, specifically in terms of the problems it introduces and the assumptions it makes, and so to show how *Between the Acts*, answerable to the dynamics of Woolf's personal development, intimates and thematizes the phenomenological attitude or imagination. This is to say, further, that my

interest in phenomenology centers less on its methodology than on its way of apprehending and interpreting the ontological relations between self and world: its grid, so to speak. Methodologically, phenomenology may be interpreted, variously, as the attempt to achieve a pure description of its subject (see Edward S. Casey's *Imagining: A Phenomenological Study* [Bloomington: Indiana University Press, 1976]); as the empathetic receptiveness of the critic to the work of the author he is engaged with, his merging with the author's consciousness (the aim of the Geneva School of critics); as the process whereby reader and text together bring the literary work, "the aesthetic object," to birth (see Wolfgang Iser's *The Act of Reading: A Theory of Aesthetic Response* [Baltimore and London: The Johns Hopkins University Press, 1978]); or, finally, as the consistent and deliberate understanding of the writer in terms of his or her subjectivity (see Roger Poole, *The Unknown Virginia Woolf* [Cambridge: Cambridge University Press, 1978]).

In his suggestive and important essay, "The Philosophical Realism of Virginia Woolf," in *English Literature and British Philosophy: A Collection of Essays*, ed. S. P. Rosenbaum (Chicago: University of Chicago Press, 1971), pp. 316–56, Rosenbaum sets out to demonstrate the relevance of G. E. Moore's philosophy to an understanding of Woolf's work. Rosenbaum denies that Woolf was an idealist (p. 323), and his remarks on the final novels suggest a position radically different from mine. In them, he maintains, "Virginia Woolf is less preoccupied with consciousness and perception than in her four preceding ones. . . . In each the content of consciousness is more important than the act" (p. 355).

14. "Indirect Language and the Voices of Silence" (hereafter referred to as *IL*) appears in the collection of Merleau-Ponty's work called *Signs*, trans. Richard C. McCleary (Evanston, Ill.: Northwestern University Press, 1964), pp. 39–83. In its original form, the essay comprised the central chapter of the posthumously published work *The Prose of the World*, ed. Claude Lefort, trans. John O'Neill (London: Heinemann, 1974). (The book will be referred to hereafter as *PW*.) Merleau-Ponty extracted and, as Lefort says, "considerably modified" the chapter (p. x), which appeared in *Les Temps modernes* in 1952.

Others have noted or implied the resemblance between Woolf's work and Merleau-Ponty's. See Harvena Richter, *Virginia Woolf: The Inward Voyage* (Princeton, N.J.: Princeton University Press, 1970), p. 245; Iser, *The Act of Reading*, p. 169; and Poole, *The Unknown Virginia Woolf*, p. 198. Poole's "postphenomenological" study (p. 4), to which I shall return, is the most elaborate attempt to provide a reading of Woolf in terms of her "embodiment." According to Poole, "In Virginia Woolf, indeed, phenomenology found its novelist" (p. 198); and up to a point his study proves remarkably illuminating, both of Woolf herself and of (some of) her fiction. Poole's tendentiousness, however (most notably the attempt to cast Leonard Woolf in the role of villain in the drama of Virginia's life), leads to extremely partial interpretations and at times, as we shall see, to misreadings of her fiction.

15. Poole, *The Unknown Virginia Woolf*, chap. 16 and, especially, chap. 17.

16. Virginia Woolf, *Between the Acts* (London: Hogarth Press, 1941), p. 140.

17. I have explored this aspect of the book briefly in *Horizons of Assent*, chap. 1.

18. See, for example, Phyllis Rose, *Woman of Letters: A Life of Virginia Woolf* (New York: Oxford University Press, 1978), p. 233.

19. Alex Zwerdling, "*Between the Acts* and the Coming of War," *Novel* 10 (Spring 1977):232.

20. Maria DiBattista, *Virginia Woolf's Major Novels: The Fables of Anon* (New Haven and London: Yale University Press, 1980), pp. 209 and 208.

21. Merleau-Ponty, "Introduction" to *Signs*, p. 14.

22. Compare the statement by Pierre Thévenaz in *What is Phenomenology? and Other Essays*, ed. James M. Edie (Chicago: Quadrangle Books, 1962), p. 50: "The world gives itself to consciousness which confers on it its meaning."

The fact that in this scene "there was no longer a view" (pp. 245–46) seems to me to indicate not that La Trobe has succeeded in erasing the world but that her interaction with it is now elemental, radical, earthy. Surrendering control, she achieves something more.

23. Woolf, *A Writer's Diary*, p. 279.

24. See Christopher Caudwell, *Romance and Realism: A Study in English Bourgeois Literature*, ed. Samuel Hynes (Princeton, N.J.: Princeton University Press, 1970), pp. 97–119.

25. Merleau-Ponty, "On the Phenomenology of Language," in *Signs*, p. 89. Geoffrey Hartman deals suggestively with the idea of the novel's gaps in "Virginia's Web," in *Beyond*

Formalism: Literary Essays 1958–1970 (New Haven and London: Yale University Press, 1970), pp. 71–84.

26. Commenting on this passage, B. H. Fussell writes (in "Woolf's Peculiar Comic World: *Between the Acts*," in *Virginia Woolf: Revaluation and Continuity*, ed. Ralph Freedman [Berkeley and Los Angeles: University of California Press, 1980]): "The vase, symbolic of art, within a room, symbolic of life—both distill images of the abyss at the center of consciousness and of reality" (p. 273). To which one wants to respond, in Merleau-Ponty's words, that "an abyss is not nothing; it has its environs and edges. One always thinks of something. . . . Even the action of thinking is caught up in the push and shove of being" ("Introduction" to *Signs*, p. 14).

27. According to Vincent Descombes in *Le Même et l'autre: quarante-cinq ans de philosophie française (1933–1978)* (Paris: Editions de Minuit, 1979), Merleau-Ponty's philosophy represents at the last an "idéalisme *réformé*, mais non *surmonté*" (p. 88; an "idealism *reformed* but not *overcome*"). But even if that is the case, there is no doubt but that in his work (and Woolf's) the world and consciousness have been granted a new substantiality and freedom.

Death, Grief, Analogous Form:
As I Lay Dying

Eric J. Sundquist

> You know that if I were reincarnated, I'd want
> to come back a buzzard. Nothing hates him or
> envies him or wants him or needs him. He is
> never bothered or in danger, and he can eat
> anything.—Faulkner, 1956 interview

Faulkner's desire to be reincarnated as a buzzard[1] may appear to betray the kind of grotesque humor that *As I Lay Dying* has been rightly
accused of indulging. It is a noteworthy gloss not simply because the
novel's own buzzards pose a constant threat to the rotting corpse of Addie
Bundren as it is borne on its funeral journey to Jefferson, but also because
Faulkner's identification with the birds, when viewed in the context of the
problems of narrative form posed by the novel, indicates immediately a
grand, if macabre, detachment from his materials. Such a detachment from
materials that are both dead and yet potently living—or to be more exact in
terms of the book, from materials that are in the process of dying—
suggests an analogy that is probably relevant to all of Faulkner's work
(and, from the vantage of 1956, to his great fictional design itself) but has
particular interest for *As I Lay Dying* since the novel itself seems curiously
detached from his other major works. Though its mood is that of savage
burlesque, and thus represents a continuation of the intimate family
brutalities Faulkner had already explored in *The Sound and the Fury* and
would make more violently shocking when he revised *Sanctuary*, *As I Lay
Dying* is rather a tender book. It can, more than any of his novels, be read
independently, and it is his most perfect and finished piece of fiction. On
the other hand—and perhaps because of this—it is nearly a compendium
of the problematic techniques that Faulkner had discovered in the sudden
creative illumination of *The Sound and the Fury* and would relentlessly pursue throughout the remainder of his career. It is, in fact, a virtual textbook

of technique, one that displays all his talents and their inevitable risks as they support and drive one another to the perilous limits of narrative form that Faulkner would require for his great novels on the prolonged tragedy and grief of the South.

Complaints about Faulkner's rhetoric—its gratuitous contortions, its motiveless expanse, its tactless mix of pathos and ridicule—are common even among his admirers. Most often, such complaints proceed from one of two assumptions: that the author or narrator (the two are easily confused) has fallen victim to his own fantasies of technique; or that a character or speaker (these two are also easily confused) has been allowed a command of language utterly incommensurate wih his place in the novel's realistic or representational scheme. In some notable instances the two difficulties are merged, as in the following passage from *As I Lay Dying*, in which the young boy Vardaman, "speaking" both as one of the book's fifteen main characters and as one of its equal number of narrators, describes an encounter with his brother's horse in the barn:

> It is dark. I can hear wood, silence: I know them. But not living sounds, not even him. It is as though the dark were resolving him out of his integrity, into an unrelated scattering of components—snuffings and stampings; smells of cooling flesh and ammoniac hair; an illusion of a co-ordinated whole of splotched hide and strong bones within which, detached and secret and familiar, an *is* different from my *is*. I see him dissolve—legs, a rolling eye, a gaudy splotching like cold flames—and float upon the dark in fading solution; all one yet neither; all either yet none. I can see hearing coil toward him, caressing, shaping his hard shape—fetlock, hip, shoulder and head; smell and sound. I am not afraid.[2]

Vardaman's narration presents an outrageous example of the kind of writing that has understandably led Martin Green to complain that Faulkner's rhetoric often appears to exist *"in vacuo,"* that there is a "gap between it and the writer" so apparent as to leave him completely "alienated" from it.[3] What Green's complaint assumes, however, is in this case exactly what the form of *As I Lay Dying* so astutely challenges—a narrative consciousness formed by a supposed union between the author and his language, a union formalized and made conventional by the standard device of omniscient, or at least partly omniscient, narration, which the novel explicitly discards and disavows.

Vardaman's episode with the horse insists that we experience it as alienated language—alien in the sense of being disembodied, traumatically cut off from the conscious identity of character on the one hand and author on the other. The episode is remarkable but, in the context of the book's other unique rhetorical problems, not extraordinary. And in fact it has thematic significance insofar as the book is obsessively concerned with problems of disembodiment, with disjunctive relationships between character and narration or between bodily self and conscious identity. At extremity, Vardaman's trauma leads to the novel's shortest and most comically wrenching chapter—"My mother is a fish"[4]—and therefore suggests an intimate analogy between the absence of an omniscient narrator, a controlling point of view, and the central event of the book—the death of Addie Bundren, with respect to which each character defines his own identity. The relationship between absent omniscient narrator (or author) and dead mother does not, of course, consist of an exact parallel. Addie Bundren appears in the book, not only dying but in fact speaking her own story in one chapter that appears more than a hundred pages after her literal death. It is important here to distinguish literal from figurative death, for the book's title—its adverb capable of being construed as "while," "how," or even "as if"—endorses the fact that Addie's death as it is experienced (one might speak of the phenomenology of her death) occurs over the course of the book and in relation to each character, thus rendering the distinction both necessary and hazardous. The title contains this possibility, moreover, by intimating an elegiac past tense where the collected acts of individual memory (the speaking "I" of each narrator) are disembodied and merged with the dying "I" of the mother, and by playing on the colloquial use of "lay" as an intransitive verb, so as to blur further the distinction between past and present events, a blurring sanctioned and exacerbated by the mixing of narrative tenses among the book's fifty-nine chapters. The action of the book occurs, that is, as Addie *lies* dying and as she *lay* dying, with each narrative "I" participating in the dissolution of her "I" by reflecting and partially embodying it.

It is in this respect that the dying maintains a figurative power far succeeding the literal event of Addie's death; and the chronological displacement of her single monologue alerts us to the possibility not only that we must understand the death itself to function as an act of temporal and spatial disembodiment, but that Addie's speech, as it were logically disengaged from the corporeal self that could have uttered it, is an extreme example of the way in which the novel's other acts of speech should be interpreted—as partially or wholly detached from the bodily selves that appear to utter them. One thinks for immediate comparison of Whitman's "Crossing Brooklyn Ferry," in which the speaker's violation of temporal and spatial boundaries generates the frightening sense of a truly disembodied, ever-present voice; but more so than Whitman's poem, the voices of *As I Lay Dying*, because they get detached even more obviously from a bounded authorial self, raise doubts concerning the propriety of referring to the novel's narrative acts as monologues. Such doubts are readily apparent in the example of Vardaman's encounter with Jewel's horse, where the utterance seems disembodied from the conscious identity of author and narrator alike. It also works to enforce our understanding of Vardaman's

traumatic reaction to his mother's death, however, and by doing so provides an analogy for the narrative form of the entire novel. The horse that
is resolved "out of his integrity, into an unrelated scattering of components
. . . an illusion of a co-ordinated whole of splotched hide and strong bones
within which, detached and secret and familiar, [there is] an *is* different
from my *is*," is emblematic, even symptomatic, of the body of Addie, in
process of being resolved out of her integrity, the *"is"* of her self-contained
identity; and it is emblematic of the "body" of the novel, itself disintegrated
and yet carefully producing the "illusion of a co-ordinated whole."

Because the relationship between the bodily self and the conscious
identity of Addie remains an issue throughout the book, because the self
must continue both *to be* and *not to be* the corpse carried along on its self-
imposed journey to Jefferson (a possibility disturbingly underscored by
Anse's comic refrain "her mind is set on it"), one is tempted to speak of the
body of the book as existing in an analogously fragile state and maintaining
its narrative form despite the apparent absence of that substance one might
compare to, or identify with, a central point of view embodied in an omniscient narrator. The horse's phenomenal dissolution and "float[ing] upon
the dark" recalls other instances in the novel in which objects experienced
are detached from their fixed physical limits—for example, Addie's face in
death, which "seems to float detached upon [darkness], lightly as the
reflection of a dead leaf," or the flooded ford, where the road appears to
have "been soaked free of earth and floated upward, to leave in its spectral
tracing a monument to a still more profound desolation"—all of which
contribute to our experience of the novel itself as an object whose uttered
parts are radically detached from fixed limits and fully identifiable sources.[5]
The novel, like the family whose story it tells, is held together in the most
precarious fashion, its narrative components adhering and referring to an
act that is simultaneously literal and figurative, just as the body of Addie is
neither exactly corpse nor conscious self. The logic thus presents itself of
speaking of the novel too as a corpse, as a narrative whose form is continually on the verge of decomposition and whose integrity is retained only by
a heroic imaginative effort.

Some early readers, misunderstanding the nature of Vardaman's reaction to his mother's death, took him to be another idiot, like Benjy Compson. Though one would not need Faulkner's own certification to deny such
a claim, the explanation he once provided is important. Vardaman reacts as
he does, Faulkner pointed out, because he is a child faced with the intimate
and perplexing loss of his mother, because "suddenly her position in the
mosaic of the household [is] vacant."[6] This is true for all members of the
novel's family, for whom Addie, at least in the portion of their history
presented in the novel (the portion detached, as it were, from the fuller one
we imagine by interpretive projection), is the center that no longer holds,
that is defunct and yet lingers in stages of tenuous attachment. Varda-

man's confusions between his mother and the fish, and between her seeming imprisonment in the coffin and his own recollection of being momentarily trapped in the corn crib—

> It was not her because it was laying right yonder in the dirt. And now it's all chopped up. I chopped it up. It's laying in the kitchen in the bleeding pan, waiting to be cooked and et. Then it wasn't and she was, and now it is and she wasn't.

> "Are you going to nail her up in it, Cash? Cash? Cash?" I got shut up in the new crib the new door it was too heavy for me it went shut I couldn't breathe because the rat was breathing up all the air. I said "Are you going to nail it shut, Cash? Nail it? *Nail* it?"[7]

—provide the most moving instances of the psychological disorientation that affects each of the Bundrens in his own way. And they bring into focus the two central problems of bodily integrity and conscious identity with which the novel is concerned: how can a body that still *is* be thought of as *was?* how can I, whose self has depended upon, and been defined in relation to, another self, now understand the integrity of my own identity? Vardaman, child though he is, consistently asks the most difficult and sophisticated questions about death in the book. He asks where Addie has gone: he in effect questions the farcical funeral journey that is founded particularly on Addie's command to Anse that she be buried in Jefferson and sanctioned generally by the technically absurd and paradoxical notion on which funeral ceremonies are based—that the corpse both *is* and *is not* the self of the person; and he alone, innocently though of course mistakenly, assigns an agency to Addie's death by blaming Doctor Peabody, whose visit coincides with her death no less reasonably than the chopping up and eating of the fish.

Peabody's role in the novel is important quite aside from the comic relief provided when his obese body—again tangentially calling our attention to the importance of corporeal form in the novel—must be hauled up the steep hill to the Bundren house by means of a rope; important because, as Faulkner himself remarked, it gives "a nudge of credibility to a condition which was getting close to the realm of unbelief." Bringing in Peabody from what Faulkner called "comparatively the metropolitan outland" allows the reader to admit of the Bundrens that "maybe they do exist. Up to that time they were functioning in this bizarre fashion almost inside a vacuum, and pretty soon you wouldn't have believed it until some stranger came in as a witness."[8] Faulkner's explanation is a perfect index of one of the novel's more instrumental effects: that in the absence of a controlling narrator the characters, who as narrators themselves participate in the dissolution of the book's integrity and yet by that very act define and maintain its fragile form, do indeed, as Darl says, "sound as though they [are] speaking out of the air about your head"[9] and appear to be acting in a virtual vacuum—the vacuum left both by the "author" who is not, as it were, present and by the integrated form that we as a consequence imagine would be there if he were. Without attaching too much importance to Faulkner's remarks we might nonetheless consider Peabody's appearance, apart from its other functions, in some measure a response to Faulkner's anxiety about the vacuum created by his own authorial absence, one that is bound up with the vacuum created by Addie's death. That is to say, the need to imagine a narrative rendered coherent by the controlling presence of an author—an authoritative *voice*—is not unlike the need to imagine, and the stricken reluctance to let go belief in, the integrated self of one who has died. Both needs may well be spoken of as conventional, as being formed by prior or habitual expectations, though it is precisely for that reason that both are so psychologically demanding.

Though Peabody need not necessarily be thought of as a figure for the author (a conventional way of meeting this demand), part of his role as witness consists of a most telling remark about the action of death in the novel: "I can remember how when I was young I believed death to be a phenomenon of the body; now I know it to be merely a function of the mind—and that of the minds of the ones who suffer the bereavement."[10] Of the two qualifications by which Peabody's remarks proceed, the second is the most striking and the most definitive with respect to the form of the novel; for while the distinction raised by the first—that body and consciousness may present separable forms of identity—is one simultaneously entertained and held in abeyance by the book, the insistence that death demands the intimate participation of other minds virtually explicates the reactions of Addie's family to her demise and, correspondingly, the disintegrated yet tenuously coherent form of the novel. What dies in death, Peabody suggests, is not simply the body nor even simply the mind attached to the body. Rather—and here again one might speak of the phenomenology of death—what dies are the connections between one mind and others. Thus it is that Addie dies not within a single, temporally bounded moment, but rather lies dying throughout the book, in that her death is not complete until the book ends. But even this is not a satisfactory way of putting it. For although one could claim that her death is complete once she is buried, once her command is fulfilled, this would ignore the fact that many if not almost all the monologues, whether they are in the present or past tense, need to be understood as occurring, or continuing to occur, *after* the chronological end of the action. The process of detachment that grief involves must, that is, be understood as continuing beyond the physical limits of the story.

Peabody's definition suggests, moreover, that the mind that dies, the integral "I," depends on others for its dying (a metaphysical version of

Addie's devoutly upheld command), and thus also undergoes a process of detachment. If this is so, then the self or the "I" existing prior to physical death is a self composed of others. Such a self is not isolated or solitary but communal; or, one should say, its integrity depends upon being integrated and its identity upon being constituted by identification, by a form of psychological or emotional analogy that works to extend the boundaries of identity. It is in death, as the novel tells us time and again, that this paradox is made manifest, that the need to imagine an integral self becomes most apparent even as the possibility of doing so passes away, a passing physically symbolized, as in Addie Bundren's case, by a decomposing corpse. And it is the action of grief, the refusal to let go those connections which once formed an integral self, that most painfully attests to the illusion of identity upon which our notions of self are founded. The "I" that lies dying, then, is the "I" of Addie and it is not; it is the "I" of each family member and it is not. As in the case of Anse, of whom Dewey Dell says, "he looks like right after the maul hits the steer and it [is] no longer alive and dont yet know that it is dead,"[11] it is the "I" that each in his connection to her has formed and that now resists its own detachment and isolation even as it takes place. These paradoxes have their perfect analogous expression in the narrative form of the book, which both insists upon and yet prohibits our imagining that the fragmentary, disembodied episodes are—or to be more exact, *were once*—connected to the body or self of a story presented by a single controlling narrator. In taking this further risk, Faulkner perfects the formal strategy that the story of Caddy, lost in the grief-stricken maze of *The Sound and the Fury*, had suggested: like Addie, *As I Lay Dying* is both integrated and disintegrated; like each member of the family, each narrative episode participates in composing that integrated self at the same time it works out its own psychological detachment from it.

The theatrical collection of voices that the novel resembles not only reminds us that consciousness is largely memory, that the self is a fusion between a body with clear limits and a mind with unpredictable ones, and that the psychological chronology of our lives is easily more chaotic than that of the conventional novel; but it does so by reminding us as well that although the novel, like any system of belief, offers an illusion of integrated form which may well be an improvement upon life, it is one that is precarious and requires our belief in things that do not exist. Or, as William Gass has remarked, "theories of character are not absurd in the way representational theories are; they are absurd in a grander way, for the belief in Hamlet (which audiences often seem to have) is like the belief in God—incomprehensible to reason—and one is inclined to seek a motive: some deep fear or emotional need."[12] *As I Lay Dying* is an exemplary case, for it is markedly a book in which characters exist on the basis of the briefest and most fragmentary physical descriptions and in which dialogue is constantly reported and often dislocated by narrative voices that, while they are careful to record identical dialects differently, nonetheless seem utterly severed from the peculiar bodily selves that ostensibly produce them. Vardaman's willingness to confuse the body of his mother with the body of a fish begins as a matter of temporal comparison (before the fish was "not-fish" Addie was still "is"[13]) but issues eventually in a spatial or corporeal integration of the two, dislocating one and the other from fixed limits in order to conceive a new form of identity. Vardaman's notion is absurd; and yet it is only an extreme and traumatic form of the logic of analogy on which the book depends, a logic demanded by Faulkner's presenting his characters with powers of articulation that are literally inconceivable, by his splicing of reported action and dialogue with stream-of-consciousness narration, and, of course, by his dislocation of conventional prose limits through frequent violation of the rules of grammar and punctuation.

Among the three children most disturbingly affected by the death, Vardaman, perhaps because of the mechanism of transference, seems in some respects best able to maintain a hold on his own identity. He does so by a continual, prosaically simplified enumeration of his connections to, and understanding of, the actions around him. On the other hand, Darl seems technically his opposite and stands in much the same relation to him as Quentin does to Benjy in *The Sound and the Fury*. Though his sympathy with Vardaman becomes so pronounced that they ultimately listen together to the coffin, where Darl says Addie is "talking to God" and "calling on Him to help her lay down her life," Darl moves uncomfortably toward the tormented self-conscious posturings of Quentin Compson. Unable to contain his consciousness within the boundaries of sanity, Darl expresses his madness through hallucination and clairvoyance. As Tull puts it, "It's like he had got into the inside of you, someway. Like somehow you was looking at yourself and your doings outen his eyes."[14] In his clairvoyant knowledge of Dewey Dell's pregnancy and Jewel's illegitimacy; in narrating the events of Addie's actual death from a physical point that makes it impossible; and at last, on his way to a Jackson insane asylum, in speaking of himself in the third person, Darl tempts us to identify him with the omniscient author. But while Faulkner himself on one occasion associated Darl's visionary madness with artistic power,[15] it is important to note that this too is an instance of the novel's reluctance to meet the anxiety of omniscience. That is, by suggesting a link between omniscience and madness, Faulkner reveals what the novel backs away from as a form of disembodiment so extreme as to be terrifying and debilitating.

In fact, the tranquil side of Darl's madness, subtly and exactly expressed in his contention that "it would be nice if you could just ravel out into time," is countered by the more nightmarish character who, as Dewey Dell reports, "sits at the supper table with his eyes gone further than the food and the lamp, full of the land dug out of his skull and the holes filled with distance beyond the land." In psychological terms, the person of Darl offers the danger that the conventional boundaries between internal and external will become irremediably confused; while in terms of the novel, the character of Darl, who as Tull remarks "just thinks by himself too much," offers the danger that Addie's dying will be swallowed up by his consciousness, that her "I" and those of the other characters will become inseparable from his own.[16] Darl's omniscience is thus presented as a paradox that parallels, and takes its cue from, the paradox of death as it is explored in the novel: just as Addie's death calls into question the boundaries of the self by defining that self as a series of connections that appear even as they are disintegrated, Darl's intense consciousness, like that of an omniscient author-narrator, defines a self whose identity risks being lost in the act of becoming saturated with the ability to be connected to other minds.[17] The very form of the novel requires, of course, that the characters be understood as minds, as instances of narration or storytelling, but by constantly exposing as impractical our desire to fix the limits of each character's conscious identity, the novel also constantly refers us to the one identity, the one mind—that of the author—that has become so illusive as to be felt to be missing altogether.

In speaking of a corpse like Addie's that continues to seem both dead and alive, the difficulty of choosing between grammatical forms—"she" and "it," "is" and "was"—keeps in view the central problem of bodily integrity, a problem explored insistently by the novel's blurring of boundaries between the animate and the inanimate, as in Anse's monologue on roads, Darl's on the river and the wagon, or Dewey Dell's on the dead earth. There are other examples we must turn to, but in all cases such blurrings increase our dependence on the rhetorical terms of the novel, preventing us from doubting the legitimacy of the absurd ritual journey as it unfolds and keeping us attached to the startling possibility of Addie's continued integral power. In this respect the most unnerving yet effective device is the sudden appearance more than halfway through the book, and chronologically (though it makes little sense to speak of it so) some four days after her death, of Addie's single monologue, one of the most emotionally charged pieces of writing in the novel and perhaps the one that comes closest to stating internally a theory of its narrative form.

The importance of Addie's diatribe against "words"—and particularly the word *love*—lies not simply in her belief that "words dont ever fit even what they are trying to say at," that we have "to use one another by words like spiders dangling by their mouths from a beam, swinging and twisting and never touching,"[18] for these remarks add virtually nothing to the overwhelming effect already generated by the novel that this is the case. Nor does Addie's enumeration of her pregnancies and the manner in which each balances out or revenges another accomplish much more than provid-

ing a partial key to the various relationships of antagonism and devotion
that exist among her children. While these relationships are important and
finally have much to do with analogies one might draw between the family
and the book as integrated forms, the instructive and instrumental
significance of Addie's monologue arises rather in those sections of her
utterance which may be said most to resemble the brooding, silenced voice
of the narrator (or author) and which are therefore most likely to be mis-
read as moments of sheer invention for the sake of invention on Faulkner's
part. The implied or explicit correlation between words and bodies that
appears throughout Addie's monologue recalls similar dramatizations of
Faulkner's authorial agony in *The Sound and the Fury*, dramatizations that in
each case also prefigure the intimate analogy between creation and grief in
Faulkner's most passionate explorations of wasted love and historical loss,
Absalom, Absalom! and *Go Down, Moses*.

Words like love, motherhood, pride, sin, and fear, Addie suggests, are
just "shape[s] to fill a lack," shapes that, when the need for them arises,
cannot adequately fill the void left by an accomplished act or a past event.
Words "fumble" at deeds "like orphans to whom are pointed out in a
crowd two faces and told, That is your father, your mother," and they
resemble, in Addie's mind, the names of her husband and children, whose
names and bodies imperfectly fill the lack in her bodily self they have
caused:

> I would think: The shape of my body where I used to be a virgin is in
> the shape of a   and I couldn't think *Anse*, couldn't remem-
> ber *Anse*. It was not that I could think of myself as no longer unvirgin,
> because I was three now. And when I would think *Cash* and *Darl* that
> way until their names would die and solidify into a shape and then
> fade away, I would say, All right. It doesn't matter. It doesn't matter
> what they call them.[19]

Although it might be too much to claim that the confused and sometimes
contradictory remarks of Addie's monologue immediately explain anything, they do clarify the fact that the novel, as John K. Simon has pointed
out, is "the story of a body, Addie's, both in its existence as an unem-
balmed corpse and as it was—at least partly—conceived for passion."[20]
That is, they clarify what Addie implies and what Dewey Dell, in her own
first pregnancy, has begun to discover—that the connection between sexual "lying" and lying dying is an intimate one, and that the violation is not
simply sexual but generational, as Dewey Dell understands: "I feel my
body, my bones and flesh beginning to part and open upon the alone, and
the process of coming unalone is terrible."[21]

Pregnancy for Dewey Dell and for Addie involves a confusion of identity that inverts the one expressed in the process of death, in which the
impossibility of conceiving of the self as a singular identity is made paradoxically conspicuous in the sudden need to preserve those connections

that define the self even as they pass away. Standing at the other end of death, as it were, "the process of coming unalone" initiates in their most apparent physical form the connections without which one cannot fully imagine ever having been a lone, identical self existing apart from conscious and bodily ties to others. In extremity, the "coming unalone," the becoming more than one "I," leads to a threat of utter extinction through saturation, as in the case of Darl, whom we might think of as figuratively invaded by, and thus consciously "bearing" in distorted shape, all the novel's characters and events; or it leads to an extinction in which consciousness is completely severed from its own "I," as in Darl's meditation on sleep and in the nightmare that Dewey Dell's pregnancy, in conjunction with her mother's death, leads her to recall:

> When I used to sleep with Vardaman I had a nightmare once I thought I was awake but I couldn't see and I couldn't feel I couldn't feel the bed under me and I couldn't think what I was I couldn't think of my name I couldn't even think I am a girl I couldn't even think I nor even think I want to wake up nor remember what was opposite to awake so I could do that.

It is this predicament that Addie speaks of metaphorically when she cannot remember the shape of her body when virgin, cannot even articulate the word that might describe it. Words, that is, are inadequate not so much because they fail to "fit even what they are trying to say at," but because they fail to describe or fill the blank space that only the act of conceiving the need for a word can make manifest as irreparably lost or passed. Words are for something we are not or can no longer be: or as Peabody remarks, in a humorous variation on this potent analogy, when "it finally occurred to Anse himself that [Addie] needed [a doctor], it was already too late."[22]

As I Lay Dying speaks pointedly to the need for establishing and maintaining conscious attachments symbolically incorporated in bodily ties by constant reference, in both actual and formal terms, to the loss of the originating mother. Darl's claim that he has no mother and that the illegitimate Jewel has a horse for a mother; Dewey Dell's psychological merging of death and childbearing (both in her rhetorical association with Addie as mother and in her conceiving of the funeral journey as a means to get an abortion); Cash's obsession with Addie's coffin, as though its perfection and preservation will somehow save the bodily integrity of Addie; Jewel's heroic actions to save that coffin and its body from flood and fire; and Vardaman's transfiguration of mother into fish[23]—all of these reactions reflect the fact that grieving is foremost a process of detachment, of disembodiment, in which the act of *expression* is central. Supported by the chaotic chronology of the novel, which prevents us from knowing "where" the characters are speaking from, the community of voices itself participates in the paradoxical action that grieving is, an action that expresses connections in order both to make them and let them go. Like the voices of the women singing at the wake described by Tull, the voices of the novel that tell Addie's story (including her own) seem to "come out of the air, flowing together and on in sad, comforting tunes. When they cease it's like they hadn't gone away. It's like they had just disappeared into the air and when we moved we would loose them again out of the air around us, sad and comforting."[24]

This is true whether we conceive of the characters as talking, as thinking, or—in some instances—even as writing their stories; and the confusion as to which is the more appropriate conception is integral to the fact that grief seldom has an appropriate form or a distinct chronology. What Faulkner once spoke of as characteristic of his entire work is particularly relevant to *As I Lay Dying:* "The fact that I have moved my characters around in time successfully, at least in my own estimation, proves to me my own theory that time is a fluid condition which has no existence except in the momentary avatars of individual people. There is no such thing as *was*—only *is*. If *was* existed, there would be no grief or sorrow."[25] The form of the novel keeps *is* from becoming *was* as Addie's corpse is kept dying beyond the physical death and—since the stories have no fixed temporal origins but rather are desperately detached from them—even beyond the supposed chronological end of the action, Addie's burial and Anse's remarriage. Grief itself seems disembodied from its object precisely because the boundaries of that object have ceased to have specific meaning and now receive abnormally deliberate, if displaced, attention. The dislocation of conscious attention that grief can produce makes Vardaman's psychological transferences from mother to fish, for example, or Cash's from body to coffin plausible and even necessary, and helps explain what André Bleikasten has referred to as Faulkner's possession by the "demon of analogy" in the novel.[26] The action of grief responds to and reflects the demand for analogy, for the possibility of relocating the lost integrity of one object in another as a way of expressing the maintenance of emotional connections that are threatening to disappear.

Since the novel refuses to settle on a point of view, a narrative focus that gives immediate coherence to the story, but on the contrary forces us to develop that coherent identity by an act of imaginative identification, piecing it together from disparate parts, it too might well be regarded as a family without a mother, as it were, without a single source from which we can clearly say the parts have sprung. And yet of course we do say just that: we say Faulkner is the author, these all are parts of him, products of his creation. To say this, however, is both necessary and speculative, for the parts—disembodied from the act that apparently produced them—are in their own way as much orphaned as Addie's own children or the words that she speaks of as filling a lack left by a deed that has passed. The self that produced them, or the integral point of view that we imagine as controlling them, has "come unalone" in that act, which is now a lack filled by shapes. We know and need it only in retrospect; and because this is the case, the process of grieving that the Bundrens undergo—a process in which their breaking of connections with Addie at once defines her self as composed of them yet requires each of them to lie dying along with her—is analogous to the narrative unfolding of "Faulkner's story," a process in which the shape of the book is built up by accumulation and connection but paradoxically participates in the disintegration of that imagined single form, leaving each episode in isolation, tenuously attached to the others and at the same time orphaned—referring to, yet failing properly to "fill" and complete, the lack that they make manifest. Because they exist in the novel's form as disembodied both from the bodies that utter them *and* from the one body that we must understand as having once produced them, the narrative episodes do indeed seem a collection of voices in the air.

As I Lay Dying is best understood, then, as a book in which death is the story and the story is a death, a book in which the authorial "I" also lies dying; that is, he is dead as Addie is dead, dead as a single identity but still alive in the episodes that continue to refer themselves to that identity and continue to constitute it even more emphatically in our desire to locate Faulkner's own "language," his own "story," in the voices of his characters. To speak of the book as a corpse, a *corpus*, is to recognize that such an expression is at once appropriate and inadequate, for just as Addie's corpse is not what dies (except on one occasion) in the book, the words that fill the book, like the family that continues to fill and be filled by Addie Bundren, are alive, however disembodied, fragmented, and comically bereaved. The expressions of grief that work out their own disembodiment from a lost, decomposing object by the insistent desire for analogous experience find analogy in the novel's form, which like the action of grief relocates the limits and power of that object in the stories of which it is now composed. Those expressions continue to have and to acquire meaning, and continue to make connections, despite the absurdity of doing so and despite the fact that they appear to act, as Faulkner recognized, in a virtual vacuum.

It is a measure of the novel's magnificent power that it leads us to recognize Faulkner's mastery in the very situation in which we are tempted to say he has surrendered control of the book, has himself become disembodied as "author." Wright Morris has spoken quite rightly of such examples of stylistic power in Faulkner's work as moments in which "the technique is so flawless that the effect is incandescent. Craft and raw material are in such lucid balance that it seems the craftsman himself is missing."[27] A more appropriate way of characterizing *As I Lay Dying* is difficult to imagine, for Faulkner is indeed missing—missing as Addie is missing, nonetheless commanding our attention and our attempts to account for his seemingly invisible control. His own notorious remarks (in the preface to *Sanctuary*) about the ease and speed with which he wrote the novel are no doubt slightly overstated; but Faulkner's admission on another occasion that the novel is an example of that creative situation in which "technique charges in and takes command of the dream before the writer himself can get his hands on it"[28] corresponds to our sense that the book's craft and material, its form and substance, like the form and substance of Addie, are working in brilliant accord, at once engagingly distinct and emotionally inseparable.

It is such power, charged by the activity of grieving that expresses itself analogically, that compels us to seek analogues for the author in the work, connections between Faulkner and Peabody, Faulkner and Darl, Faulkner and Addie, for example—or perhaps just as appropriately, as the lucidity of Faulkner's technique may suggest, between the author and Cash, the patient, meticulous builder of Addie's coffin. Faulkner's many references in letters and interviews to himself as a craftsman, as a user of "tools" and materials and a virtual builder of tales, make the analogy unavoidable; and though this analogy is not so immediately central as the formal analogy between Faulkner and Addie, it amplifies that one by bringing into focus the relationships between body and coffin, and perhaps more notably between coffin and book as objects of extraordinary fragility and devotion. Against flood, fire, and scavenging buzzards the coffin, though hiding it from view, preserves its rotting cargo long enough to get it buried in Jefferson—preserves the integrity of the object it both literally contains and figuratively renders absurd *as* an object in the same way that the form of the book, elaborately pieced together, both literally contains its central event, Addie's death, and figuratively renders absurd the physical limits of that event. Darl's early characterizations of his dead mother's body as "spent yet alert," "volitional," or "lightly alive, waiting to come awake,"[29] as well as the novel's continual unpredicated reference to the coffin and its body as "it" (or to both as "her"), all work to blur the distinction between body and container, the animate and the inanimate, in a fashion that is completely analogous to the novel's formal blurring of distinctions between its own structure of expression and the ongoing event that is expressed. The coffin "contains" the object of the family's quixotic devotion as absolutely and precariously as the book "contains" the dying of Addie Bundren. Like the book, the coffin is both the shape filled by the fragile self of Addie and a "shape to fill a lack," the lack that death makes manifest and, in fact, *is*, but in which those of whose minds it is a function refuse fully to believe.

The coffin and the book, each in its way, maintain the integrity of Addie's bodily self. But if we keep in mind the example of gentle Cash, who admits that there is "a fellow in every man that's done a-past the sanity or the insanity, that watches the sane and the insane doings of that man with the same horror and the same astonishment," the coffin and the book must also be seen as maintaining, in moral terms, the integrity of the funeral journey—and against rather overwhelming odds. For quite aside from the preposterous physical threats to the journey, the family's own intentions are continually betrayed as shallow and self-serving. Anse wants new teeth and a new wife; Dewey Dell wants an abortion; Cash wants a gramophone; and Vardaman wants to eat bananas and see a toy train. Only Jewel and Darl seem immune from mixed motives for reaching Jefferson, the one determined to complete the burial, the other determined to prevent it. And although the effort may succeed precisely because of these base intentions, it is also the case—as in Vardaman's wish to see the train, which he says "made my heart hurt"—that the intentions themselves may have become bound up with the forms of analogous experience and expression that grief both makes possible and necessitates. There seems no other explanation for Faulkner's most masterful stroke in the novel, the complete deletion of the actual burial of Addie, the act that her command set in motion and to which the entire action of the book is devoted. Yet as Vardaman unwittingly suggests early on when he asks Dewey Dell, "did [Addie] go far as town?"[30] it is not the burial that matters but the journey, the heroic effort to sustain the fragile community of the family in the face of physical and psychological trauma. Each of the Bundrens participates in the journey as he participates in the dying of Addie; each journeys and each dies, and in doing so testifies to the continued integrity of the dead mother, memorializing the passing of the body by expressing the emotional ties that continue to compose the self.

The novel's treatment of the corpse of Addie must thus be understood in the same light as Vardaman's boring of holes through the coffin into her face—as an act of love whose grotesque expression is at once perversely comic and at the same time utterly sincere. What the book poignantly exposes is the precarious nature of ritual expression, particularly that of funeral rituals, in which an absurd possibility—that the corpse of the person nonetheless *is* the person—is maintained not because anyone believes it but because no one can immediately, emotionally deny it. The trauma of grief, in which death most clearly *is* a function of other minds, makes the irrational conventional; and the elegy that the expression of grief may become must itself, as the novel certainly does, harbor the eventuality of seeming comic or grotesque. It is "only when the ritual is disengaged from its symbolic function," Olga Vickery has remarked of the novel, "that the comic aspect becomes apparent." Vickery goes on to note that the distinction between empty and significant ritual is not, in fact, unlike the distinction Addie's monologue draws between words and deeds,[31] an analogy that is completely appropriate if—and only if—we understand words to be capable of more than Addie admits; that is, only if we understand words, the shapes that fill a lack, as the possible expression of an identity that is

most intensely and passionately present even as it passes away. The ritual
of the book threatens at every point to become disengaged from its symbolic function and thus to appear simply absurd or grotesque; and yet this
is perfectly in keeping with the various characters' precarious and
traumatic attachment to the central object of the ritual, and moreover in
perfect keeping with the novel's formal disengagement of its narrative
expression from a controlling consciousness, a consciousness that would
more clearly and conventionally stabilize the meaning of the death and its
ritual enactment. The absurdity of the characters' reactions, as well as the
absurdity of the journey itself, register in unmediated form the paradox of
death that the book struggles so hard to contain.

At one point Darl describes Anse's face as having been "carved by a
savage caricaturist [in] a monstrous burlesque of all bereavement."[32] If one
is tempted to say that this applies equally well to each of the characters,
and that Faulkner's modern parable produces only a travesty of its characters' efforts and a virtual parody of itself, it must be kept in mind that, since
parody works by a form of analogy which is more successful the more
fragile are the boundaries between the mockery and the object, the tale of
the Bundrens is one that preserves that fragile equilibrium and, in fact,
continually expresses it formally in the extenuated distinctions between
voice and character, between corpse and self, and in this case most of all
between the conventions of ritual and their burlesque. "There's not too
fine a distinction between humor and tragedy," Faulkner once remarked,
for "even tragedy is in a way walking a tightrope between . . . the bizarre
and the terrible."[33] It is difficult, of course, to read *As I Lay Dying* as
tragedy; but its bizarre and terrible humor keeps before us the fact that
comedy itself is often a means of releasing pressure and relieving anguish.
The contortions of language that break down boundaries between the outrageous and the awful, that is to say, are not unlike the emotional trauma
associated with death, for the instability of the expression of grief makes it
particularly susceptible to the potential comedy of analogy.

Such contortions tend easily toward the tall tale; but then Faulkner, in
an age dominated by *The Waste Land* and by Hemingway's cold-blooded
and often futile heroism, might well have felt the necessity of exaggeration
in order to render a parable of heroic effort in the modern world. Of course
all of Faulkner's novels tend toward the tall tale, but what is extraordinary
about *As I Lay Dying*, particularly when we recall that it follows *The Sound
and the Fury* and falls between the composition and revision of *Sanctuary*,
Faulkner's most unrelentingly brutal parable of the modern world, is that
the comedy itself could come to seem the finest, most passionate expression of grief and—with precarious extremity—of love. In this respect, the
novel projects a world of tragic compassion Faulkner would not find again
until *Absalom, Absalom!* and *Go Down, Moses*, where the intimate entangle-
ment of grief and love, and the scattered family passions they reflect, are so

anguished as to appear almost beyond redemption. For the moment, however—perhaps the only certain moment in his career—Faulkner's own compassion became brilliant, powerful, and unabashedly moving.[33]

Notes

1. "William Faulkner: An Interview," with Jean Stein, *Paris Review* (Spring 1956), reprinted in *William Faulkner: Three Decades of Criticism,* ed. Frederick J. Hoffman and Olga W. Vickery (New York: Harcourt, 1963), p. 72.

2. William Faulkner, *As I Lay Dying* (New York: Vintage-Random, 1964), p. 55.

3. Martin Green, *Re-Appraisals: Some Commonsense Readings in American Literature* (New York: Norton, 1965), p. 174.

4. *As I Lay Dying,* p. 79.

5. Ibid., e.g., pp. 29, 31, 109, 49, 136.

6. *Faulkner in the University,* ed. Frederick Gwynn and Joseph Blotner (Charlottesville: University of Virginia Press, 1959), p. 110.

7. *As I Lay Dying,* pp. 62–63.

8. *Faulkner in the University,* pp. 113–14.

9. *As I Lay Dying,* p. 19.

10. Ibid., p. 42.

11. Ibid., p. 58.

12. William Gass, "The Concept of Character in Fiction," *Fiction and the Figures of Life* (New York: Knopf, 1970), p. 37.

13. *As I Lay Dying,* p. 52.

14. Ibid., pp. 204–5, 119.

15. See *Faulkner in the University,* p. 113: "Who can say how much of the good poetry in the world has come out of madness, and who can say just how much of super-perceptivity the—a mad person might not have?" Faulkner even appeared to have apprehended an unconscious power in the character of Darl that, instead of leading to a fuller identification between author and character, rather disengaged them. "You can't make [a character] do things once he comes alive and stands up and casts his own shadow," Faulkner claimed. "I couldn't always understand why [Darl] did things, and when we would quarrel about it, he always won, because at that time he was alive, he was under his own power" (ibid., pp. 263–64).

16. *As I Lay Dying,* pp. 198, 26, 68.

17. In one of the best essays on the novel, Calvin Bedient speaks quite rightly of Darl's "vacuum of identity" and notes that, "although Darl is invaded by others as the mystic is innundated by God and the novelist possessed by his characters, those who occupy Darl do not replenish him." See "Pride and Nakedness in *As I Lay Dying,*" *Modern Language Quarterly* 29 (1968):67. For a further theoretical consideration of the problems of voice and identity, see Stephen M. Ross, "'Voice' in Narrative Texts: The Example of *As I Lay Dying,*" *PMLA* 94 (1979):300–310.

18. *As I Lay Dying,* pp. 163–64.

19. Ibid., pp. 163–66.

20. John K. Simon, "The Scene and Imagery of Metamorphosis in *As I Lay Dying,*" *Criticism* 7 (1965):14.

21. *As I Lay Dying,* p. 59.

22. Ibid., pp. 115, 41.

23. André Bleikasten suggests an interesting approach to the fish analogy by noting that "it is perhaps not going too far to consider it also as a regressive image of the child. Is a fetus not physiologically a fish in its mother's womb?" If so, "the image should then be read as an expression of prenatal nostalgia, an emblem of the primal union of child and mother Vardaman is unconsciously yearning for." This seems perfectly plausible, though there is no reason to insist that the wish for union is wholly unconscious; on the contrary, the desire to be reunited with Addie, whether as pre- or postnatal mother, is what so much of the book's rhetorical power depends on. See *Faulkner's As I Lay Dying,* trans. Roger Little (Bloomington: Indiana University Press, 1973), p. 97.

24. *As I Lay Dying,* p. 86.

25. Stein, "William Faulkner: An Interview," p. 82.

26. *Faulkner's As I Lay Dying,* p. 39.

27. Wright Morris, *The Territory Ahead* (1957; reprint ed. Lincoln: University of Nebraska Press, 1978), p. 177.

28. Stein, "William Faulkner: An Interview," p. 72.

29. *As I Lay Dying,* pp. 50, 91, 75.

30. Ibid., pp. 228, 206, 63.

31. Olga Vickery, *The Novels of William Faulkner: A Critical Interpretation* (Baton Rouge: Louisiana State University Press, 1959), p. 53.

32. *As I Lay Dying,* pp. 73–74.

33. This essay was revised at a time during which I held a fellowship from the American Council of Learned Societies; I am grateful to the Council for its support.

The Approximations of Romance: Paul Ricoeur and the Ironic Style of Postmodern Criticism

Daniel T. O'Hara

I can see plainly that there are two sides to the matter but unfortunately I can occupy only one of them.—Joyce, from a letter to Grant Richards (5/5/06)

I
"The Gaze of His Disciple": The Romance of Interpretation

"Two Gallants," the centerpiece of James Joyce's *Dubliners*, concludes with a street scene. Lenehan has caught up finally with his pal, Corley, and now awaits the revelation of what Corley has extracted from his new girl friend, a young serving maid:

> Corley halted at the first lamp and stared grimly before him. Then with a grave gesture he extended a hand towards the light and, smiling, opened it slowly to the gaze of his disciple. A small gold coin shone in the palm.[1]

Needless to say, Lenehan is satisfied, even as the reader feels a bit short-changed. For we have been led by Joyce to expect the sign of a sexual, not a financial climax: the girl's key, not her money. The tradition of romantic gallantry that extends back through the heroic adventures of Dumas to the courtly epics and that repeatedly has been echoed in the story, could not have sunk any lower into the modern world of perennial adolescents always on the make for the easy touch, a "fall" that has ironically revealed its "essential" nature.

The severe disjunction between reader expectation and perverse textual fulfillment focuses attention on the final metaphor and image, that of

183

"the gaze of his disciple" and the "small gold coin" shining in Corley's grimy palm. After an initial surprise with regard to this figurative conjunction, the scene takes on added dimensions of meaning that the entire story and its position in this collection of accounts of "spiritual paralysis" reinforce. Quite simply, Corley and Lenehan have betrayed Ireland and all her heroic, chivalric, and religious traditions, and thereby they have betrayed themselves. They have become the unwittingly ironic, even self-parodic supplements of these diverse traditions of a dying culture. That is, they have become what they unknowingly beheld: the clownish, motley representatives of a coarse, commercialized society, the wave of the future in Ireland at the time. That Corley's act of betrayal has repeated in a cruder tone Judas's betrayal of Christ, or that Joyce in his letters of this period felt that the Irish people usually betray their genuine poets and heroes in just this fashion, especially in modern times, is more fuel for the semantic conflagration Joyce has set here and into which he has betrayed us, willing martyrs all, certainly, of such an ironically metaphoric auto-da-fé.

I have begun with this scene from Joyce because I want to contrast its savage, multidimensional irony with the simplified and idealized critical version of such irony found in the established interpretation of the story. In his essay on "Two Gallants" in the Viking critical edition of *Dubliners,* A. Walton Litz, one of the leading American Joyceans, reads the final scene as an example of Joyce's power as a creative artist. Starting from the startling denouement of the story, Litz shows how the dramatic patterns of realistic imagery in the text paradoxically compose a symbolic structure of stress and counterstress that is, in fact, resolved by this unexpected climax. The final reflexive vision or "epiphany" is symbolic primarily of the text's own projected "organic" unity, a kind of order available in the modern world only within the ambiguous confines of modernist "autotelic" art:

> But after the initial surprise has been assimilated the reader realizes that the "denouement" was inevitable, that the entire story tends towards this shocking conclusion. The gold coin—probably stolen . . . from the servant girl's employer—is a final symbol of debased "gallantry," but it is also a fitting climax to related motifs of Ireland's political, economic, and spiritual degradation. It is a true epiphany, a showing forth of hidden reality, and like all of Joyce's epiphanies it is wholly dependent upon its context.[2]

By reading from the end, and in light of the total context of the story and collection, Litz "assimilates" the shock of the climax to his celebration of Joyce's creative, revelatory power. The piercing gap between expectation and ironic fulfillment, between sordid realism and complex symbolic allusiveness, that the story builds up is obscured by an idolatrous figure of Joyce the masterful creator of "true" epiphanies. This figure is shaped according to the dictates of what is essentially "New Critical" interpretive practices which celebrate "irony." Such a figure of Joyce now occupies the alien territory of semantic difference. As such, Litz's Joyce is a "true" epiphany of the modernist critical "god."

In his act of reading Litz redescribes Joyce's story and Joyce himself in accord with the "New Critical" understanding of the creator. Litz himself, a scholar of the "New Criticism," identifies the genealogy of this vision in his introduction to the section of *Modern Literary Criticism* devoted to T. S. Eliot. He quotes as central to any reading of Eliot and the discursive practices he inaugurated Coleridge's Romantic Image of the poet from chapter 14 of *Biographia Literaria*. Eliot had orginally quoted this passage himself, for his own purposes, in his essay on Andrew Marvell's poetry of "wit" in 1921:

> The poet, described in ideal perfection, brings the whole soul of man into activity. . . . He diffuses a tone and spirit of unity, that blends, and (as it were) *fuses*, each into each, by that synthetic and magical power, to which we have exclusively appropriated the name of imagination. This power . . . reveals itself in the balance or reconciliation of opposite or discordant qualities: of sameness, with difference; of the general, with the concrete; the idea, with the image; the individual, with the representative; the sense of novelty and freshness, with old and familiar objects.[3]

What Litz has done, as a scholar trained in "New Critical" methods of reading, is to transform Joyce's biting irony into another wheel in the smoothly running machine for producing such readings of irony.

This lucid "New Critical" interpretation of irony obscures the radical discontinuities of the reading experience with heroic images of the creator. Rhetorical differences are interpreted by the "New Critic" as antithetical meanings, which the text shapes into a heterocosm that, like the appearance of design in the heavens, conjures up the image of a divine creativity, "the poet, described in ideal perfection." The providential order no longer available in the world of modern science can thus still be found in the ironic work of art. Such "New Critical" irony has been exposed for what it is, aesthetic evasion, by contemporary criticism, particularly in the work of William V. Spanos and Paul A. Bové. The dialectic of the romance of interpretation found in other critics' texts is allowed to play itself out in theirs. Yet, paradoxically enough, this exposure has allowed such an understanding of irony as found in the "New Criticism" to become what now it must be: a self-consciously programmatic feature of contemporary critical discourse, an object of parodic imitation, with mock-heroic or, more often, purely absurd, images of the critic substituting for images of the creator:

> it is indeed possible to find in Bloom's work the major contemporary continuation of the ironic, aesthetic vision classically located in the

New Criticism. . . . The important parallel between Bloom [as a representative case in contemporary criticism] and the New Critics is . . . in
a consideration of their analogous desires to create machines or models or metaphors for reading which trope against time by playfully
substituting a variety of figures within a well-controlled, unques-
tioned, powerful theoretical and practical critical apparatus. In fact,
one can even go further and assert that . . . this freeplay within fixed
boundaries, which represents an aspiration to power conceived as
"absolute freedom," reveals itself as a subjective projection which
ends in a critical self-parody revealing the deathly stillness of ironic
play.[4]

In short, in terms of my argument, the disciple (the critic) would become
the master (the ironic creator as envisioned by the "New Critics"), thanks
to the intensity of the critical gaze, but he has, in fact, become more like
one of the master's clowns. That is, the postmodern critic can exploit now
the "New Critical" conventions of interpretation—its technique of close
reading—in such a way that even as he would revise or rebel against those
conventions his own acts of reading, his texts, would reenact the drama of
irony, ambiguity, and paradox, all so that the image of the critic as creator
might displace that of the literary artist. Unfortunately, however, for the
critics involved, the scene that results is more like the staging of Bottom's
dream and its aftermath than like the performance of Peter Quince at the
clavier in Stevens' unsurpassable poem with that title.

For example, take Harold Bloom. Bloom, trained in the American
brand of *explication de texte,* began his career as a systematic theorist of the
anxiety of influence in 1970 with his book *Yeats.* There he read into the
intertextual spaces between Yeats's visionary poems and those of his precursors (largely Shelley and Blake) a modern form of Gnosticism (a visionary or tragic historical determinism) that Bloom condemned at that
time, only to come full circle in *The Flight to Lucifer: A Gnostic Fantasy* (1979)
and embrace the great original of Yeats's supposed Gnostic Sophia he
formerly had scorned. Bloom has given birth to himself, via his precursor's
apparent muse, in the form of the Yeats he had seen: he has become what
he beheld. Similarly, in *Orientalism* (1978), Edward W. Said reinvented the
discipline of Mid-Eastern Areas Studies by seeing in its hegemonic conceptual and rhetorical discontinuities and disjunctions endless variations on
Flaubert's obsession with Kuchuk Hanem, an Egyptian courtesan, all so
that Said might give birth to himself as the contemporary renovator of the
discipline, in skeptical emulation and radical revision of his powerful,
heroic father-figure in the field, Massignon.

Michel Foucault, a highly sophisticated thinker with no direct links to
American "New Criticism," nevertheless falls victim to his own variety of
critical irony (probably derived from Flaubert, Valéry, and Proust). In such
texts as "The Fantasia of the Library," "What Is an Author?," "Nietzsche,

Genealogy, History," as well as at the conclusion of *Les Mots et les choses*—with that infamous "death of man" Dionysian dance—Foucault dissolves the site of representation into the theatrical space of the Archive, unravels the discursive network that supports the idea of the author, and exposes the sterile instrumentality of conventional history-writing. But the result is that in the very act of genealogical suspicion, archival denial, and archaeological self-immolation the latest self-idolatrous phoenix rises from the ashes of the will-to-knowledge, murmuring over and over again in the indifferent twilight, Foucault's last recognizable words from "What is an Author?" as he slips down the rabbit-hole of discourse: "What matter who's speaking?" This is a climactic repetition of a question from Beckett's *Stories and Texts for Nothing* that Foucault opens his essay with.[5] Foucault, like Bloom and Said, cannot resist the charms of his own rhetoric, the critic's phantasmagoria. That Bloom, Said, and Foucault, each in his own notorious way, scorns the supposed sublimations of metaphor, is a fitting irony.

Even Jacques Derrida, that most suspicious of post-structuralist writers, has obliged Foucault with a possible answer to Beckett's seemingly impossible question. In *Spurs: Nietzsche's Styles,* Derrida constructs an aporia out of Nietzsche's conflicting remarks on woman, an aporia of undecidability between understanding those remarks as the defensive polemics of an insecure man and reading them as one reads the cryptic citation from the Nietzsche Archive: " ' I have forgotten my umbrella.' " Which is to say, with an exuberant shrug of the shoulders. Derrida suggests that the pietistic devotion of the scholars who preserved this scrap from the dancing pen of the would-be master of woman just may have provided us with the key for unlocking the mystery of Nietzsche's myriad "styles" of writing. For if the scholars are like perfect eunuchs guarding the harem of Nietzsche's productions, then perhaps Nietzsche's protean style is more like the hermaphrodite than terrible Turk. After all, "What if Truth were a woman, what then?" is the question with which Nietzsche opens his preface to his *Beyond Good and Evil* and a celebration of Dionysus effectively rounds off the book. So, now, to escape becoming the unwitting dupe of the metaphysics of presence, one must actually *be*—in one's writing, of course—perverse, radically perverse.

My intention in surveying this bizarre spectacle of postmodern criticism is not to provoke finger-wagging. Rather, it is to argue that like Cyril Graham in Oscar Wilde's "The Portrait of Mr. W. H." the contemporary critic is hard at work counterfeiting his thinly disguised idealized or de-idealized self-portraits, self-consciously, even self-contemptuously (herein lies the distinction between Bloom and company and Litz and the "New Critics"). The purpose of this romance of interpretation is the establishment of the critic's ironic authority, so that he might guarantee to himself the permanence of his possible sublimity, and replicate through his students his image of truth, and so, like Satan, secure his sphere of influence. In the absence of any major creators of the stature of Joyce or Valéry or Mann who could reform our view of the tradition, the contemporary critic, under the impact of continental developments in linguistics, anthropology, pyschoanalysis, and philosophical hermeneutics, leaps into the void and seeks to populate it with his own monuments, in a self-conscious parody of the great modernist masters of the Anglo-American, French and German traditions, as they were represented by the former generation of critics. Consider, for instance, Derrida's *La Vérité en peinture* (1978). The last third of this writing consists in a deconstructive interrogation of Heidegger's "The Origin of the Work of Art" done in the mock-catechetical and encyclopedic style of the Ithaca chapter of Joyce's *Ulysses*, the favorite section of the novel for dedicated Joyceans.[7]

My point is this: whether or not Harold Bloom's description of the internalization of quest-romance is accurate as a portrayal of the essential movement of Romantic poetry, it has become all-too-prophetic of the dialectic of the romance of interpretation in postmodern criticism:

> The poet takes the patterns of quest-romance and transposes them into his own imaginative life, so that the entire rhythm of the quest is heard again in the movement of the poet himself from poem to poem. . . . The hero of internalized quest is the poet himself, the antagonists of quest are everything in the self that blocks imaginative work, and the fulfillment is never the poem itself but the poem beyond that is made possible by the apocalypse of imagination.[8]

One just has to make the necessary substitutions.

Postmodern criticism exploits the current fascination with the interstices of the text and those which exist between texts within the discursive formation of an epoch, to insert in these recently cleared spaces of representation, as if by sleight-of-hand, self-reflecting images of the critic caught in the act of misreading. In short, whereas Litz says he sees Joyce the creator occupying the space of representation, that disjunctive interface between the archetypes of literary history and the scrupulous realism of Joyce's modernism, Bloom would say he sees himself as that Joyce—or, perhaps more accurately, his Shelley or Byron informing such a figure of Joyce. Such honesty conflicts, of course, with the devotional practice of the last generation of critics, who so often appeared to claim that one should go to the text on one's knees. Postmodern criticism, however, eschews such hypocrisy and so, from one perspective, traces a "fall" from the propriety, the critical decorum of a former age. Yet this "fall" discloses, in a manner akin to that enacted in Joyce's story, the essential features of a destructive ideology idealized as a form of Romantic or aesthetic humanism. Our fate now is to see the inescapable consequences of Bloom's kind of honesty, to exchange "New Critical" devotion for a grimy palm and a shiny coin. This is a fate that none of us seems able to evade indefinitely, no matter how we would woo our freedom from the texts of the past, no matter how expertly we keep the game of criticism going. In reading the ironic disjunctions constituting texts, our criticism cannot help but appear to be approximating the internalization of quest-romance as defined by Bloom.

The result of such critical displays is the abandonment of the scene of instruction that mediates, for students, the works of literature to "New Critically" trained interpreters and scholars and their journalistic ephebes. Consequently, the questions raised by figurative language, by such ironical metaphoric disjunctions as that in Joyce's "Two Gallants," must remain in the oblivion of self-evidence for most readers. Even in the work of the two leading, if antithetical, theorists of metaphor, Jacques Derrida and Paul Ricoeur, the founding conditions of the possibility of their discourse appear to ensnare these powerful self-conscious figures in the nets of the romance of interpretation. I would contend that perhaps only by returning to a renewed interrogation of the great modernists might today's critics learn to master their own ironies enough so that they would be able to instruct the present in the living powers of the past.

What I hope to do in what follows is to suggest how both Derrida and Ricoeur, each in his own way, does get ensnared in the romance of interpretation, but with a saving difference in the case of Ricoeur, a difference that I hope to show, when I return to an example from Joyce, would make Ricoeur, rather than Derrida, a better Ariadne for the labyrinth of the master ironist.

II
The Vicarious Image: Metaphor Between Derrida and Ricoeur

Recall now Derrida's position on figurative, particularly metaphoric, language—a tautology, for Derrida. It can be reduced to two statements, not his own, both of which he acknowledges in "White Mythology." The first statement is Nietzsche's from *The Birth of Tragedy*. According to Nietzsche, for a genuine poet, that is, for a madman, "metaphor" is not a rhetorical figure but "a vicarious image that he actually beholds in place of a concept." That is, for the poet, metaphor is a linguistic means for knowingly conjuring up an only apparently extralinguistic presence that would mediate between the disjunctions of philosophical speculation. Hence the madness or "folly." The other statement is Heidegger's from *Der Satz vom Grund* that "the metaphysical exists only within the boundaries of metaphysics." That is, this metaphoric conjuring act is a sleight-of-hand trick done in the service of a metaphysics of presence that condemns writing to a submissive role in the play of domination and surrender of speech and writing that has been enacted from Plato to Husserl in the Western tradition. The power of figuration is repressed, brought to a halt and made to bow down before one of its own vicarious images that has been idolized in the interest of securing the belief in a "transcendental signified," an extralinguistic Absolute, a god-principle of some kind, whether it be called God, Reason, Nature, Culture, Being, Self, Myth and so on, all so that the dominant power structure of a particular epoch can give itself a form of justification.[9]

Derrida via Heidegger and Nietzsche accepts Kant's conception of aesthetic representation from *The Critique of Judgement* (1790) that it is an instance of representation "which induces much thought, yet without the possibility of any definite thought whatever, i.e., concept, being adequate to it, and which language, consequently, can never quite get on level terms with or render completely intelligible."[10] But unlike Kant, of course, who like the New Critics in their own way, celebrates this formal vacancy for its almost infinite semantic possiblities as the provocative stimulus of the imagination to represent artfully the world, Derrida shows how aesthetic representation, in the form of "dead" metaphor, animates even the most abstract and logical of philosophical or speculative discourses. Thus, such discourse, despite its pretensions to rationality, reality, and responsibility, is an example of human, all-too-human, folly. For, to follow Heidegger's lead, metaphor in philosophy functions in a covert way to transpose the sensible into the nonsensible (seen as the supersensible), in the name of some first principle of Reason that is never recognized for what it really is: the inherently foolish, spectral reformulation and repetition of "differance," the pale ghost of the frivolous trace. Like Nietzsche's ironic revision of the divine child of Heraclitus in "Philosophy in the Tragic Age of the Greeks,"[11] who plays before the waters of mortality, repeatedly building up and then destroying (before completing) castles of being, the self-deluded philosopher worships a first principle or god-concept designed to put an end to this play (temporally) and created in the image of all he lacks and would become—that is, virtually out of nothing at all—but which the philosopher, unlike the young Zeus, takes all-too-seriously as a masterful representation of that which is.

Derrida's position is critical of the self-deceptions of reason, especially when it thinks its categories for representing its formulation of experience grasp a real presence external to any of those formulations, as if the circle in encompassing its center assumed that the latter were the essence of being. Derrida, then, is critical of reason much in the same way as Kant was critical:

> There exists, therefore, a natural and inevitable Dialectic of pure rea-
> son, not one in which a mere bungler might get entangled from want
> of knowledge, or which a sophist might artificially devise to confuse
> rational people, but one that is inherent in, and inseparable from
> human reason, and which even after its illusion has been exposed, will

never cease to fascinate our reason, and to precipitate it into momentary errors, such as require to be removed again and again.[12]

But where Kant attributes error to the (false) dialectic of pure reason (the play of rational categories produces the idea of an unknown something that can be known beyond the confines of the mind), Derrida recognizes the comic script of language.[13]

Ricoeur's position in *The Rule of Metaphor* can also be reduced to two statements, not his own, one of which he acknowledges, but the other of which he does not. For Ricoeur, one begins with Aristotle's definition of metaphor from the *Poetics* as "giving the thing a name that belongs to something else; the transference being either from genus to species, or from species to genus, or from species to species, or on grounds of analogy." Then Ricoeur submits this definition of metaphor to the many and various interrogations of it found in the history of philosophy and criticism, from Classical rhetoric to modern semiotic, semantic, philosophical, linguistic, and "deconstructive" studies, only to end with a renewed understanding of Aristotle's view that the poet is a master of metaphor, who sees similarity amidst differences and who creates fictions that redescribe reality, unleashing the potentialities of the real, as is best summarized (for Ricoeur) by Aristotle's statement from the *Metaphysics* that the poet, like the Platonic Eros, reaches into that "source of the movement of natural objects called *physis*, being present in them somehow, either potentially or in complete reality." The poet for Ricoeur, following Aristotle's alogical, explicitly mythical formulation here, is he "who perceives power as act and act as power . . . who sees whole and complete what is sketchy and in process, who perceives . . . things as not prevented from becoming, seeing them as blossoming forth . . . every form attained as a promise of newness."[14] This beautiful compensatory vision of the poet argues that the metaphorical power of his visionary "as" supplements things as they are with fictions of what they might be in a manner akin to Yeats's famous celebration of the poet's creative power at the conclusion of "Among School Children," that other statement which Ricoeur does not quote but which is wholly appropriate to his position:

> —O Presences
> That passion, piety or affection knows
> And that all heavenly glory symbolise—
> O self-born mockers of man's enterprise;
>
> VIII
> Labour is blossoming or dancing where
> The body is not bruised to pleasure soul,
> Nor beauty born out of its own despair,
> Nor blear-eyed wisdom out of midnight oil.

O chestnut-tree, great-rooted blossomer,
Are you the leaf, the blossom or the bole?
O body swayed to music, O brightening glance,
How can we know the dancer from the dance?[15]

Ricoeur, in short, wishes to preserve for the speculative metaphors of the philosopher and the poet the power to reorganize and to expand our conceptual world. If Derrida's deconstruction is allied, indirectly, with Kant's critique of pure reason, then Ricoeur's hermeneutic phenomenology is allied with Kant's celebration of the creative imagination, that "art [of synthesis] hidden in the depth of the human soul, the true secrets of which we shall hardly ever be able to guess and reveal."[16]

How might Derrida and Ricoeur read our opening metaphor from Joyce—"the gaze of his disciple"? Judging from how antithetically they read the metaphor of the sun's creative, unseen action at a distance ("sowing a god-created flame") that Aristotle draws from Homer to discuss in the *Rhetoric*, it might go something like the following. Derrida would see Joyce's metaphor as laying bare the process of transcription and transfiguration inherent in metaphor. Stupid Lenehan, Corley's self-conscious lackey, becomes invested figuratively with all the trappings of spiritual discipleship, but all so that, whatever Joyce's intentions, he may appear unworthy and the metaphoric process may be ironically seen for what it is: a metaphysical conjurer's trick, in which the "sensible" or material (Lenehan's "gaze") is translated into the "supersensible" or nonsensible ("of his disciple"). This, of course, makes Corley into an unwitting shanty-Irish Anti-Christ, an inverted priest of love. Ricoeur, however, on an analogy with Gilbert Ryle's notions, would see Joyce's metaphor as an intentional, creative "category mistake" that transfers an attribution, that of discipleship, from one realm (the spiritual realm), and applies it to the material realm, that of Corley and Lenehan, all so that even in its fallen modern forms the world of Joyce's Dublin may be seen as manifesting what Aristotle might call, according to Ricoeur's understanding of him, a living if self-degrading being whose very degradation sketches out alternative possibilities. In other words, Derrida and Ricoeur would provide the basis for a critic to read Joyce's metaphor as a regional instance of one of their beloved and antithetically defined positions. So both Derrida and Ricoeur in their critiques of metaphor provide more evidence of the romance of interpretation at work by showing how their respective methods of interpretation and argument produce insights that reflect and harmonize with those methods. To put it another way, the theoretical positions of Derrida and Ricoeur are *like* self-fulfilling prophecies of what one must find when examining other texts by their particular lights.

Even so, the differences between Derrida and Ricoeur as interpreters and theorists could not be more glaringly apparent than in their different positions on metaphor. Derrida's method of reading, which his under-standing of metaphor justifies, is to destroy metaphysical syntheses by reduction to aporias, aporias that he demonstrates are generated by the formulas of language and not the categories of pure reason. For example, in his analysis of Lévi-Strauss's *Triste Tropiques* in *De la Grammatologie* Der-rida demonstrates that the opposition in Lévi-Strauss's text between nature and culture is not simply a methodological assumption, a convenient fiction assumed by Lévi-Strauss in order to categorize his observations, but rather this opposition, licensed by the metaphysics of presence, especially as it operates on Lévi-Strauss via Rousseau's influence, has been produced necessarily by the differential play of writing in an epoch when all styles of inscription are determined by this metaphysics of presence.

For Derrida, the interpreter should produce the repressed deconstruc-tive play of *écriture*, in which any writer's discourse, no matter how self-conscious the writer, no matter how idealized the discourse, must be implicated, within the theater of the interpreter's own text:

> The writer writes *in* a language and *in* a logic whose proper system, laws, and life his discourse by definition cannot dominate absolutely. He uses them only by letting himself, after a fashion and up to a point, be governed by the system. And the reading [of any writer's text] must always aim at a certain relationship, unperceived by the writer, be-tween what he commands and what he does not command of the patterns of the language that he uses. This relationship is not a certain quantitative distribution of shadow and light, of weakness or of force, but a signifying structure that critical reading should *produce*.[17]

This "postmodern" critical trace of the writer implicated in the web of his text and its networks of figures could not contrast more strikingly with the Romantic Image of the poet proclaimed by Coleridge and endorsed in somewhat revised form—Donne and Marvell replacing Milton and Wordsworth as the model of the poet—by Eliot and his American disciples. The aim of the interpreter is, for Derrida, to expose "difference" at play, that mock "presence disappearing in its own [mock] radiance," that "oblit-eration of the face of being" which all inscription, particularly metaphoric inscription, presupposes and would deny.

Ricoeur's method of reading, on the other hand, which his theory of metaphor validates, is an open-ended dialectical interrogation that aligns in a single vision the history of thinking on a classic philosophical di-lemma, so as to spiral back from a contemporary impasse to those first annunciations of the critical problem under discussion as it existed on the original shifting boundaries between speculative discourse and myth. Ricoeur prefers to differentiate in a systematic way the conflict of interpre-tations that is raging in the human sciences by distinguishing between the hermeneutics of suspicion, as practiced by the disciples of Marx,

Nietzsche, and Freud, and the hermeneutics of recuperation, as seen in the work of Hegel, Bultmann, and Eliade. Ricoeur's own method of interpretation, as seen in *Freud and Philosophy* and *The Rule of Metaphor* is *critical* and *dialectical* in the original strong Kantian sense.[18] There is a first phase in which Ricoeur articulates the differences that exist in the philosophical tradition between opposing sides of an issue, in the language of the thinkers themselves; then there is a second phase in which Ricoeur demonstrates the conceptual and metaphorical affinities between opposing thinkers in a contemporary debate and then between these present opponents and their precursors in the tradition; and, finally, there is a third phase in which Ricoeur speculates on the nature and structure of a possible future synthesis of all these opposing lines of thought that the very activity of thinking seems to promise, a synthesis, modeled upon an ancient symbolic formulation that has mythic dimensions. Such a speculative synthesis, proposed in the critical language of philosophy but modeled upon an ancient prereflective symbolic or mythic paradigm, this critical fiction, is always proposed as such by Ricoeur, but also only proposed as a regulative or limit idea, never affirmed as the "truth."

For example, in *The Rule of Metaphor* Ricoeur concludes with a meditation upon the vision of the poet as a master of metaphor found in Aristotle. He then speculates on the nature of metaphor as a creative imitation of reality that portrays as complete and active, *as living*,[19] what the technological imagination would see as parts of the universe of death. This idea of creative imitation that redescribes reality in terms of the possibilities of becoming, liberating the real from bondage to what now is and setting it free toward a future of what may be, is the synthesis of the different views on metaphor proposed by Ricoeur as worthy of renewed questioning. Deferring all final or absolute synthetic resolutions and maintaining a critical stance toward them allows Ricoeur to resist the temptation to succumb to either comforting myths of wholeness, unity, and order, or self-indulgent visions of apocalypse, of the "end" of this, that, or the other. Unlike Derrida, then, Ricoeur is an example of the modern ironic thinker par excellence who has, apparently, mastered his irony. For when he returns to the contemporary impasse from which he started, after reflecting on the history of the problem and a possible synthesis suggested by that history, he does not propose any final solutions or some absolute answer— not even this critical hesistancy is taken programmatically as one by Ricoeur. Instead, he refocuses the discussion on the prereflective symbolic and mythic dimensions of language, which philosophical and critical thinking still cannot control or exhaust. In essence, then, Ricoeur seeks to recuperate traditional questions, not traditional answers, even as Derrida seeks to dispel such hoary enigmatic giants into the jocular windmills of textuality. Ricoeur, like Heidegger, is nostalgic for the old questions; Derrida, like Nietzsche, would be prophetic of new ones. Or of none at all.

I quote now two representative sets of assertions in this connection. First, Ricoeur from *History and Truth:*

> I shall not try to construct a systematic answer to this question by starting with a dogmatic principle. Rather, I shall proceed by a series of *approximations* wherein the solutions reached at one level will be rectified by bringing the initial question back into question.[20]

Now, Derrida from "White Mythology" and then from "Structure, Sign, and Play":

> Metaphysics . . . has effaced in itself that fabulous scene which brought it into being, and which yet remains, active and stirring, inscribed in white ink, an invisible drawing covered over in the palimpsest of Western metaphysics.
>
> Here there is a sort of question, call it historical, of which we are only glimpsing today the *conception,* the *formation,* the *gestation,* the *labor.* I employ these words, I admit, with a glance toward the business of child-bearing—but also with a glance toward those who, in a company from which I do not exclude myself, turn their eyes away in the face of the as yet unnameable which is proclaiming itself and which can do so, as is necessarily the case whenever a birth is in the offing, only under the species of non-species, in the formless, mute, infant and terrifying form of monstrosity. . . . I do not believe that there is any perception.[21]

And yet, and yet. . . . What, after all, does this imagery of monstrous birth from Derrida's now notorious essay suggest? What does Ricoeur's apotheosis of Aristotle's vision of the poet upon the scaffold of Gilbert Ryle's notion of a category mistake really intend? Surely, not that some revelation is at hand; surely not that the Second Coming is at hand, although Yeats's apocalyptic poem of that name does seem to be echoed by Derrida in particular. Are not both these visions, that of Ricoeur and that of Derrida, mirror images of each other, like the Gnostic Demiurge and his shadowy female reflection upon the roiling waters of primal darkness? To what species of nonspecies can such highly ironic, antithetical versions of the romance of interpretation give birth? In short, do not both Derrida, despite his deconstructive *double-entendres* that explode all seriousness into the laughter of the trace, and Ricoeur, despite his pedantic self-effacement and scrupulous demurrals, do not both of these representative, consciously antithetical thinkers, engage, each in his own way, in his own ironic style of the romance of interpretation, ritually producing from the traces of the ancestral religion the two-faced coin of the ontotheological tradition—on the one side of which is inscribed the motto "the light of the world," and on the other side of which is inscribed its companion piece, "the dark night of the soul"?

Even more significantly, do not Derrida's and Ricoeur's texts invariably gravitate toward a first principle—whatever its name, however self-consciously mocked or slyly proposed, whether it is called myth or "differance"? With Ricoeur, there seems to be little question that this is so. After all, Ricoeur *is* a believer still. But what about Derrida? After all, does not he put into radical question all such procedures, as in "That Dangerous Supplement" chapter of the *Grammatology?*

Well, yes, of course. But he does so, I would argue, in a way that repeats, with ironic variations, the trace of the traditional perversion—something that he obviously knows:

> Not only is differance irreducible to every ontological or theological—onto-theological—reappropriation, but it opens up the very space in which onto-theology—philosophy—produces its system and its history. It thus encompasses and irrevocably surpasses onto-theology or philosophy.[22]

What is this "differance"? How is it functioning here in Derrida's text? Certainly as an instrument for reinventing origins, in Derrida's own terms. How is it essentially different, then, in its function as a reimagined first principle, a god-trace if you will, from its companions in other philosophers' texts, such as Ricoeur's prereflective conditioning ground of philosophical discourse that he has identified variously in his career as "myth," "symbol," "metaphor," or discursive "surplus of meaning"? Granted, Derrida's "difference" is not unitary, static, and pristine. But then, neither is Ricoeur's "symbol," or Kierkegaard's "Christ," or Hegel's *Geist*, or the Trinity, for that matter. And Derrida's apparently greater ironic self-awareness, his self-conscious recognition of the provisional, makeshift nature of his "conceptions," his "bricolage," seems of no help here. The form of Derrida's statement on "differance" repeats, ironically, the ruling dialectic of the very tradition it would expose and subvert. In a similar way, consider how what Derrida says about *woman* in Nietzsche's text (from *Spurs*) transforms that term into an ironic version of the very thing he would avoid:

> There is no such thing as the essence of woman because woman averts, she is averted of herself. Out of the depths, endless and unfathomable, she engulfs and distorts all vestige of essentiality, of identity, of property. And the philosophical discourse, blinded, founders on these shoals and is hurled down these depthless depths to its ruin.[23]

As Nietzsche himself puts it in *The Twilight of the Idols:* "I fear that we are not getting rid of God, so long as we still believe in grammar."[24] That is, as long as we believe in *any form* of determinism, even the most radical of linguistic determinisms that would seem to explode all of our ruling ideas and values, hurtling them into the innocence of becoming, we are repeatedly in danger of reestablishing the tradition we would overturn—of course, in a more ironic form. That is, we are constantly in danger of appearing to be like Corley and Lenehan in the realm of criticism.

The question raised by the examples of Ricoeur and Derrida is this: must we all be condemned to being, whatever our degree of self-consciousness, "god's buffoons" and "parodists of world-history" (Nietzsche's phrases from *Beyond Good and Evil*),[25] to being members in too good standing of what Derrida himself calls "a priesthood of parodist interpreters"? Must we always now be haunted by a last laugh, first laughed by Nietzsche in *Zarathustra*, that had no end for him but the eleven years he spent staring at a blank wall inscribing and reinscribing there in his deluded mind's eye the names of his "chosen" masks: "Dionysus/The Crucified One."[26]

> Nietzsche . . . studied the deep pool
> Of these discolorations, mastering
>
> The moving and the moving of their forms
> In much-mottled motions of blank time.
>
> His revery was the deepness of the pool,
> The very pool, his thoughts the colored forms,
>
> The eccentric souvenirs of human shapes,
> Wrapped in their seemings, crowd on curious crowd,
>
> In a kind of total affluence, all first,
> All final, colors subjected in revery
>
> To an innate grandiose, an innate light,
> The sun of Nietzsche gildering the pool,
>
> Yes: gildering the swarm-like manias
> In perpetual revolution, round and round.[27]

III
The Irony of the Critic's Metaphors

Let us return now to Joyce to see how he glosses the romance of interpretation by offering a critique of critical metaphor of his own that supplements both Derrida's deconstructive and Ricoeur's hermeneutic understanding of the ironic relation between figurative language and the act of philosophical or critical reflection and speculation based upon that language. Consider the opening paragraph of "The Sisters," the programmatic introduction to the argument of *Dubliners:*

There was no hope for him this time: it was the third stroke. Night
after night I had passed the house (it was vacation time) and studied
the lighted square of window: and night after night I had found it
lighted in the same way, faintly and evenly. If he was dead, I thought,
I would see the reflection of candles on the darkened blind for I knew
that two candles must be set at the head of a corpse. He had often said
to me: *I am not long for this world,* and I had thought his words idle.
Now I knew they were true. Every night as I gazed up at the window I
said softly to myself the word *paralysis.* It had always sounded
strangely in my ears, like the word *gnomon* in the Euclid and the word
simony in the Catechism. But now it sounded to me like the name of
some maleficent and sinful being. It filled me with fear, and yet I
longed to be nearer to it and to look upon its deadly work.[28]

The young boy is fascinated by every unfamiliar word as it inscribes itself
in his mind. Such words as *paralysis, gnomon,* and *simony* provoke in him an
uncanny conjunction of diverse associations that function to undercut,
ironically, the boy's reading, that imaginative repetition, of those signs
which would tell him the meaning of what he sees. Yet such irony, at the
expense of the young boy's critical pretensions, also finally and paradoxically confirms his strange, presumptuous associations. He himself is like a
"gnomon," the figure that is left after another, larger figure of the same
kind has been taken away. So, too, it is clear from the rest of the story, was
the dead priest like a "gnomon" in relation to his own ideal of the priesthood. And the young boy's periodic deliveries of snuff to the old priest, in
return for which the latter instructs the former in the "mysteries" of the
Church in a savage unwitting parody of such ritual, do constitute acts of
"simony"—the exchange of material goods for spiritual knowledge and
power, the transfer of significance from one realm to another in the human
economy of meaning.

So how do we read Joyce's irony? It is not simply destructive, under-
mining the boy's insights from the lofty perspective of the authorial pup-
peteer. Nor is it purely recuperative, endorsing the latent creative and
metaphoric conjunctions of the boy that, despite his ignorance or the fallen
status of his world, do "see" into the heart of things. Does this mean that
the critic should reify the image of Joyce the ironic creator who has mastered his irony and insert that glorified image into the space of representation, into the gap between these different semantic possibilities
evoked by the text and so bring the process of reading to a halt before an
idol of one's own devising? To do so would be to ignore the last third of
this opening, in which Joyce anticipates such a possible reading by exposing to us how the boy's immature mind, to put an end to the play of
figurative associations and critical speculation and to unify them under a
single sublime metaphorical figure, imagines that the word *paralysis* stands
for a "maleficent and sinful being," a demonic agent, whose dreadful fas-

cinating work he would examine. That is, Joyce prophetically shows us the ironic operations of critical metaphor from the initial disjunction between opposing semantic possibilities to the sublime apotheosis of a demonic creator-figure behind such "work." Joyce recommends only that we keep our distance and examine the entire process of art's potentially fatal shaping of life.

Like Derrida, then, Joyce would expose how we become what we behold as we allow the play of grammatical inscriptions to produce the fictions of presence that transform us into all-too-willing slaves of our own vicarious idols. And like Ricoeur, Joyce's ironic metaphorical conjunctions redescribe reality by filling in the sketches of our would-be self-portraits traced by past impressions, the way Joyce suggests the mind of the creator behind the young boy's ironic observations.

My point, then, is simply this: that "postmodern" criticism does not represent the same kind of breakthrough into a radically different conception of man's temporality that "postmodern" poetry and fiction apparently do.[29] "Postmodern" criticism is largely a self-conscious application, to the critical domain, of the inventions, techniques, stances, and ironic style of literary modernism as conceived by the New Critics. As Paul De Man has recently put it, concerning this inevitable dialectic of literary history that simultaneously constitutes and subverts the critical sense of identity as difference:

> The discourse by which the figural structure of the self is asserted fails to escape from the categories it claims to deconstruct, and this remains true, of course, of any discourse which pretends to re-inscribe in its turn the figure of this aporia. There can be no escape from the dialectical movement that produces the text.[30]

This dialectical movement, which De Man calls "allegory of reading," Bloom calls "the anxiety of influence," and I would call "the romance of interpretation," necessarily produces from the play of textual inscriptions either a god or a demon made in the image of what the critic must become like, no matter what his intentions may be.

A final question: what can we conclude about the uncanny necessity of such a situation? Perhaps only this: that Ricoeur, because of his historical orientation and hermeneutical perspective, would be a more helpful guide to tracing our genealogies among the great modernists. In addition, his understanding of figurative language and the "ancillary" stance of his method of interpretation, his putting the prereflective discourse first, allows us to see contemporary criticism for what it, alas, must be: "the gaze of his disciple," haunted by an all-too-familiar uncompounded ghost.

In the final analysis, then, it is Ricoeur rather than Derrida who would be our best guide to, say, the maze of Joyce's texts. For Ricoeur would appreciate Joyce's insight into what is still the modern dilemma: how all of us still occupy positions similar to that of the young Joyce with regard to the tradition. I quote Stephen Dedalus here from the Nestor chapter on this topic. Stephen is meditating, while teaching a history lesson with half his mind, upon the nightmare influence on his students in particular, of what Stevens in "Sunday Morning" calls "the dark/Encroachment of that old catastrophe":[31]

> Here also over their craven hearts his shadow lies and on the scoffer's heart and lips and on mine. It lies upon their eager faces who offered him a coin of the tribute.[32]

Via Ricoeur we can see how the approximations of romance in the ironic postmodern style of criticism begin, inevitably perhaps, to reconstitute the traces of such a shadow. Perhaps we can also expect now to learn that a few of our most notable avant garde critics have espoused the old faith in some new, more fashionably esoteric form. If so, may not one be permitted a Joycean smile?

Notes

1. Robert Scholes and A. Walton Litz, ed. *James Joyce: Dubliners: Text, Criticism, and Notes* (New York: Penguin Books, 1976), p. 60.

2. *Ibid.*, p. 377.

3. Lawrence I. Lipking and A. Walton Litz, eds. *Modern Literary Criticism, 1900–1970* (New York: Atheneum, 1972), p. 69.

4. Paul A. Bové, *Destructive Poetics: Heidegger and Modern American Poetry* (New York: Columbia University Press, 1980), p. 23. For the clearest statement of Spanos's position, see "Modern Literary Criticism and the Spatialization of Time: An Existential Critique," *Journal of Aesthetics and Art Criticism* 29 (1970): 87–104.

5. Cf. Michel Foucault, "What Is an Author?" in *Textual Strategies: Perspectives in Post-Structuralist Criticism*, ed. Josué Harari (Ithaca, N. Y.: Cornell University Press, 1979), pp. 141–60.

6. Cf. Jacques Derrida, *Spurs: Nietzsche's Styles*, trans. Barbara Harlow (Chicago: The University of Chicago Press, 1979).

7. For example, see Hugh Kenner, *The Stoic Comedians* and his discussion of Joyce. See also Litz's contribution to *James Joyce's Ulysses: Critical Essays*, ed. Clive Hart and David Hayman (Berkeley, Calif.: University of California Press, 1974), pp. 385–406.

8. Harold Bloom, "The Internalization of Quest Romance," *The Ringers in the Tower: Studies in Romantic Tradition* (Chicago: The University of Chicago Press, 1971), pp. 15 and 19.

9. Cf. my review-essay in *Journal of Aesthetics and Art Criticism* 36 (Spring 1978): 361–65 for further discussion.

10. Cf. also *Kant: The Critique of Judgment*, trans. James Creed Meredith (Oxford: At the Clarendon Press, 1928), pp. 175–76.

11. *Philosophy and Truth: Selections from Nietzsche's Notebooks of the Early 1870's*, trans. and ed. Daniel Breazeale (Atlantic Highlands, N. J.: Humanities Press, 1979), pp. xlvii and xlviii.

12. Immanuel Kant, *Critique of Pure Reason*, trans. F. Max Müller (Garden City, N.Y.: Anchor Books, 1966), p. 224.

13. See my review-essay of Derrida's *Of Grammatology* in *Journal of Aesthetics and Art Criticism* 36 (Spring 1978): 361–65, for further discussion of the Kantian dimension of Derrida's project.

14. Paul Ricoeur, *The Rule of Metaphor: Multi-disciplinary Studies of the Creation of Meaning in Language,* trans. Robert Czerny (with Kathleen McLaughlin and John Costello, S.J.) (Toronto: University of Toronto Press, 1977), pp. 23 and 43. See my review-essay, "The Irony of Being Metaphorical," in *Boundary 2* 8 (Winter 1980).

15. *The Collected Poems of W. B. Yeats* (New York: Macmillan, 1966), p. 216.

16. Kant, *Critique of Pure Reason,* p. 123.

17. Jacques Derrida, *Of Grammatology,* trans. G. Spivak (Baltimore, Md.: The Johns Hopkins University Press, 1977), p. 158.

18. For a discussion of this idea, see my essay "The Prophet of Our Laughter: The Irony of Understanding Nietzsche," in *Boundary 2* 9 (Winter 1981).

19. See "Self-Born Mockery: The Irony of (Self)-Reflecton in Yeats," in my *Tragic Knowledge: Yeats's Autobiography and Hermeneutics* (New York: Columbia University Press, 1981).

20. Paul Ricoeur, *History and Truth,* trans. Charles Kebley (Evanston, Ill.: Northwestern University Press, 1965), p. 37.

21. Jacques Derrida, "White Mythology: Metaphor in the Text of Philosophy," *New Literary History* 6 (Autumn 1974):69; and "Structure, Sign, and Play in the Discourse of the Human Sciences," in *The Structuralist Controversy,* ed. Richard Macksey and Eugenio Donato (Baltimore, Md.: The Johns Hopkins University Press, 1970), p. 265.

22. Jacques Derrida, "Differance," in *Speech and Phenomena and Other Essays on Husserl's Theory of Signs,* trans. David B. Allison (Evanston, Ill.: Northwestern University Press, 1973), pp. 134–35.

23. Derrida, *Spurs,* p. 51.

24. Friedrich Nietzsche, *Twilight of the Idols,* trans. R. J. Hollingdale (Baltimore, Md.: Penguin Books, 1968), p. 40.

25. Friedrich Nietzsche, *Beyond Good and Evil,* trans. Walter Kaufmann (New York: Vintage, 1967), p. 150.

26. Cf. the letters from the period of Nietzsche's breakdown in Turin in early January 1889 collected in Charles Middleton, trans. and ed. *Selected Letters of Nietzsche* (Chicago and London: The University of Chicago Press, 1969), pp. 344–48.

27. *The Collected Poems of Wallace Stevens* (New York: Knopf, 1954), p. 342.

28. Scholes and Litz, *James Joyce,* p. 9.

29. For a discussion of this issue of "postmodernism," see my review-essay "The Freedom of the Master?" of Gerald Graff's *Literature Against Itself: Literary Ideas in Modern Society* (Chicago: The University of Chicago Press, 1979), in *Contemporary Literature* (Fall 1980).

30. Paul De Man, *Allegories of Reading: Figural Language in Rousseau, Nietzsche, Rilke and Proust* (New Haven, Conn.: Yale University Press, 1979), p. 187. For a discussion of De Man's conception of irony as it relates to modern literary and critical forms, see my essay "The Power of Nothing in *Women in Love,*" in *Bucknell Review* (forthcoming).

31. Stevens, *Collected Poems,* p. 67.

32. James Joyce, *Ulysses* (New York: Random House, 1961), p. 26. For a further discussion of "the romance of interpretation" as it appears in postmodern criticism, see my essay "The Romance of Interpretation: A 'Postmodern' Critical Style," in *Boundary 2* 8 (Spring 1980).

Going On and Going Nowhere: Wittgenstein and the Question of Criteria in Literary Criticism

Charles Altieri

I

A decade of intense literary theorizing has left us with little more than an acute sense of the problems we have as a discipline and a dim fear that what unites us is only our sense of the inevitability of these problems. This fear, however, may be necessary only to the extent that we lack any theoretical way to reach agreement on how we reach agreement. Our disputes may prove that we simply are not addressing the same criteria, both in our close readings and in our concerns to show how texts may be used for larger cultural purposes. Yet there seem to be virtually no efforts to see whether such differences are necessary. The most common theoretical positions (even among those who despise theory) are radically relativistic. Among historicists we see two sharply opposed forms of this idea that oddly duplicate the same logic. Against conventional claims that we can never know the past unless we thoroughly bracket modern assumptions, we find Gadamer insisting that we can rely only on modern needs and questions as a condition of giving life and meaning to the past. Then there are many analytic, skeptical arguments that treat all criteria to which we might subject disputes as relative to the needs, desires, or wills to power of their proponents. The best modern minds, like Foucault, often mix from these a complex and potent brew. But neither seems an adequate account of criteria for understanding. None can explain how we might value the modern significance of works from the past precisely because we understand on many levels how they differ from our ordinary assumptions. And the skeptical position, at least, seems to make all acts of persuasion or even of compromise into acts of domination. This is probably counterintuitive and it definitely raises serious questions about bothering with discourse at all, especially discourse "explaining" the skeptical view. I am not likely to agree if I know I will be considered a dupe (although even thinking that already means I am a dupe, ad nauseam).

Under such pressure, and perhaps faced with such images of futile labor, some contemporary theorists are tempted to take on an opposite tack and to develop their model of criteria from the hypothetical-empirical inquiry employed in natural science. One preserves a clear role for discussion and debate, but it is extremely difficult to decide on the specific forms of coherence or of testing that apply to literary hypotheses. If one insists on testable hypotheses about intentions in order to have determinate meaning, one still has the problem of showing what possible laws will dictate general patterns of coherence for inferring the agent's complex purposes. We do not have clear empirical evidence for falsifying plausible alternatives about intentions (they are banned from extensional languages) and we have no established methodology for framing the argument functions of our hypotheses. Similarly, if we try to use scientific models for establishing cultural significance, we not only lack rules, but we also run the risk of treating all texts as testable generalizations, although many literary works are intended to be seen as resonant particulars with nonpropositional means for becoming representative. Many writers, for example, are not concerned with the descriptive or general "truth" value of what they construct. Their aim is to create a possible or potential, ideal way of acting. I do not see how models of discourse developed to test how instances are explained by laws can also provide what might be called an inferential calculus for judging works or interpretive hypotheses as more or less relevant or satisfying or illuminating with respect to possible forms of action. There may be a descriptive component in such discussions, but isolating it will not easily lead to the desired overall criteria. Probably the clearest instance of this impossibility is theory's need to explain how critics can value competing imaginative versions of roughly the same state of affairs, say by Balzac, Flaubert, Rousseau, and Tolstoy. Carnap was no fool in banishing metaphysical attitudes from the provenance of scientific method, as attempts even in the social sciences to rely on its criteria for dealing with persons and actions might by now have shown us.[1]

The anomalies and contradictions both within and between these positions are serious enough to warrant our exploring other possible criteria for making many of the judgments we need or would like to be able to make about literary texts. I want to argue here that taking certain abstractions from Wittgenstein's later work can bring us a long way toward locating the criteria we need because he treats criteria in essentially dramatistic rather than scientific terms, and thus allows a good deal of pluralism while still providing a considerable range of shared judgments. Wittgenstein establishes a pluralism that is not a purely tolerant relativism but what W. J. T. Mitchell once called a way of living with less than security but more than insecurity. This attitude depends on what I call a consensual or grammatical pragmatism where criteria derive from deeply embedded cultural practices that produce contexts and expectations for judging competing claims. Such proceedings require our seeking forms of representativeness that involve complex notions of individuals and types rather than the lawfulness demanded by Popperian methodology. The reliance on individual cases provides Wittgenstein's link to classical pragmatism, while the idea of representativeness creates a view of results that is less practical and more formal than is typical of pragmatism. The aim is not the discovery of what works in an empirical sense but of what allows agents to agree on what might count as significant practical results. Thus for Wittgenstein the concrete test of understanding involves imagining a way of sharing processes. One can then abstract as his basic norm a test of the power any model has to allow us to go on in connection with situations, purposes, and shared cultural frameworks or grammars that are extremely flexible:

> Try not to think of understanding as a mental process at all. For *that* is the expression which confuses you. But ask yourself: what sort of cases, in what kind of circumstances do we say, "Now I know how to go on, when, that is, the formula *has* occurred to me?" (PI, 154)[2]

Passages like this, I hope to show, lead well beyond dispute about criteria. By demonstrating a way of reaching agreements that does not depend on scientific models, Wittgenstein's understanding of understanding will eventually allow us to give cogent support to traditional claims that literary works serve distinct cognitive and normative roles. First, however, we need to clarify Wittgenstein's treatment of criteria for understanding by asking what kind of cases in theory seem to require his particular way of going on. I shall take as my example a specific, and I think representative, critical argument by Stanley Fish that makes consensual pluralism lead to what seems to me a seriously flawed radical relativism. I do not want to prove that Fish's case is "false." Instead I shall try to draw contrasts between it and the perspective I take from Wittgenstein in order to show how much we cannot do from Fish's stance (while remaining within conditions where agreement is possible) but can from Wittgenstein's. In other words, contrast here will reveal how criteria can themselves be judged by the very test Wittgenstein proposes—their capacity to allow us to go on and show how descriptions of literary phenomena are plausible and connect to other forms of life.

II

The obvious contrastive strategy to demonstrate the value of Wittgensteinian models is to set them against radically different positions like

Positivism on the one hand, Derrida on the other. I shall touch on these as we proceed, especially the need to find alternatives to the unholy brotherhood of the two positions I mentioned as they live one another's life and die one another's death over the question of whether arguments can refer to an isolated *propre sens*. However, this level of argument tends to be so general that one never sees how Wittgensteinian criteria actually work and lead to literary issues. Therefore I shall begin here on a very different tack. Instead of global contrasts, I shall try to show what Wittgenstein can help us do by setting him against a position that shares the consensual model but does not in my view fully appreciate how cultural grammars work. By narrowing the area of discussion I hope also to show that the contrast is not merely an academic one, because how we understand the grounds and uses of consensus will shape what we can say about value, community, and literary education. From my perspective, even framing the relevant issues requires that we develop a form of relativism that can explain levels within culture and thus show how differences can still be judged within fairly stable criteria.

Stanley Fish's essay "Normal Circumstances . . . and Other Special Cases" is the most concise, intelligent defense of a radical conventionalism and thus a good indication of its problems.[3] His fundamental claim is one held also by most deconstructionist thinkers (if only as a strategy): descriptive statements cannot be taken as observations of facts but stem from an interested position and are mediated through representations that depend on social conventions. Then, because descriptions are not determined by natural laws and because judgments on conventions take place within conventions, one can treat terms for judgment as "arbitrary." There can be no *propre sens* that is not someone's property, so all claims about "literal" meaning or "normal" pragmatic contexts must be seen as the product of contextually dependent frameworks of questions and expectations. We can produce interpretive stability for our judgments, but they are "stable in more than one direction, as a succession of interpretive assumptions give it a succession of stable shapes" (629). What is literal about a text, or even what constitutes the relevant intention shaping a text, will depend on criteria of evidence that are established coherently but differently by competing theories or cultural contexts. And, I infer, there is no way for competing theories to be judged on any common ground. From Fish's perspective, then, one can explain agreement, as long as conventions and constraints are shared, while also explaining how meanings and views of relevant evidence change as cultures or interests change.

If, however, one has adopted the spirit of Wittgenstein's later thought, there is something suspicious about Fish's confident, sweeping assertions. The temptation is not so much to disagree, because that would only produce counterclaims on the same level of discourse, as to call attention to a wide discrepancy between the neatness of theory and the complexity of actual practice. Is it really the case that we can usually characterize the specific questions and expectations that differentiate one culture's interpretations of meanings from another's? Are there not some elements that are more resistant than others to changes in fashion or ideology and that then make demands on competing theories? Wittgenstein, for example, reminds us of cases where emotions seem lodged in a face, so that there are some relatively constant features of portraits even in opposing interpretations. Similarly, Richard Schiff points out that while critics contemporary with Cézanne differed radically in their interpretations of the rationale for his work, they agreed in describing his fundamental stylistic traits and, I infer, the effect of specific paintings.[4] Or, to put the case more generally, one could argue that once Fish tries to explain everything by a concept of conventions of inquiry he really explains nothing. For now he must still use "convention" in order to explain such apparent differences as why some sentences or procedures seem more ambiguous or more readily construed than others or why his view of criteria is superior to others. There must be degrees of convention and thus levels on which some principles will serve to assess particular competing positions. Fish offers what we might call a single-thread model of cultural phenomena, which I think require instead analytic concepts like Quine's of networks of connections more delicate and changeable at the periphery than in the fairly stable assumptions that constitute the densely interwoven interior.[5]

An extended example will establish the specific differences between Fish and the version of networks one can develop from Wittgenstein. Fish offers a legal case to illustrate the bad faith inherent in positions that deny his relativist stance. The judge must decide whether a man can receive an inheritance from someone he has killed. The letter of the law makes no qualifications on inheritance from a properly documented will, so if the appeal is to be denied the status of the letter of the law becomes problematic. In Fish's case the judge decides against the claimant because it is "one of the 'general fundamental maxims of the common law' that 'no one shall be permitted to profit by his own fraud . . . or to acquire property by his own crime' " (633). Fish finds this reasoning highly suspect. It results, he suggests, from a condition of desire rather than a dictate inherent in the law or legal reasoning. Here the judge seems to set the "literal" meaning of the law aside. Because the judge wants "to find a way of reading the statute so as to bar the inheritance," he conceals the obvious meaning and posits as objective in the law implicit intentions that justify his case. So under the guise of objectivity we find another form of literal objectivity being set aside, without any self-consciousness about the sleight of hand. But all self-consciousness would do is make us aware of how there is in fact no determinate literal meaning: only by first projecting a purpose on and for the law can we posit any literal meaning (634). We construct our objectivities.

Even if we grant Fish's epistemological point, however, it does not necessarily support the purely relativist ethics and positivist legal theory at least strongly implicit in Fish's position. Although purposes are not objective, they may have considerable support in traditional and conceptual forms of going on strongly in legal institutions (although often never literally present "in" the specific law). The problem is clearest in Fish's apparent assumption that both purposes facing the court have no value connection independent of the specific existential moment of choice. Both purposes seem to exist on the same level. But this is not how law or society works. The law must have, and society tends to have, levels of embedding among priorities and principles that allow recursive justifications that are not all subject to change at the same rate and thus not all equally dependent on the same kinds of purposes. Law must work like Quine's network, not like Barthes' onion. So the finding of implicit intentions based on higher, inclusive principles is not merely one among possible choices or priorities but one based on the fundamental possibility of ever resolving competing interpretations without pure arbitrariness, that is, on the very idea of law. Fish is right that inheritance law *could* outweigh an unlawful-gain provision if the highest priority of law were the disposition of property, but the embedded principles would be different; we would then have another kind of society, again with levels of embedding. What Fish ignores brings us to the heart of Wittgenstein's vision—that for some of the basic principles in social institutions to change, the society itself would have to emphasize different forms of life. In this particular case, for the property consideration to outweigh constraints against violent gain one would have to envision a society bound procedurally to versions of the person and of fairness very different from those commonly affirmed in Western culture. Such changes are possible, but they will not alter as fashions do or as Nietzschean wills desire, nor will they depend on or explain the choices of a single judge.[6]

The probable reasons for Fish's seeking so simple an explanation make a very important contrast to Wittgenstein. He sets up an absolute opposition between categories like literalness, with fixed and hence dependable criteria, and categories that depend only on will or convention. This brings him very close to assumptions like Bertrand Russell's, and that in turn explains why Derrida is attractive to Fish since Derrida's "scandal" depends on ironically subverting Russellian demands for *propre sens.* Yet neither Russell's form of philosophy nor its skeptical inversions can handle cultural institutions like law because they have no way of dealing with levels of embedding and the forms of practical, not analytic, judgment they require. Fish's basic argumentative strategy is a perfect instance of this problem (and a perfect instance of how Derrida creates temptations for literary theorists). Fish bases his radical relativism on the demand that any opposing position produce a fixed definition or proper sense for concepts like "normal" or "literal." In effect he insists upon analytic or scientific grounds for refuting the claim that all systematic models or cultural conventions are "arbitrary." This allows him to treat even the oddest scenario as a counterexample sufficient to demonstrate that the ideas of normalcy or literalness are not legitimate. However, it is not such facts but the conditions imposed on the inquiry that support his arguments. Normalcy is not the kind of concept that involves necessary and sufficient conditions and hence it cannot be deemed "arbitrary" in particular cases by relying only on isolated counterexamples. Normalcy is either statistical or grammatical; in either case it is a function of ways of measuring probability not possibility. In Wittgenstein's work the ground of norms is grammatical: they are expectations that derive from the ways we learn to use language in contexts. So judging normalcy involves not definitive descriptions of states of affairs that can be falsified but the probabilistic evaluation of which situation types best combine for understanding appropriate contexts and embedded values.[7] Thus it will not do to make Fish's leap from the correct assumption that coherence is relative to the problematic one that all the terms that establish coherence are equally relative. Where conditions of coherence depend on regularities or probabilities rather than rules or laws, one must be careful to distinguish between isolated situations and adjustments based on embedded procedures. Wittgenstein, in fact, would probably completely reverse Fish's arguments here. The philosophically salient feature of discussions of normalcy would be the degree of transparent cleverness, and hence of atypicality that goes into inventing the counterexample. The more elaborate the invention, the more likely it is that the counterexample is relevant only to philosophical concerns for necessary and sufficient conditions. Ironically, the elaborate counterexample indicates, if it does not quite prove, how deeply embedded and "normal" is the procedure one is trying to deny. And because of this marginal status, the counterexample reveals the power of criteria of going on to make significant discriminations. There are simply not many connections one could make if one assumed such cases as typical.

III

We need now to see how we can describe a general model of understanding and possible agreement based on probabilistic criteria like those we have been discussing. We must, in other words, find a way of accounting for the possibility of agents agreeing on some matters while disagreeing on others, or of agents from different cultural or historical contexts reaching common purposes in specific areas. Ideal cases here would consist of agents from different cultures acknowledging some authority or process that would lead them to criticize and revise their course of activity. In order to rationalize these possibilities of self-criticism, Wittgenstein first tried the protopositivism of the *Tractatus*. When he recognized that there were more areas of secure agreement than could be accounted for by truth-functional operations, he briefly flirted with explanations based on natural law. But one does not need such ontological grounds if one can provide behavioral descriptions sufficiently subtle to specify how agreement and fit are recognized.

I shall try to show briefly how he satisfied these needs through the criterion of going on elaborated in the *Investigations*—first, because the criterion provides an alternative to the endless regress of defining norms only within philosophy or only in truth-functional terms, and second, because his account correlates with a plausible image of how we get educated into and operate in terms of networks of cultural practices. This analytic discussion will lead to my speculating on how Wittgenstein's own discourse embodies his view of criteria and exemplifies the cognitive status one can attribute to literary texts.

The obvious way to begin analyzing the treatment of criteria in the *Investigations* is by the virtually ritualistic act of recounting Wittgenstein's criticism of the *Tractatus*. Like most rituals, this one deals with a crucial boundary—here between the authority of philosophy to dictate norms for valid statements and some more flexible, and more problematic, sense that philosophy itself requires justification in terms of broader dimensions of cultural life. That one must suspect philosophically derived criteria that end up proclaiming the absolute critical authority of philosophy is the cutting edge for recent claims that truth standards are only constructs of wills to power. Wittgenstein's achievement was to see the problem clearly but not to jump to some alternative absolute like wills to power or arbitrary conventions. Instead of shifting from one set of grounds for truth claims to another, Wittgenstein tried to change our general ideas of the place criteria have in our experience and of how we can discover the ways we recognize and acknowledge constraints on our discourses.

Wittgenstein's reflections on the *Tractatus* are paradigms of self-criticism that at once raise questions of how self-criticism is possible and demonstrate the necessity of such acts:

> The more narrowly we examine actual language the sharper becomes the conflict between it and our requirement. (For the crystalline purity of logic was, of course, not a result of investigation; it was a requirement.) . . . the requirement is now in danger of becoming empty. (PI, 107)

> F. P. Ramsey once emphasized in conversation with me that logic was a 'normative science.' . . . In philosophy we often *compare* the use of words with games and calculi which have fixed rules, but cannot say that someone who is using language *must* be playing such a game. But if you say that our languages only *approximate* to such calculi you

are standing on the very brink of a misunderstanding. For this it may look as if what we were talking about were an *ideal* language. . . . Whereas logic does not treat of language or of thought in the sense in which a natural science treats of a natural phenomenon, and the most that can be said is that we *construct* ideal languages. But here the word "ideal" is liable to mislead, for it sounds as if these languages were better, more perfect than our everyday language; and as if it took the logician to show people at last what a proper sentence looked like. (PI, 81)

I shall take up the problem of specifying the grounds for this self-criticism later when I discuss second-order aspects of "going on." Now the important issue is realizing that what seemed to be obvious logical criteria are in fact imposed norms as soon as one asks about the ways philosophy connects to common life. Wittgenstein had to play for himself the role Callicles plays for Socrates in *Gorgias:* he proposed the problem that while there are rules for making claims as a philosopher within philosophy, there are no obvious forms of authority that allow the philosopher to impose his conclusions or methods on those not bound to the philosopher's ways of proceeding. This does not mean that explanatory schemes do not make sense or do work. But it does make us aware that it is easy to overextend our schemes without clarifying the grounds for applying them. We cannot lose sight of the possibility that philosophy itself is condemned to disease as long as it needs to hypostatize other diseases—vagueness and multiplicity—as the general cultural source of the symptoms it can cure. Wittgenstein defined, then, what has become a general dilemma in modern writing—that any interpretive language or second-order discourse about human actions faces very difficult problems of authorizing its relationship to the multiple forms of first-order practices. How does one decide whether it is the practices that need the rational order of explanatory systems or the systems that are only symptomatic restructurings and evasions of practices that are in order as they are?

These problems lead well beyond philosophical consequences to questions of how we use the past, understand cultural authority, and structure our educational goals. But it may be that coming to terms with the philosophical problems provides us with new ways of thinking about culture, authority, and education. Consider the probable source of Fish's errors—not faulty empirical research but relying on too generalized an idea of criteria and too abstract a notion of evidence. And these tendencies take hold because of what Wittgenstein calls a strong temptation to predicate of a phenomenon "what lies in the method of representing it" (PI, 104). Then what lies in the method seems to support a generalized abstraction like that of "convention." As we find ideal terms we tend to displace actual determinations. Consider, Wittgenstein asks us, a typical philosophical temptation: " 'This sentence makes sense.' 'What sense?' "This set of words is a sentence!' 'What sentence?' " (PI, 502). "Sentence" and "sense" seem comparable entities, and "sense" seems the more useful category since it can be attributed to all meaningful expressions. But "sense" is an odd, ideal entity; we do not make "sense," we make sentences that as sentences can be used in various circumstances. Once we abstract a category like "sense," we are tempted to propose rules and calculi for it that make the category a somewhat arbitrary norm for how we understand sentences. And once we have a norm, it is hard to avoid thinking that meanings are arbitrary unless rationalized in a coherent model of sense. Once "sense" is introduced and rationalized, the desire to achieve regularity and coherence creates instead an entity whose nature and lines of relation to the world we begin to doubt. We then extend our doubt from the explanation to the phenomenon. We put ourselves in a situation where the ideal of clarity encourages skeptical denials that anything makes coherent "sense." And we argue about that issue instead of looking at sentences. We create pictures that are idle because we ignore questions of the work they might do, and in philosophy as in life, idleness is an impetus for making trouble (PI, 288–91).

Now we should be able to see the force of the criterion of going on in relation to questions of meaning. The criteria are located in the web of cultural practices whose grammar one learns when one is educated within a society. These constitute forms of life or, in more neo-Kantian terms, "the possibilities of phenomena" (PI, 90). Forms of life in turn constitute a level for interpretation where one can illustrate an alternative to rigorous logical or empirical criteria. For in many cases the possibilities of phenomena inhere in the ordinary cultural practices that allow us to get things done or reach agreement on the basis of situations and contexts of expectation. "Sense" then depends on conditions of appropriateness or fit. In these cases, utterances, and acts, have meaning to the extent that we find them having a function in contexts. And we test hypotheses about the meaning simply by seeing whether a person can go on to make the desired connections by initiating or continuing a practice that produces the desired results or degrees of mutual understanding. Going on is a behavioral consequence of fit or appropriateness. One makes sense of the idea of sense, then, by shifting one's terms of inquiry from trying to specify grounds to examining practical conditions and consequences attendant upon an utterance:

> *Hearing* a word in a particular sense. How queer that there should be such a thing.
> Phrased *like this*, emphasized like this, heard in this way, this sentence is the first in a series in which a transition is made to *these* sentences, pictures, action. (PI, 534)

If we refuse this shift we have no way of moving from the thin ice of logic to the rough ground from which problems emerge and on which solutions

must be tested. Staying within philosophy tends to produce an ice follies of
the mind where we are "robbed of our orientation" (PI, 2, 259).

I want to dispel two possible misinterpretations here. First, I am not
saying that there are no abstract semantic codes or conventions that make
possible lexical sense or even pragmatic sense. My point is simply one of
priorities for theoretical reflection. Because cultural embeddings are so
complex, it is dangerous to base any specific description of an utterance or
act in context on these abstract systematic properties. How they function
for ordinary behavior can be tested only by maintaining our orientation
within specific practices. Structures of lexical sense define abstract possibilities for meanings but they will not explain particular choices, uses, or
tests of adequacy. Second, attention to rules or conventions will explain
agreement in some cases—those definable by practices themselves taught
in terms of rules—but they will not adequately characterize most forms of
interpersonal behavior connected with expressions or with fluid exchanges
like conversations or complex practical work.

In order to illustrate briefly how criteria depend on practices, I shall
take up the problematic topic of judging a translation. (In other writings I
use the example of interpreting actions.) If we were to begin with some
absolute standards of adequacy, we would obviously almost never be
satisfied with a translation. Unless languages are absolutely congruent,
there will always be some problem of synonymy. And in practices, like
reading poetry, where the precision of language as a coherent internal
system (tied to the physical qualities of the words) is paramount, we in fact
find a good deal of dispute about adequacy in translation. But there are
numerous other areas of life in which we rely on translations without
worrying about distortion or more melodramatic states of *aporia* and entrapment within "arbitrary" cultural differences. The translator understands a set of constraints that govern his or her work—in the semantic
code, in the need to project a plausible intention for the writer, and in the
tasks the translation is expected to serve. Yet whether we are translating or
judging a translation in these practical contexts, our criteria rarely depend
on either rules or some original sense of an abstract meaning to be
transferred into another language. Rather, we move through a series of
concrete choices in which a feeling of being puzzled over certain expressions gives way to a sense of finding equivalents that make a coherent fit
(cf. PI, 175 and nos. 459, 597, and Z, 72–75). Local fit then merges with
one's sense of being able to move smoothly through the entire discourse
and the smoothness is in turn tested by whether the translation is judged
to serve the purposes for which it was undertaken.

The way that norms work in ordinary translations helps avoid a second possible misunderstanding of what the criterion of going on entails.
While the later Wittgenstein shares Derrida's giving priority to rhetoric
over logic, he is not required to treat referential models of discourse as

inevitably in internal contradictions that are denied in order to preserve a form of authority that maintains given interests. In Wittgenstein's case, overall demystification makes for powerful local permissions no longer requiring the infinite self-consciousness of skeptical play. The skeptical stance is not a superior or "authentic position" because it too must be justified by what other forms of activity it makes possible or knots it unties. By the same token, while a truth-functional calculus is not a sufficient overall basis for arriving at philosophical conclusions, it is an extremely powerful and valid instrument for analyzing the empirical value of descriptive propositions. If agents desire impersonal, objective measures and can agree that they do not warp the phenomenon in any way that pertains to the inquiry, they can rationally all choose to abide by the forms of life constituted in our scientific traditions.

We should by now be clear enough on the ideas of going on to begin worrying about the obvious problem we must handle if we expect the criterion to do significant work. Going on is so flexible a concept that it may be useless because a virtually infinite set of possible ways to go on seems at hand in any given case. How then do we make discriminations among ways of going on without relying on conventions or returning to the normative authority of philosophy? One needs to explain at least two conditions—one specific and the other more general. First, when different particular arguments are offered, the relevant norms are what practices they allow or admit and how that connection of practices conforms to one's overall purposes in the project. Then, when it is not specific choices but criteria themselves that are in question, when we are judging, say, a particular practice, the relevant norm becomes the general fit with other cultural values that a given stance allows. The more general we get, the more dispute we can expect, but it may be a serious illusion to demand of philosophy that it resolve reasoned discussion about values. What matters most is getting us to clarify, for ourselves and each other, what is involved in and might follow from our choices. Both kinds of criteria come to bear on one of Wittgenstein's clearest treatments of this issue. How, he asks, are we to judge concepts of fear derived solely from the behavior of animals? Clearly, the concept facilitates some ways of going on, but just as clearly the choice of a model or picture involves obvious limitations. Because it contains predicates only grammatically connected with our ways of speaking about animals, this concept "would have no first person and none of its forms would be an expression of fear" (Z, 524). Animals do not say "I am afraid"; they only exhibit fear and thus do not give any role to a responding discourse interpreting or allaying the fear. To judge the specific model then, we must hold it up against our sense of the tasks we want it to do and the grammatical expectations allowing or blocking the desired transitions. Thus the animal model facilitates transitions to other physiological aspects of behavior and a unified scientific reductionism, but it simply does not fit our usual patterns of human interactions unless we are willing to make radical adjustments in our general sense of what we take a person to be and how we deal with him or her. These adjustments, in turn, open some ways of acting, block others. Whether they are deemed worth making depends on very complex hierarchies among attitudes, often decidable only by choosing a general community one wants to identify with.

If we shift to a literary example we can see more clearly where sets of grammatical expectations come from and how they work to indicate the relative use value of a critical statement. If one makes the claim that all one has in interpreting a literary text are conventions or codes, one immediately encounters several difficulties arising from a history of discourses about these texts. For if we respect them we find it hard not to assume that certain texts have properties of depth or complexity or significance that require a concern for purposes and expressive qualities not usually predicated of behavior according to conventions or codes. Similarly, a history of close readings will indicate dense aspects of diction, theme, and structure that require a very complex view of conventions. One could try to supplement the failure of one's convention-based account to handle these features. One could deny the claim to depth or try to explain depth or insight, and so on, as a property of ways of using conventions. But the effort is likely to reveal the poverty of the original conceptual commitment. Epicycles are not the best way to develop explanations.

Practical criticism affords similar examples of how we rely on implicit grammatical standards for measuring ways of going on. I think it is reasonable to claim that most well-educated readers of poetry from Pope to the present could agree on at least some instances of inferior criticism.[8] These works are likely to be reductive or to get so caught up in ideological or methodological concerns that all texts begin to look the same. In both cases the problem is clear: the inadequate work of criticism does not allow sufficient connections by which to give a fairly full life to stylistic or thematic aspects of the text. One cannot imagine the text having the value readers give it on the basis of the path for going on that the critic provides. Now we reach what is for me the clinching feature of Wittgenstein's line of thinking on this issue. Suppose that one wants to make explicit criticisms of the inferior reading or try to educate its author. One could not simply offer the author a theory that contradicts him. For what would justify the theory? One might use theories in the educational process, but these are less norms for specifying constraints on the critic than heuristic ways of indicating how one might begin reading texts more complexly. There need not be a single correct reading one teaches, but there are realms of expectations one tries to illustrate. From this perspective, theory itself becomes less a means for seeking true descriptions of some essential properties of texts than an abstract way of establishing or organizing conceptually what a literary culture constitutes as expectations for rich readings and what possible analytic terms a critic can consistently share with those practicing other disciplines. (One might say that Harold Bloom provides terms for rich readings, but in so inconsistent a way that no other discourse can follow from his descriptions.)

IV

One could proliferate endless examples of going on, but each would require elaborate contrastive discussion in order to make the consequences of competing choices clear. More important, this exercise would not get us to that feature of Wittgenstein which I think is most useful for understanding literary phenomena. This feature is not the specific use of going on but the analysis of how one can understand second-order, general principles or perspectives that clarify the need for and use of the criteria of going on in specific cases. One possible critical response here is that Wittgenstein's uniqueness consists in his refusal to countenance such second-order questions because they produce endless regress. Certainly, Wittgenstein does not base anything on second-order propositions or some "rational" foundation for philosophy (whether we derive our terms for reason from the mind or from objective properties in the world). But in order to demonstrate, or, better, to illustrate, the limits of such positions, Wittgenstein elaborates what I think can be seen as an alternative model for second-order thought that enables us to recover some basic cognitive and ethical features of literary texts. Instead of relying on the authority of "philosophical" ideals of criteria for understanding, Wittgenstein bases his later method on distinctions between stating and showing developed in the *Tractatus*. Showing becomes the principle for making second-order assessments, and reliance on showing requires imaginative tests of going on that lead beyond philosophy to at least discussion of pragmatic consequences. The *Investigations* gives content to the act of showing by proposing as an alternative to logical formalism and empiricist standards of description an appeal to perspicuous representations that imaginatively manipulate our ways of looking at phenomena:

> A main source of our failure to understand is that we do not *command a clear view* of the use of our words. Our grammar is lacking in this sort of perspicuity. A perspicuous representation produces just that understanding which consists in "seeing connexions." Hence the importance of finding and inventing *intermediate cases.*
> The concept of a perspicuous representation is of fundamental significance for us. It earmarks the form of account we give, the way we look at things. (Is this a "Weltanschauung"?)
> For we can avoid ineptness or emptiness in our assertions only by presenting the model as what it is, as an object of comparison—as, so

to speak, a measuring rod; not as a preconceived idea to which reality must correspond. (PI, 131)

> I wanted to put that picture before him, and his acceptance of the picture consists in his now being inclined to regard a given case differently; that is to compare it with *this* rather than *that* set of pictures. I have changed his *way of looking at things*. (PI, 154)

Philosophy finds a way to live with circularity, then, by organizing its reflections into imaginary attitudes that invoke considerations of the practical paths and limitations attendant upon the chosen stance.

The process Wittgenstein exhibits can, I think, best be seen as making exemplification rather than description the basis of philosophical method. I take the terms needed to give resonance to this idea from Nelson Goodman, who treats description and exemplification as two fundamental forms of denotation.[9] Where descriptions denote by pointing to states of affairs, exemplifications denote the labels they exemplify. If I give you a swatch of red and say, "this is the color of that dress," I denote that color and make a proposition. But if I tell you to use this piece of cloth to pick out other pieces of the same shade, I use the cloth to denote some properties it exemplifies. (See for Wittgenstein's version of this, PG, 274–76; Z, 294). In the latter case the sample is a perspicuous representation. Thus we can extend Goodman to argue that insofar as we view ways of looking in terms of perspicuous representations they serve exemplary functions. They clarify what is involved in the use of a form of organizing the world that brings with it grammatical expectations and typical possibilities and consequences. Then we can further modify Goodman by acknowledging two different kinds of labels—those invoking fixed predicates and those articulating fresh combinations of available terms. The red swatch can be either a familiar shade of red or something a designer creates that one has never seen before. In the latter case we are speaking of a constitutive rather than a regulative example, and we approximate better the status of many literary texts and of Wittgenstein's own second-order reflections. Regulative examples remind one of established ways of going on—"it is done like this"—while constitutive examples suggest that one try to do it like this and see what connections become possible. Notice how careful Wittgenstein is to adopt Kantian aesthetics as his means for preserving these constitutive features of examples: "So what the picture tells me is itself. Its telling me something will consist in my recognizing in it some sort of characteristic arrangement; its telling me something consists in its own structure" (PG, 165, 169; see also Z, 158–60, 175, 279–95).[10]

This Kantian model enables Wittgenstein to show how even constitutive examples do not collapse into covert philosophical propositions. The example brings with it "a characteristic arrangement," so that it implicates dramatic expectations of characteristic procedures and consequences. It has a family history (PI, 583) and thus orients behavior by projecting connections between phenomena, attitudes, and practices embedded in cultural life. Even the simplest example like the perspicuous remark, "A man can pretend to be unconscious; but conscious" (Z, 395) reminds us that we usually act as if mental life contained levels of thinking that require us to distinguish between pretense and awareness of pretense. This suggests in turn one way of showing how models of mental life that ignore levels of reflection will be tangled in contradictions. More elaborate examples (such as Wittgenstein's discussions of reading) lead us to understand what it means to speak of the familiar or being guided. This example works simultaneously in two directions, calling attention to reading as an activity learned when one gets educated in a culture, and as a process within that culture that contains characteristic signs indicating whether one is successfully engaged in it. When one knows an activity, one also knows what it means to lose one's way. Both aspects therefore serve to tie an abstraction like understanding to a behavioral nexus of processes and practices. We may be no closer to an abstract explanation or even description of understanding, but we have a sense of behavioral norms. This in turn provides the crucial contrastive basis for our recognizing the characteristic marks of not understanding and for our seeing how the aporia could conceivably be resolved.

It becomes possible now to make the example of reading a metaphor for the overall working of Wittgenstein's later philosophical style. Wittgenstein does not intend to provide accurate representations or explanations of specific phenomena that can be stated as propositions. He is concerned primarily with exploring possibilities and stances, not with proving specific theses, hence his basic effort is to dramatize forms of thinking that can engage traditional problems in ways that enable us to escape aporia and engage in processes that can elicit public agreement. When he takes up first-order analysis of specific philosophical problems, Wittgenstein tries to clarify contrasts that stem from the pictures or expectations one brings to a situation. A resolution occurs when one can project consequences that allow one to continue the desired task or discourse without endless adjustments or self-justifications (which are psychological versions of epicycles). This same process occurs more self-reflexively on second-order levels of analysis. Here what is at stake is not ways of looking at things or situations but ways of looking at our ways of looking. There are here no clear behavioral norms for going on. Thus there are no specific claims Wittgenstein can make. Instead, philosophy becomes something very close to the highest forms of art. Its justification as a second-order "way of looking" consists in several forms of internal coherence. Wittgenstein's text presents a dramatic contrast between two ways of viewing the world. The first measure of value is the contrast in practical situations between the exemplified attitudes of the logical philosopher and the flexible grammarian who dissolves problems. These contrasts are ultimately between dramatic consequences. In second-order, self-reflexive tests of values, the crucial criterion is not practical effects but the qualities of a person or a text made possible by how one represents one's ways of going on. Going on here is a question of how one integrates positions and how we can assess one's modes of acting in the practical order by constructing reasons (or images) for them that in turn invite judgments in relation to models of the person or of behavior honored by a culture. If I interpret a series of my actions as pursuing magnanimity, I create both an image of myself as a person and a set of cultural terms in which to judge the adequacy of my action with regard to my projected ideal. Going on makes possible an ethics of choosing identities in relation to a given ethos. In this way one can speculate upon a dimension of going on that leads beyond even practical ethics to ultimate questions of cultural and religious identity based on the identifications one makes with specific attitudes. How we imagine the forms of going on relevant for interpreting and judging our actions determines what cultures, historical or transhistorical, we can claim identification with. This vision reminds us of what Wittgenstein shares with Kant and Hegel, and thus it makes their visions of cultural identity seem somewhat more concrete and perhaps even plausible.

V

Some ways of going on also lead into the intense inane. I want to draw back from such speculations in order to clarify possible contributions of Wittgenstein's thinking on criteria to two major areas of literary theory—the concern for cognition, or how literary texts contribute to our understanding of the world, and the concern for establishing criteria of meaning and significance that enable us to claim public, cultural consequences for the actions that texts present.

If Wittgenstein does show how the criterion of going on gives a cognitive role to exemplification, it is easy to extend that discussion in order to clarify how literary texts can become forms of knowledge. Most views of understanding require that any claim to knowledge be supported by an account of how the statement refers to what it names. But it is difficult to say how literary texts name and how imaginative worlds refer. We must be indirect and, following Wittgenstein, shift from a philosophical analysis of knowledge claims to grammatical investigation of the practices that lead to such claims. If we turn to Western literary traditions and try to recover their force, or the modes of going on they sustained, we see that the basic cognitive claim says nothing about reference. The claim is only that texts are useful because they instruct as well as delight. Instruction need not entail ideas of propositions and reference, and what theorists sought by ideas of mimesis need not depend on principles of verisimilitude or principles of moral reason (Aristotle's *theoria*).[11] What we have seen of exemplification as a principle of instruction and mode of affecting understanding involves only our mastering how texts project possible existential implications. Texts do not "refer" but project examples of grammatical beliefs and expectations that may be used in subsequent situations as terms of a referring statement. In the literary text, examples are simply possible scenarios.

One can clarify this approach to issues of cognition by briefly developing two concepts—an idea of what Keats called stationing, so that we can handle exemplification, and an idea of situating, by which we can discuss representativeness without relying on ideas of picturing or copying or idealizing. Stationing entails treating a text as the exemplification of an attitude or stance toward specific aspects of experience. Stationings are possible ways for an interpreting or desiring consciousness to dispose itself: they project a given process of going on by looking at things in a specific way. Situating, then, is the process by which readers test the projective power of imaginative stationings. In situating a text, a reader tries to identify with the attitude presented while at the same time critically constructing scenarios that would allow the text to represent a form of going on. Thus understanding *Madame Bovary* entails first seeing how Emma's attitudes are plausible ways of responding to her version of her situation and then testing their values and limitations. The same process then must take place on the more general level of situating the basic attitude projected by the author. Now the representative situation will be much larger, including psychological, social, and literary contexts.[12] But we still preserve the idea of cognitive content as an example whose possible uses are being explored. We are concerned for representativeness, not specific denotations, so that the cognitive issue for the literary text is simply whether in its role as label it is sufficient to help us interpret and structure subsequent experiences. The cognitive role of the text is to make it possible for us to go on with certain qualities of understanding and empathy because of representative properties in the example.

This model of making connections to possible forms of going on leads easily into hypotheses of how we judge the significance of specific literary texts and the general cultural role literary institutions serve. Significance, E. D. Hirsch's term for the use value of texts, is essentially a matter of judging the connections a text makes available. Significance is a measure of how a text, or a way of reading a text, establishes ways of going on that make transitions to other texts and concerns in relation to qualities the critic tries to show are valuable. Where one mode of situating emphasizes centripetal relations in which knowledge of the world deepens one's appreciation of the text as a specific experience, a second mode of situating establishes significance by describing the centrifugal relations a work illuminates.[13] In this respect literary texts serve as fundamental constituents of what might be called a grammar for making discriminations with respect to categories like depth and quality. Even the simplest grammar, as Charles Fillmore shows, develops because agents learn to situate terms in relation to typical scenarios for using them in practical contexts. Literary works offer similar exemplary scenarios for self-reflexive attitudes and stances that might be projected in complex moments within cultural life.[14] Insofar as one possesses appropriate images of how people can go on under such circumstance, one has a way of understanding others' behavior and possible ways of engaging it. Wittgenstein leads us to a view of cultural life that recovers a somewhat domesticated version of Hegel: the constitutive force of culture consists in its composing a range of expressive acts and possible second-order relations among those acts which are at once the source of our power to make complex discriminations about experience and the grounds of our ultimate identity as reflective beings.

All these cognitive and cultural claims depend to some extent on assumptions about the semantic or ontological status of literary texts. One cannot do very much with claims about knowledge or culture if one cannot locate public terms for discussing literary texts or recovering meanings from the past. These needs bring us back to questions I partially avoided in my discussion of Fish: how can we expect agreement on hierarchic relations among a text's semantic features or lines of relation to the world when there is little evidence, historically and synchronically, of specific shared rules, paradigms, and expectations among readers? One can hypothesize competence, but it is difficult under most models of understanding to describe competence without a circular process of defining competence relative to one's claims about a text. For behind the semantic issues lies the difficulty of establishing what principles, logic, or set of statistical analyses has the authority to adjudicate among competing views.

The criterion of going on will not resolve any of these abstract issues, but it will ground obvious ways of limiting or qualifying indeterminacy and competing ideologies. The crucial principle here is one we have already observed. Even if grammars and conditions of competence are relative to cultures and communities, cultures and communities are not monolithic but consist of levels of possible understandings and paths for making connections. We can to a large extent choose provisional cultural roles or identities that allow us to take up stances that partially bracket contemporary prejudices. (Gadamer ignores the fact that having a grammar by which to identify prejudices probably indicates our partial freedom from them.) In this light one can easily make a strong case for reconstructing authorial intentions, since then we treat texts as human artifacts and preserve historical differences within a broad pluralism. But I want here to concentrate on how the flexibility of culture affects critical intentions. I grant the claim that there is no *propre sens*, no essence of literature or form of a given text that determines how we should read. Yet even when we cannot expect single answers, we can rely upon expectations about going on in order to focus differences, suggest tests for resolving them, and, above all, spell out the consequences of certain ways of looking at literary works. Thus, while one cannot insist that there are separate inquiries necessary for analyzing meaning and significance, one can show that a failure to make this distinction will greatly reduce what one can take to be significant. A critic devoted to contemporary terms of analysis perforce finds only his own culture reflected in what he reads. He has no principle for finding writers like Dante significant precisely because the meanings they offer suggest alternatives to the confining perspective of a purely contemporary framework.

On a more general level, attention to criteria for going on within a cultural heritage enables us to shift our attention from large ideological areas where we disagree to two possible spheres of partial agreement—one based on practical assumptions inherent in common ways of learning to read and a second based on historical identifications one makes when one chooses the questions and standards one will accept for one's criticism. The first sphere of agreement is apparent as soon as we suggest intermediate cases. It is hard to imagine someone being considered a competent reader who does not respect accuracy to overt features of a text's language or who feels no obligation to address a text's emotional or structural properties. We might then further narrow the range of disagreements by asking about the relationship of a given reading of a text to the history of readings a culture or a discipline preserves. Because this history dictates the filiations possible to a given way of going on, it enables disputants to shift the burden of argument from descriptive categories to the realm of ethos. In both cases the crucial questions become—do you want to be able to claim affiinity with a set of writers and theorists, and how will you project the value of your way of going on in relation or in opposition to these historical filiations? Once one chooses a historical identity, some of the most perplexing issues of criticism become mutually discussable if not easily resolved. For example, a tradition of evaluations creates the burden on a critic of explaining or living up to the terms of appreciation—a banal reading of Shakespeare cannot be adequate, while a complex one on Joyce Kilmer's "meanings" is probably wrong; a history of reading discloses dense patterns of internal relationships that a critic must account for if he or she identifies with that history; and the development of terms for thematic or historical readings and appreciations provides a grammar of qualities for critical languages that affords ways of judging the coherence, complexity, and depth of a specific performance or theoretical position. One need not accept these constraints, but if one does not produce an alternative set of cultural affiliations it will become very difficult to give decent reasons for the possible authority or use of one's critical practice. We must expect a case for tradition to breed corresponding arguments defending a need for transgression. But even a case for transgression that seeks to explain itself will need the same historical stage. And a stance that refuses to attempt legitimizing itself has obviously dangerous social consequences because it denies the social practice of offering justifications and accepting criticisms.

By equating Wittgenstein with Hegel, I am obviously ignoring his alienated critical voice suspicious of all pieties and generalized beliefs. Wittgenstein becomes here almost a convert to Eliot's romance with high culture, if not with priest and king. Yet while he would not sanction such a move, it seems to me a plausible consequence of his attacks on logic and his recovery of the force that culture wields as the ground of our grammars. In my view, if not in Wittgenstein's, an attack on *logos* that does not turn into skepticism will put an enormous burden on *ethos*. Constraints are not on one's descriptions but on one's fidelity to models and practices sustained by a culture. We saw some implications of this shift in grounds when we discussed the kinds of agreement and authority practical critics might seek.

I want to conclude this essay by speculating on implications relevant to literature of connections among exemplification, *ethos,* and the kinds of issues where criteria of going on are most significant. The guiding principle for these speculations will be the notion that when we have no clear rules or empirical norms, our judgments are based less on concepts than on images or examples. We make decisions by projecting the kind of person one becomes through making choices that involve cultural filiations, which themselves are based on a history of discourses about their probable consequences in several dimensions. It is precisely in their power to give vivid determinations of such images and consequences that imaginative works affect behavior by affecting identifications, even if only to make Emma Bovarys of us all. Wittgenstein's model of understanding helps explain this common feature and recurrent theoretical claim in Western literary traditions because he shows the need for and place of imaginative identifications.

The more important issue here is how the realm of *ethos* and projected identifications pertains to the second-order aspects of critical theory we have been discussing. If we view critical positions as forms of stationing, we have a way of discussing their possible significance even though we cannot rely on descriptive criteria. We cannot ignore standards of accuracy, conceptual coherence, and consistency to accepted empirical beliefs, but literary theories tend to make normative claims not reducible to these tests. We find ourselves having to choose, and having to judge, among several positions that equally satisfy the standards mentioned. So we need tests for how theory projects ways of going on through what the theoretical discourse exemplifies. I propose as the measure for the discussions that arise questions of what features or powers of a person the theory can plausibly produce by its ways of reading and posing significance for its readings. It is in fact the case that most literary theories that get much attention project these qualities in terms of what I call text-psyche correlations. Any literary theory will privilege some way of constructing hierarchies among the features of a text, and theories typically do this by relying on images of psychic powers produced by attending to such features. Aristotle correlates probable plots with powers of judging actions; Wilde imagines a sense of artistic form as an analogue to the power to escape bourgeois society and give form to one's life; Richards draws comparisons between textual structures and a complexly balanced psyche; modern response theories claim to produce a sense of freedom; and even neostructuralists connect deconstruction with powers to escape the trap of believing in arbitrary sign systems and thus to preserve the only forms of autonomy left to Romantic man. Correspondingly, we find even the most ironic critics paradoxically faithful to a literary heritage in which imaginative constructs are seen as testing, qualifying, and affirming ways of acting not susceptible to explanatory arguments.

These projections of plausibly ideal persons correlated with a theory are perhaps no more likely to elicit agreement than are elaborate arguments. But they can at the very least help us to recognize and respect the coherence and possible appeal of positions we disagree with. Moreover, once we acknowledge their place in our theorizing, we will begin to ask theorists to be explicit about the grounds and consequences of their normative projections. This may mask as much as it unmasks, but it should keep us aware of the complex grounds and levels of embedding that underlie our choices and rejections of literary theories. Then, contra Fish, we shall have in focus not simply a single level of coherence but the entire stage on which we debate in order to display ourselves to ourselves.

Arguing for a sense of *ethos* as fundamental to theoretical work puts an uncomfortably self-conscious frame around one's discourse. If only for the sake of *ethos*, I must acknowledge my awareness that it is moralistic positions like mine that justify Edward Said's warning about the self-congratulatory nature of claims proposing to articulate and defend humanistic values.[14] But Said's ironic strictures against narcissism only return us again to the necessity of cultural foundations for affirming values and of the projections of plausibly ideal persons underlying normative discourse. One can recognize the danger of making self-congratulatory claims, but I doubt that very many people formed by Western literary traditions can avoid congratulating themselves for recognizing the danger of self-congratulation. We probably cannot escape the personal or the ideal in our critical discourses about literature, at least if we are to talk about significance or perhaps to talk significantly, so it is about time that we began examining how we can take responsibility for those contexts. In order to go on, we could do worse than begin recognizing what Wittgenstein has to offer to a discourse hopelessly muddled in the humanity of its practitioners and the complex historical webs constituting the terms by which that humanity becomes intelligible.

Notes

1. The Popperian approach has many ways of defending itself that I do not mention—for example, it can use genre as a form of covering law. But writers use, and alter, genres while agents must exhibit, not interpret, the forms of behavior that covering laws can explain. All the options seem to me to depend on assuming rational categories for interpreting actions, while I suspect that one needs the looser ground of grammatical categories that Wittgenstein develops. I will return briefly to this topic below, but for a much fuller account of issues raised here that are not directly involved with the question of criteria, see my *Act and Quality: A Theory of Literary Meaning* (Amherst: University of Massachusetts Press, 1981). I shall often presume on that book and essays published in the course of working on it because my purpose here is to clarify a general schema that underlies and extends the discussions of specific theoretical issues. I need then to allude to specific issues without getting bogged down in them, and I need to rely on a general philosophical critique of Derrida I develop there on the theme of replacing *propre sens* by appropriate sense as a model of meaning.

2. Ludwig Wittgenstein, *Philosophical Investigations*, trans. G. E. M. Anscombe (New York: Macmillan, 1958), no. 154. I shall abbreviate references to this work hereafter *PI* and give paragraph numbers. Other citations to Wittgenstein will be *Zettel*, ed. G. E. M. Anscombe and G. H. von Wright (Berkeley: University of California Press, 1970), *Z*; and *Philosophical Grammar*, ed. Rush Rhees (Berkeley: University of California Press, 1974), *PG*. My opposition of consensual to referential or ontological models of criteria derives from Chaim Perelman and L. Olbrechts-tyteca, *The New Rhetoric* (South Bend, Ind.: University of Notre Dame Press, 1969). This opposition derives largely from my desire to escape what Derrida does to referential criteria. The relevance of rhetorical criteria to Derrida can be seen in two essays by Newton Garver, "Preface" to Derrida's *Speech and Phenomena* (Evanston: Northwestern University Press, 1973) and "Derrida on Rousseau on Writing," *Journal of Philosophy* 74 (1978):663–74. Finally, what I try to do by locating norms in rhetoric, other critics of Derrida attempt through political analysis along lines developed by Foucault. See especially Edward Said, "The Problem of Texuality: Two Exemplary Positions," *Critical Inquiry* 4 (1978):673–714. However, my argument against Fish below can, I think, be applied to Foucault's position on power because Foucault ends up unable to defend by discourse a critical stance that is not itself reducible to a will to power. The thinker closest to my concerns, but not to my attempt to posit consensual grounds, is Jürgen Habermas on norms and legitimization.

3. The full title of Fish's essay is "Normal Circumstances, Literal Language, Direct Speech Acts, the Ordinary, the Everyday, the Obvious, What Goes Without Saying and Other Special Cases," *Critical Inquiry* 4 (1978):625–44.

4. Richard Schiff, "Seeing Cézanne," *Critical Inquiry* 4 (1978):769–807.

5. Quine's most accessible formulation of this model is near the conclusion of his "Two Dogmas of Empiricism." One could make a similar point against Fish by claiming that his discussion ignores what David Lewis calls the "salience" factor of a convention. See David Lewis, *Convention: A Philosophical Study* (Cambridge, Mass.: Harvard University Press, 1969), pp. 36–38.

6. Fish's position on the law is more radically relativist than even a typical Marxist analysis of the ways laws are influenced by a class desire to gain or maintain power. Gordon Wood offers in this respect a concise summary of E. P. Thompson's view: "The law was 'something more than . . . a pliant medium to be twisted this way and that by whatever interests already possess effective power.' The law existed in its own right, had 'its own characteristics, its own independent history and logic of evolution.' It was the aggregate product over a long period of time of countless judicial decisions and agrarian practices, backed up by 'norms tenaciously transmittted through the community.'" See Gordon Wood, "Intellectual History and the Social Sciences," in John Higham and Paul Conkin, eds., *New Directions in American Intellectual History* (Baltimore, Md.: Johns Hopkins University Press, 1979), p. 37. For an excellent discussion paralleling this view of cultural constraints and

change but devoted to literary theory, see Ralph Cohen, *The Art of Discrimination* (London: Routledge and Kegan Paul, 1964). And for a more elaborate account of how the nature of actions complicates any simple case for relativism by requiring discriminations among levels of an act, see my "The Hermeneutics of Literary Indeterminacy: A Dissent From the New Orthodoxy," *New Literary History* 10 (1978):71–99.

7. For the concept of situation types see M. A. K. Halliday, *Language as Social Semiotic: The Social Interpretation of Language and Meaning* (Baltimore, Md.: University Park Press, 1978). One use of concepts of types is to allow us to distinguish levels of generality that may be appropriate to a required task. As we saw in Fish's essay, the question of levels is, then, central to what criteria of going on will reveal. Literary theorists often make crippling mistakes because they do not see that the levels of going on that follow from a general proposition are much too simple to handle specific problems. Most response theorists, for example, never reflect on the likelihood that once you equate meaning with response you cannot easily account for all the aspects of discourse that led critics to distinguish the two ideas. The equation cannot explain why it makes no sense to even raise issues of authorial intent or education unless response is dialectically related to some other property attributable to the utterance as focusing or guiding response. Another version of this error occurs when true general categories are applied without a range of complex subcategories that would allow meaningful distinctions. It is probably true to say that literature is intertextual. But intertextuality is a useless category until one can specify differences between conscious, unreflective, and clichéd echoes of other works in a text.

8. Any hypothetical case for agreement among readers must invoke a competence condition, but the problem arises that it is viciously circular to invoke a competence condition that produces exactly the set of readers who will agree on the claim you use their agreement as evidence for. There are, however, two strategies that my line of thinking can propose to temper this circularity by employing tests of how readers would go on. First, I would define *well-educated* simply in terms of readers who are familiar with a fairly standard canon of Western literary works and who could give plausible accounts of why these texts have been valued. *Plausible* depends on the judgment of other *educated* readers, but it is loose enough to allow agreements among those who would disagree on other issues. And I do not select an arbitrary canon; we know the general cultural community associated with some basic texts like Shakespeare's. Thus my standard involves levels of judgment—standards of competence are not equivalent to sharing specific value claims and interpretations. I loathe Milton's *Paradise Regained*, but I cannot deny that he understands the cultural tradition he rejects. My second claim depends on the difference between consensual and referential criteria. In claiming competence I am not describing an independently testable condition (although such tests may be possible). Rather I am making the rhetorical claim that this projected community involves for me a sufficiently broad and respected set of procedural standards that I am content to assume them and their standards as the audience establishing my practice. This audience allows assessments on any of the ways of going on I think necessary for criticism. One can reject this audience for another as long as one accepts the consequences. I develop this view of communal standards at length in "Nietzsche's *Ecce Homo*: Narcissism, Power, Pathos, and the Status of Autobiographical Representations," *Boundary 2* 9 (1981):389–413. This argument and some of my later points on second-order questions derive from Charles Taylor, "Responsibility for Self," in Amelie Rorty, ed., *The Concept of Persons* (Berkeley: University of California Press, 1976), pp. 281–300.

9. I am freely modifying Goodman here, so I only acknowledge his influence without presuming on his authority. For a defense of my modifications see my *Act and Quality*. The relevant texts of Goodman's are *Languages of Art* (Indianapolis, Ind.: Bobbs Merrill, 1968), pp. 50–67 and his *Ways of Worldmaking* (Indianapolis, Ind.: Hackett Publishing Co., 1978), Chaps. 1, 4, 7. I apply Goodman to poetry in "Presence and Reference in a Literary Text: The Example of Williams's 'This is Just to Say'," *Critical Inquiry* 5 (1979):489–510.

10. One might make a strong case that Wittgenstein's concern during the 1920s with aesthetic issues helped develop a sense of constitutive force, form, and exemplification that enabled him to define his differences from the *Tractatus*.

11. For a good critique of problems in the concept of mimesis, see Murray Krieger, *Theory of Criticism* (Baltimore, Md.: Johns Hopkins University Press, 1976), pp. 67–97.

12. In the essay "Presence and Reference in a Literary Text," I give an extended example of differences involved in situating represented and authorial acts.

13. I am restating here Northrop Frye's distinction between centripetal and centrifugal ways of viewing texts. See his *Anatomy of Criticism* (Princeton, N.J.: Princeton University Press, 1956). I should also acknowledge a debt to Frye's discussions of principles of authority within a culture. See his *The Stubborn Structure* (London: Methuen and Co., 1970), pp. 241–56 and *passim* in part one.

14. Said, "The Problem of Textuality," p. 714.

Marx after Derrida

Gayatri Chakravorty Spivak

To go via Derrida toward Marx can be called a "literary" reading of a philosophical text. Yet such a gesture also questions disciplinary nomenclatures and boundaries such as "literature" and "philosophy." The reading is "literary" only insofar as it recognizes that what Marx produces is also a book, written in language. What such a reading emphasizes, however, is that Marx devalorizes mere "philosophical" justice and elegance by prying them open with the asymmetrical wedge of practice.[1] In other words, using the strategies of a radically "literary" approach, such a reading does not seek to reduce Marx to "mere" literature in one of its most powerful disciplinary definitions: a self-reflexive verbal text that irreducibly narrates its own constitution.

The constitution of the Marxian text remains untotalizable because it must articulate more than its verbal (if such a clean distinction were indeed possible) textuality. It is here that I must take issue with the diagnoses of critics such as Fredric Jameson or Edward Said. These critics understand the Derridian suggestion—"there is no absolute extra-text"—through a reduction of "textuality" to the narrowly verbal/visual text (an indefinite proliferation of codes on the part of both the reader and the read, "the narrative text as a free-play of signifiers," the reduction of "everything we think of as having some extratextual leverage in the text to a textual function").[2] While the textualist ideology of American "literary" criticism might have welcomed and developed the Derridian intervention in the field of "philosophy" in this spirit (and therefore Derrida's argument cannot be "exculpated" from the possibility of such a supplementation), Derrida's argument implies a rather different position as well: that the so-called "outside" of the verbal text is articulated with it in a web or network: "it was never our wish to extend the reassuring notion of the text to a whole extra-textual realm and to transform the world into a library by doing away with all boundaries . . . but . . . we sought rather to work out the theoretical and practical system of these margins, these borders, once more, from the ground up."[3]

Like all morphologies or methodologies, then, Derrida's work remains forever alterable by critical practice. A statement such as the following: "each time that the question of the proper emerges in the fields of economy (in the restricted sense), linguistics, rhetoric, psychoanalysis, politics, etc., the onto-hermeneutic form of interrogation shows its limit," for example, would remain contingent upon its critical situation.[4] It was to consider such matters, somewhat in the spirit of an apologist, that I undertook to present a version of the present essay at the 1978 Convention of the Modern Language Association of America. After my presentation a brilliant young scholar said to me with, I think, some bitterness: "You are forcing a reading on Derrida to make him consistent with Marx." The essay in its present form is also a reflection on that remark. It is a reflection as well on words I read nearly a year later, in 1979: "Once the amalgam [of Marx and Derrida] is accomplished, the appropriation incorporated, we hear that 'deconstruction' is to be abandoned, since Marx had already said it."[5] I hope it will soon become clear that nothing could be farther from the program of this essay.

I

There is a long footnote on Marx in Derrida's "The White Mythology."[6] There he praises and criticizes Marx for at once opening and leaving "the questions of 'reality,' of 'the proper,' of 'the abstraction' and the concept (the name of reality in general) of the proper." In a certain passage in *The German Ideology*, Marx and Engels scold Stirner for suggesting that property *(Eigentum)* is irreducible on the grounds that man must be defined in terms of his properties *(Eigenschaften)*. If, they suggest, one remained content to say no more than this, one need not study the economic heterogeneity of the development of private property in the production of different forms of society. Property in idealist etymological speculation and in materialist social production "are not the same thing."

Deconstructively speaking, there is one point in Marx's favor here, and one against. It is because of this perhaps that the long quotation from the *Ideology* in Derrida's footnote breaks into two.

Marx seems pre-critical when he emphasizes the binary opposition between the "social" fact of private property on the one hand, and the "natural" fact of "having" (possessing, therefore, as property) a stomach ache, or the "metaphysical" fact of predication or definition by property, on the other. He seems not to accept that what seems the pure natural or metaphysical origin or goal of unalienated "property"—the body's self-proximity in its pain or the concept's self-possession in its definition—is worked and undermined by the same self-differentiation as the so-called social alienation in possessing a thing outside of oneself. The latter is not an incident that befalls the former. This is how Derrida argues, for example, against Lévi-Strauss's differentiation between societies with and without writing. It is our longing for transcendence that makes us posit a proper situation of self-proximity or self-possession against which to measure our own fallen state—to posit, in the language of the early Derrida, speech against writing.

Marx's consideration of money, as he circles that theme in the collection of notebooks posthumously published as the *Grundrisse,* can be read in terms of the polemics of speech against writing.[7] (I am not, of course, launching an analysis of money in its various forms of appearance, or in its transformation into capital, but merely remarking upon how Marx represents the concept-metaphor *money.*)

Considering the emergence of the specific materiality of money, for instance, Marx writes: "Thus the signs [*Zeichen*] for words, for example, have a history, the alphabet etc." (*Gr,* 145). Until the encroachment of money in its specific historical-material support—what Lacan, in the case of discourse, speaks of as the "letter"—the fixing of value is *ad hoc* and inconvenient.[8] Although value in exchange always conceals a social relation (who makes what why and how and who needs what why when), and thus already shares the rusing character of a sign that conceals the presence of the thing it means, in the situation of mere exchange and the circulation of commodities before the emergence of the money form as such, the concealment is always precarious and imperfect. Once the appropriate material of money permits its transformation into pure (ideal) conventionality, money is pure form without content, pure difference rather than identity: "Money as medium of circulation becomes coin, mere vanishing moment, mere *symbol* of the values it exchanges. . . . As the most superficial (in the sense of driven out onto the surface) and the most abstract form of the entire production process [money circulation] is in itself quite without content" (*Gr,* 790). Money, like writing, is thus the sign of a sign, the possibility of the exchange of signs, not merely language but a *foreign* language (*Gr,* 163).

Money makes manifest the principle of alienation already immanent in property. "Because money is the *general equivalent* . . . everything therefore is alienable, or indifferent for the individual, external to him [*sic*]. Thus the so-called *inalienable, eternal* possessions, and the immovable, solid property relations corresponding to them, break down in the face of money" (*Gr,* 838; italics Marx's). It is precisely this necessary and immanent alienation, the ever-recuperable chain of the negation of immanent contradiction, that Derrida has rewritten as the open-ended graphic of supplementarity.[9] Thus when Marx writes: "The sphere of circulation has a gap in it, through which gold (or silver, or the money material in general) enters as a commodity with a given value,"[10] Derrida would add: if circulation carries a gap, that is already a trace that is in complicity with, that welcomes, the so-called unwelcome interloper. And, perhaps, because sublation is not openly carried through into supplementarity in Marx's text, the idea, with reference to money, not merely of contingency, but even of interloping or usurpation peculiar to the received structure of writing, makes its appearance. "The first form of appearance" of exchange value—the origin of money—"arises by chance . . . and is determined by accidental needs, whims, etc. But if it should happen to continue . . . then little by little, from the outside, and likewise by chance, regulation of reciprocal exchange arises" (*Gr*, 204–5). "From its servant-shape, in which it appears as mere medium of circulation, it suddenly becomes the lord and god in the world of commodities" (*Gr*, 221). Its very own place is necessarily displaced (*Gr*, 234).

Derrida's name for the supplement that is misrepresented as an accident is writing. And once money is seen as an (un)recognized supplement in Marx, it shows all the marks of writing. Its work is the convenience of abbreviation, through it "one can secure and stockpile a great value in a small space" (*Gr*, 237). The constitutive temporality of value (labor-time) is occluded as the material of money becomes its own measure. "Gold is therefore nominally undecipherable, not because it alone expresses an *authentic value*, but because as money it expresses *no value at all*, but merely expresses—carries on its forehead [writing "mediates" immediate and "living" expression into dead inscription or impression]—a determined quantum of its own matter, its own quantitative determination" (*Gr*, 133–34; italics Marx's).

It is the story of the oppression of a living temporality by the monstrous work of spacing—"the despotism of the eye"—what Derrida has abundantly described as the traditional account of the structure of the history of writing in *Of Grammatology*. Marx's story further recounts a violent misnaming, a situation where the circuit of the names becomes more important than the presentation of the things signified. Marx knows that "the name of a thing is quite external to its nature" (C, 195). Money corrupts what is natural and turns it, *in its natural form*, into a visible sign for the social relation of exchange: "The special difficulty in grasping money in its full determination as money . . . is here determined as a metal, a stone, as a pure corporeal thing outside them which is to be encountered as such, in nature, and which cannot, in addition, be differentiated in its formal determination, from its natural existence" (*Gr*, 239). Such a confounding of nature and sign is the result of historical processes for which the money-form is the determining condition of possibility. "Centuries of the falsification of money [*Geldfalschung*] by kings and princes have in fact left nothing behind of the original weights of gold coins but their names" (C, 194). Money is the functionary of the improper, splitting "the real content from the nominal content" (C, 222) through legitimized misrepresentation: "in fact no longer ¼ but merely ⅕ of an ounce of gold was called pound, represented money, had that name" (*Gr*, 800). The next step in the service of the improper is another step in the advancement of the technology of writing: the printing of paper money. "The purely symbolic character is still somewhat disguised in the metallic moneymark [*Geldmark*]. In paper money it stands out visibly. One sees: Ce n'est que le premier pas qui coûte" (ibid.).

Marx scrupulously introduces yet another topos in the thematics of writing. Money's work of usurpation is an agency of civilization. Comparing the "imagined" money standard of the Barbary Coast with the developed money forms of Western Europe Marx writes: "It is the same as if, in mythology, one were to consider as the higher religions those whose god-figures were not worked out in visible form but remain stuck in the imagination, i.e., where they obtain at most an oral, but not a graphic presence" (*Gr*, 795).

Yet what has one performed by showing that Marx, like the rest of us, is caught in the longing for the logos? One cannot side with Saint Max (Marx's contender in the passage quoted by Derrida) and make an end by declaring "impure" theories unfeasible. It requires at least a consideration of the relationship between theory and practice; I have attempted such a discussion elsewhere.[11] Here I shall consider briefly the point in Marx's favor that I left suspended above.

In the second half of the passage that Derrida quotes in his footnote, Marx chastises Max Stirner for romantically equating so-called synonyms— words like *value, exchange, commerce*—that can be used to describe individual as well as commercial relationships. One could of course speculate upon the irreducibly economic "metaphors" of any "metapsychology." I want rather to emphasize that the first moves of Derridian deconstruction were made by noticing what happened when the synonymity/identity of the "same" word allowed contradictory or asymmetric messages to be disguised as a unified argument.

Derrida has consolidated that move by pointing at how the exigencies of *theory* lead to a suppression of irreducible heterogeneity. And it is the inevitable suppression of the heterogeneity of individual and social transactions that is Marx's count against money. (Since Marx writes within an archaeoteleological idiom, he must see any wish to recover this heterogeneity as nostalgia; in his telos he recommends the substituting of "spacing"—*reduction* into the regular measure of the average law of general exchange—by *constitutive* temporality, money by time: "The economy of time, along with the planned distribution of labor time among the various branches of production, remains the first economic law on the basis of communal production. Indeed it becomes the law to a much higher degree. However, this is essentially different from a measurement of value . . . by labor time" (*Gr*, 175). That, however, is beside the point of this part of my argument. Tying together my anthology of quotations about the concept-metaphor of money in the *Grundrisse*, I notice something like the following formulation: Money conceals the heterogeneity of social relations irretrievably by substituting the category of (mis)-substitution for (necessarily asymmetrical) exchange. "In it [money] they [exchange-values] are all equinominal or same-named [*gleich-namig*]" (*Gr*, 189). It is along this line that Marx develops that analysis of money which (perhaps in reverse) Nietzsche's analysis of the language of truth so uncannily resembles: two things can be pronounced equal, identical, or substitutible by, first, a making equal of different things, next, a forgetting of that move, and, finally, a metaleptically created memory that conceals this genealogy. "It does not appear on its face that its determination of being money [*Bestimmung Geld zu sein*] is merely the result of social processes; it is money. This is all the more difficult since its immediate use value for the living individual stands in no relation whatever to this role, and because, in general, the memory of use value, as distinct from exchange value has become entirely extinguished in this incarnation of pure exchange value" (239–40). "The equation of the heterogeneous [*Das Gleichsetzen des Ungleichartigen*], as Shakespeare nicely defines money," and "after money is posited really as commodity, will the commodity be posited ideally as money" (*Gr*, 163, 80), will suffice here to indicate the two ends of that discourse.

Derrida radicalizes the Nietzschean position in "The White Mythology," deconstructing the opposition between metaphor and concept. The general form of the critique of Nietzsche can be used to deconstruct the opposition between use- and exchange-value and still honor Marx's instinct for heterogeneity, even as it does Nietzsche's for plurality.[12]

I am, then, speaking for a force of reading that would allow me to force a reading of Marx through Derrida. It is true that Marx, in seeing the work of money as a usurping writing-work, uses an interpretable thematic. But the steps of his analysis resemble Derrida's analysis of the exclusivist and homogenizing construction of the language of theory that is the medium of metaphysics. If we recall that Marx's description of money is not merely that it is the work of convenience of an abbreviating technology of the written sign, but also that it is the *ideal* homogenization of a heterogeneous exchange, we can see the connection more clearly by way of a common critique of idealism.

As Derrida argued in "Force and Signification," reading is constituted by its forcing. He would argue that there is no free and uncoerced reading against which a "forced reading" can be defined. As to "making Derrida consistent with Marx"—to take you back for a moment to my colleague's complaint at the MLA—("to place Derrida with Marx," so to speak), my plan and understanding—which of course cannot go very far—are to note the gap or displacement between the two that the force of a reading that wants to read both must uncover and work at.

II

The paradoxical logic of the apotropaic: to castrate oneself *already*, always already, in order to be able to castrate and repress the menace of castration, to renounce life and mastery in order to assure oneself of them; to put into play, by ruse, simulacrum, and violence, the very thing that one wishes to conserve; to lose in advance that which one wishes to erect; to suspend that which one raises: *aufheben*.[13]

Sublation or *Aufhebung* is the name of the force-gesture of the dialectic. There may be questions about the force that moves the dialectic; but about this force-gesture, which produces a new residue—the sublate, the *Aufgehoben*—there can be none. The trace of a contradiction within a thing makes it split asunder through the generation of a negation which then produces a third thing which raises, denies, suspends, and preserves the first. Force is the issue here. It is fitting that the English cognate (though not "the meaning in current usage") of *Aufhebung* is "upheaval."

Every reading is an upheaval of that which is read, not in the same way but unevenly. The slogan of "the correct reading" would deny this, or, at best, attempt deliberately to minimize the upheaval, demonstrably to produce a reading that is as closely identical as possible with the transcendent intention of the author. By contrast, and no doubt through an accident of historical polemics (I should hold such "accidents" irreducible), Marx publicized the upheaval that was his reading of Hegel, and claimed that the scientific truth of Hegel was in Marx's forced reading, the sublate that at once denied and preserved the Hegelian dialectic. The most famous of these is in the Postface to the second edition of *Capital* 1: "The Hegelian dialectic must be turned upside down [*umstülpen*], in order to uncover [*entdecken*] the rational kernel in the mystical shell" (C, 103).

In *Glas* Derrida presents his credentials as an upheaver of Hegel. He would not, of course, claim that his upheft (sublate) of Hegel is the rational kernel of Hegel. The difference between him and Marx in this regard can be plotted along the lines I have marked in the last section. Yet can that implication ever be fully absent? For what Derrida finally does with Hegel in *Glas* may be called "a setting wild [*déréglement*] of the *seminarium*" (the seed-bed of a nursery), which is an immanent contradiction in the Hegelian logic: "The nasty trick [bad turn; *mauvais tour*] of the seasons having come to unhinge [*détraquer*] the history of the spirit, the saturnalia of the *Sa* [*Savoir absolu*; absolute knowledge] would be in league with a setting wild of the *seminarium*" (Gl, 260a). Like Marx, although via Hegel, the metaphor is of the seed or germ. Only the direction has been, deliberately, reversed. For Marx, to uncover the kernel; for Derrida, to set wild the seed-bed—to dis-seminate the semes. Louis Althusser puts it this way:

[To affirm and, in the same moment, to *deny* the origin] Hegel assumed this consciously in his theory of the *Beginning* in the Logic: Being is immediately non-Being. . . . Hegel's logic is of the affirmed-denied Origin: the first form of a concept that Derrida has introduced into philosophical reflection, the *erasure*.

But the Hegelian "erasure," which the logic is from its very first word, is the negation of the negation, dialectical, therefore teleological. It is in the teleology that the true Hegelian Subject arises. Take away the teleology, and what remains is that philosophical category which Marx inherited: the category of *process without subject*.[14]

I have written at length of the Derridian erasure elsewhere. I propose to discuss the "Process without Subject" later in the essay. Here it suffices to say that I am in agreement with the opinion that Marx's rewriting of the Hegelian dialectic was his best contribution to the critique of political economy; and that, at the moment, it seems to me that Derrida's best contribution to the critique of metaphysics will be *his* rewriting of the Hegelian dialectic. In other words, it is in the area where Marx and Derrida force the reading of a philosopher who provided a description of the forcing that I force a reading and a displaced consistency. Although this is not the explicit topic of my essay, it should by now be clear that it is its point of reference.

Any extended consideration of the Hegel-Marx-Derrida conjuncture would analyze the relationship between Derrida's suggestion that

> all that Hegel thought within [the] horizon [of absolute knowledge], all, that is, except eschatology, may be read as a meditation on writing. Hegel is also the thinker of irreducible difference. He rehabilitated thought as the *memory* productive of signs. And he reintroduced . . . the essential necessity of the written trace in a philosophical . . . discourse that had always believed it possible to do without it; the last philosopher of the book and the first thinker of writing. (*Grammatology*, 26)

and Marx's contention that: "In its mystified form, the dialectic . . . seemed to transfigure and glorify what exists. In its rational form . . . it includes in its positive understanding of what exists a simultaneous recognition of its negation, its inevitable destruction" (C, 103). Such an analysis would hinge on the deconstruction of the opposition between the rational and the mystified. I shall go on to suggest that there is room for this deconstruction in Marx's own text.

III

In "Limited Inc. abc," Derrida provides an analogy between his thought and Marx's. To catch that analogy, I shall make a summary of Derrida on the "proper." Marx's analysis of the irreducible impropriety of money is tied up with a critique of the impropriety of private property. I suggested in section I that this could be "made consistent with" Derrida's analysis of the language of theory. The analogy that Derrida himself suggests is in the service of a critique of the impropriety of the proper as such.

The investigation and critique of the "proper" has been a very large part of Derrida's work. His speculations have circled about the implications of *proprius* and *prope*. Property as the distinguishing predication and as self-possession; the proper as that which is so self-proximate that it is self-adequate or self-identical; the proper name, a genealogical mark, as the most intimate legal sign of this adequate predication, this self-proximity of self-possession. Why can we not do without these conceptual practices, these hierarchical judgments? What do they conceal and reveal?

In French the *propre* is not merely proper but also clean. Derrida has written on the strange kinship between *propriété* (property, propriety) and *propre-té* (cleanliness). In "Signéponge" all these concerns are woven together.[15] "Ponge" is the poet Francis Ponge's patronymic or proper name as property-holder. The title of Derrida's essay, if broken up according to the accepted rules of wordplay, would yield: *Signe et Ponge* (sign and Ponge); *Signé Ponge* (signed Ponge), and *signe-éponge* (sign-sponge; the sign as the instrument and agent of erasure and cleanliness). How do cleanliness and the sign "connect"? If one is not attending to Derrida, the connection does not spring immediately to the eye. As follows, briefly:

The language of philosophy professes to be clean. It is the shortest distance between truth and sign. No metaphoric detours to truth are allowed there. All adventitious material (empirical or exceptional, depending on the kind of philosophy you choose) must be excluded in order to build its route. This cleanliness is not only next to, but on the way to, the godliness of truth, a truth that is vouched for in the name of the god that is its own cleanliness.

It is this obsessive "cleanliness" or rigor that Derrida questions, and points here and there at how all projects of philosophical cleanliness must conceal their own befoulment, and, more important (though this point is far less often grasped), that cleanliness is constituted by varieties of befoulment which, being implicit in all originary concepts of cleanliness, are methodologically irreducible.

The analogy between Marx and Derrida is located in a set of arguments that can be placed within this particular line of questioning. Derrida applauds J. L. Austin's inquiry into the peculiar "cleanliness" of the language of traditional philosophy. Yet he also exposes the establishment of certain "clean" contours within Austinian Speech Act Theory. The formulaic cleanliness of Austin's theory is in the service of a certain ambition to discover godliness in speech—a special speech act where Word and Deed are one, where by saying we do—the category of the Performative.[16]

Derrida's take on Speech Act theory is in two parts. The first part, "Signature Event Context," is a reading of J. L. Austin's *How To Do Things With Words*. The second, "Limited Inc. abc," is a reply to John F. Searle's critique of the first essay. In "Limited Inc." as Derrida deals with the exclusivism of the Performative, his language often becomes overtly polit-ical. For example, he calls "the system of (il- or per-locutionary) intentions and the systems of ('vertical') rules or of ('horizontal') conventions" "the language-police" or "the internal regulation through which the capitalist system seeks to limit concentration and decision-making power in order to protect itself against its own 'crisis.'"[17]

Derrida's condemnation here is based upon the Speech Act assump-tion that homogeneous intentions are neatly housed and expressed in acts of speech. Psychoanalysis has suggested that we might not be fully at home to ourselves, that the presupposition of an intending subject might be constituted by the presupposition of a radically irreducible other, that the sense of a unified self might be made up of temporally (in terms of "psychic time") unreliable (from the point of view of our picture of self, intention, and experience) animations and connections produced by the work of a psychic machine that has, in its different parts, different "objec-tives" that themselves change discontinuously. It is therefore necessary, beyond the outlines of psychoanalysis as a discipline, to entertain the structural possibility that intention is irreducibly heterogeneous. It will not do to say "why not get down to discussing the thing bang off in terms of linguistics and psychology in a straightforward fashion? . . . *after*, not before, seeing what we can screw out of ordinary language even if in what comes out there is a strong element of the undeniable" (Austin); for such a postponement leads finally to a position such as the following: "to know what an intention is, or what any other intentional state with a direction of fit is, we do not need to know the material or psychological properties of its realization" (Searle).[18]

The analogy, then, is of a language-police or capitalism of exclusivist consensus or convention based upon the convenient assumption that a homogeneous intention is neatly housed in acts of speech. The other term of the analogy may be found in a passage like the following from *Capital* 1:

> Commodities cannot go to market and exchange themselves. We must, therefore, have recourse to their guardians, the commodity-owners. . . . In order to relate these things as commodities, their guardians must relate to one another as persons whose will is housed in these things. . . . They must therefore recognize each other as owners of private property. This relationship of right, whose form is the contract . . . is a relationship of wills which mirrors the economic relation. . . . Here persons exist for one another only as representatives and hence owners of commodities. (C, 178–79)

So that the so-called exchange (inter-communication, or, simply, com-munication) of intentions (the property—in more senses than one—of the subject as voice-consciousness) can seem to take place successfully, certain conventions must be agreed upon among the custodians of language. All incursions of heterogeneity must be indefinitely postponed (*"after,* not before") or rejected out of hand ("we do not need to know"). "Persons [must] exist for one another only as representatives and hence owners of [intentions]."

This line of inquiry is a fruitful one. Derrida's analogy, a "forced" reading like mine, allows us to generalize Marx's vision of a historical alterity in the subject as the problem of ideology as well as the problem of the politico-economic determination of consciousness. Yet the following question must also be asked: are not the *grounds* of property kept secure in a most un-Derridian way in the Marxian passage? Is that not the point of Derrida's footnote in "The White Mythology"? That Marx criticizes *bad* property, the result of political economy, and contrasts it to the "intrinsic" senses of the proper?

In a certain sense this cannot be denied. I must therefore force the question a little more. In spite of the burden of evidence to the contrary, is it possible to locate an itinerary of the improper in Marx?

IV

The question of the subject was and remained a problem for Marx, not only from the point of view of man's self, but equally from the point of view of that process without subject of which Althusser writes.

That process is of course the process of the self-determination of the Idea most elaborately articulated in Hegel's *Science of Logic,* the book that Marx "by mere accident" happened "to leaf through" as he was putting together the *Grundrisse,* "the seven notebooks rough-drafted . . . chiefly for purposes of self-clarification."[19] It seems hardly necessary to say that the "subject" of this process in Hegel is indeed the Idea. As Marx's notebooks make abundantly clear, that which takes the place of the Idea (in the process) for Marx is Capital. This is where the genius of Ricardo had failed; he did not know the morphology of a concept's self-determination.

To study the development of capital as the Idea develops—this is both Marx's solution and problem. The most obvious problem is that of necessity, so obvious indeed that the charge is brought even on the most ignorant and reactionary plane against all varieties of Marxism. The Idea necessarily determines itself according to the Science of Logic. So does the idea of capital, as indeed the idea of anything. But the subject of the Hegelian science is not the idea of the Idea, or one idea among many. It is *the* idea, the Idea. Thus, although it is commonly explained that capital in Marx, in spite of being studied by means of Hegel's logic, does not carry the aura of necessity that Hegel's object of study—the Idea—does; it is also possible to say that, since Capital in Marx is *in the place of the Idea,* it is necessarily contaminated by the burden of necessity.

At least two problems arise here. First, that capital should be dragged into the circuit of irreducible necessity. To say that in order to know it one must know it in its irreducible necessity, although to act with respect to it (to do toward it rather than to know it) one must contradict that knowledge, solves the theory-practice problem in too simple a way. It is rather that Marx questions philosophical "justice" and "elegance" (and necessity) even as he uses them to establish his analysis. Otherwise Marx could not write of the extraction of surplus-value, the condition of possibility of capitalist exploitation: "this circumstance is a piece of good luck for the buyer [of labor-power: the capitalist], but by no means an injustice towards the seller [of labor-power: the worker]" (C, 301). A purely philosophical justification for revolutionary practice cannot be found.

It is because this heterogeneous concatenation of "knowing" and "doing," this possibility of a radical critique of philosophical justice, is most often recuperated within a reading *in terms of* philosophical justice and consistency, that the deconstructive moment in Marx is seen as a blind condemnation of what, according to Marx's own system, is philosophically just. To quote what I think is a representative example: "[In Marx] it is Science and Technology that fulfill the essence of Nature by indefinitely reproducing it as separated. However, they do this in the name of a finality supposed to be Nature itself."[20]

The second problematic implication of the filling of the empty place of plenitude in Logic by capital gives rise to the following question: What if the system of the logic only functioned correctly in terms of an irreducibly necessary Subject? Can one sustain the conclusions about capital as "correct" in that case?

These perplexities are at once caused by, and generate, what I call the mark of the improper. The methodology is doubted by the text, yet the grounds of a practice based on the methodology are endorsed. It is written into the practice of the theory that the example cannot be proper or adequate to the discourse.

A version of this radical impropriety is the theme of Derrida's work. Derrida suggests further that this impropriety represents itself as (a desire for) the proper. Thus the argument that all methodologies are radically improper has provoked the strongest criticism: irrationalism, nihilism, negative theology, radical skepticism, paralysis. To protect oneself against these presumed dangers, one chooses to understand as nothing but common sense, mere rhetorical gestures, or yet marginal comments Marx's own undeveloped admissions: that his analysis must use the same method that makes the object of his analysis an evil: abstracting out individual heterogeneity into a quantitative measure of homogeneous labor so that calculation may be possible: ". . . in every value-formation-process the higher labor must be reduced to average social labor. . . . One thus saves a superfluous operation and simplifies the analysis by the assumption that the worker employed by capital performs simple average social labor" (C, 306).

There is something in common between the method of analysis (reduction) and the property of capital—where the method seeks its own convenience by abbreviation (simplify the analysis). This can pose an unresolvable problem for a philosophy of action. (In fact, Baudrillard's entire critique of Marx is based upon this simple insight.) Although he criticizes the political economists for their uncritical attitude toward the capitalist mode of production, Marx is obliged to present his own participation in capital's method as no more than a necessary methodological hazard. Derrida emphasizes that such a simplification and such an alliance *constitute* the method of all theory, always giving the precritical myth of truth the lie. I have tried to suggest that it is in Marx's basic critique of the suppression of heterogeneity that the Derridian analogy is to be found. Derrida's analogy (and indeed all his work, most especially "The White Mythology" and "Limited Inc.") discloses that the method of all logic—Hegel's science of logic or the logic of the speech act—is allied to capitalism: exclusivism, a common code represented as universal, suppression of heterogeneity. It is not enough to say, as Marx and Althusser do, that freed of its idealistic burden, the method of logic can yield proper science. Putting Capital in the place of the Idea, Marx's materialism is more radical than Marx's text allows.

There are at least two ways of dealing with the situation. Both are implicated in the critic's pride of discovery. One is to go diagnostic on Marx and see where he falls short. The other is to force a reading in terms of what has enabled one to make the diagnosis in the first place: to show the power of Marx's text in terms of the supplement it asks for. In Derrida's terms, then, I have noticed how Marx's text is improper to itself, needs more than "itself" in order to be read, gives a reading here that more than matches a reading that is refused there, and uses a method that is originarily contaminated.

The itinerary of the improper in Marx does not stop here. The problem is not simply that capital, the agent of Marx's logic, is contingent and evil. It is also that it is radically im-proper. In the place of self-proximity and self-possession, it must provide itself with the mind of one class of human beings and the body of another. As Marx writes, quoting *Faust*, it is "an animated monster which begins to work '*as if* it had love in its body' " (C, 302).

The class of human beings whose mind capital must *appropriate* (*aneignen*—make its own) in order to create its monstrous self is the capitalist class. "As the conscious bearer of this movement [the movement of capital], the possessor of money becomes a capitalist. . . . The *objective* content of the valorization of value becomes his *subjective* purpose . . . and

it is only insofar as this is his sole driving force that he functions as . . .
capital personified and endowed with consciousness and a will" (C, 254).

The class of human beings whose *body* capital must appropriate is the
working class. (Here a slight but important difference must be noted. As a
"materialist" in the most colloquial sense, Marx will privilege the body over
the mind. Labor itself cannot be usurped, especially not by the transformed power of money, which derives its efficacy by the idealization of a
material gesture. It is the potential of the worker's body actualized in time
["living labor"] that capital usurps.) Time remains constitutive of value.
Capital is a determination of value. Its body is made up of the workers'
bodies in time. "Capital is dead labor which, vampire-like, lives only by
sucking living labor, and lives the more, the more labor it sucks" (C, 342).

But, paradoxically enough it is not only capital, that monster and
vampire, that has no proper being. In this schema, free human labor can be
appropriated by capital because it too can be im-proper to itself. The distinguishing *property* of labor-power is to be im-proper, in excess of self-
adequation. (This fact does not come about with capitalism; capitalism
makes use of it for the purposes of the self-determination of capital.) Even
if the body is made the privileged pole of the body-mind opposition (and
this is by no means always true in Marx), labor-power is not adequate to
itself. It is in its nature to perform more than the body's adequation or
reproduction. There is room for capital's appropriation within its nature
(just as, it can be argued, there is room for appropriation by labor in
Nature). To make labor-power adequate to the body so as to release its
potential for excess would be the *artificial* obligation of social or revolutionary justice.

Although this is clearly Marx's argument, his conclusions are not
clearly drawn. We remain caught within the opposition *Fremdarbeit*
(alienated labor) and *Eigenarbeit* (proper labor)—work for the capitalist and
for oneself. Here Derrida allows us to see that the condition of possibility of
this opposition is ever *Eigenarbeit*'s "im-propriety" or inadequation to itself.
(Perhaps I should repeat that Derrida's critique is of the concept of truth as
the concept's adequation to reality and therefore to itself; Derrida shows
that the condition of the possibility of the opposition between truth and
metaphor is the concept's "im-propriety" or inadequation to itself.) Marx's
well-known conclusions, even when the in- or sur-adequation of labor-
power to the body is most clearly articulated, is one of opposition, not
complicity: "suddenly there arises the voice of the worker. . . . 'The commodity I have sold you [my labor-power] differs from the rest of the crowd
of commodities in that its use makes value, a greater value than it itself
costs' " (C, 342). The necessary labor that is adequate to the body's continuation can always be exceeded by the body's potential, which by virtue of
time's constitutive agency is *susceptible to* idealization, that is, transformation into value, the species term of capital. It is by *an-eigen*-ing (ap-
propriating) that *Eigenschaft* (property) of labor-power that capital

generates *Eigentum* (property). ("Appropriation through and mediated by divestiture and alienation [*Ent- und Veräußerung*] is the fundamental presupposition" [*Gr*, 196].) This can be one version of the itinerary of the improper in Marx. I have not gone too far from Derrida's footnote.

(It should be mentioned here that, if Marx never makes explicit the ethical implications of labor's logical susceptibility to capital, he is of course not unaware of them. His frequent though unemphatic mention of the "justice" of the transaction between the capitalist and the wage-laborer bears witness to that.)

The itinerary of the im-proper in Marx runs also through that end-and-origin term: use-value, against which is posed the contingent circuit of exchange value. "The usefulness of a thing makes it a use-value. . . . The very body of the commodity is therefore a use-value. Thus its characteristic does not depend upon whether the appropriation of its useful properties [*Gebrauchseigenschaften*] cost men little or much time. . . . Use-value realizes [*verwirklicht*] itself only in use or consumption" (C, 126). But this body of the commodity—"iron, corn, a diamond"—signifies an exchange-situation between man and nature. It is a "good" exchange, perpetrated by the concrete individual, before the "bad" exchange organized by abstraction has set in. The presence of a version of exchange ("relationship") in descriptions of the origin of society in an identity of man and nature is to be seen even in the early writings. "The identity of nature and man appears in such a way that the restricted relation to one another determines men's restricted relation to nature, just because nature is as yet hardly modified historically, and, on the other hand, man's consciousness of the necessity of associating with the individuals around him is the beginning of the consciousness that he is living in society at all."[21] Here again Derrida's argument from supplementarity helps us. If a hierarchical opposition is set up between two concepts (identity/relationship, use-value/exchange-value), the less favored or logically posterior concept can be shown to be implicit in the other, supply a lack in the other that was always already there. Although Baudrillard sees this merely as Marx's ideological problem, whereas he can himself speak for "primitive societies," his remarks are useful here:

> The system of political economy does not produce only the individual as labor power that is sold and exchanged: it produces the very conception of labor power as the fundamental human potential. . . . The system is rooted in the identification of the individual with his labor power and with his act of "transforming nature according to human ends." In a word, man is not only quantitatively exploited as a productive force by the *system* of capitalist economy, but is also overdetermined as a producer by the *code* of political economy.[22]

The opposition between use-value and exchange-value can be deconstructed, and both shown to share the mark of im-propriety. The category of use-value is, of course, emptied of its archaeo-teleological pathos when it is used to describe the relationship between capital and labor-power. The capitalization of living labor is the realization of the use-value of labor *seen as a commodity by capital*. Here Marx's complaint may be simply that the monster bred of idealization should thus be capable of consuming and realizing the potential of the human body as a commodity. It may be the anguish of a materialist philosopher, in however restricted a sense, rather than the unexamined idealism of a self-deceived materialist.

Very generally speaking, the objective of *Capital* 1 seems always to have been to make the philosophical ground accessible to "the worker" as the considered basis for future action. In the *Grundrisse* on the other hand Marx is writing "for himself" (if that expression may be risked) and the "future action" is the writing of a book. Whereas in the *Capital* the tone is that of an outraged olympian, in the *Grundrisse* the bafflement shows, is worked at, and sometimes controlled by a gesture of postponement.

In *Capital* Marx can cover in mockery the problem that value (→money→capital) is the agency equivalent to the Idea in Hegel's logic. In the *Grundrisse* the problem remains in the background, a methodological necessity whose implications are hinted at only in rare passages. Here is the mockery in *Capital* 1:

> Value differentiates itself as original value from itself as surplus-value, just as God the father differentiates himself from himself as God the Son, although both are of the same age and form, in fact, one single person; for only by the surplus-value of £10 does the £100 originally advanced become capital, and as soon as this has happened, as soon as the son has been created, and, through the son, the father, their difference vanishes again, and both become one, £100. (C, 256)

By contrast, when Marx hints at the relationship between capital and the matrix of the self-determining concept in the *Grundrisse,* his tone is remarkably sober. Marx is speaking of capital's effort to reduce circulation time to an impossible zero, because circulation is a barrier to its development:

> The continuity of production presupposes that circulation time has been sublated [*aufgehoben*]. The nature of capital presupposes that it travels through the different phases of circulation not as it does in the idea-representation [*Vorstellung*], where one concept turns into the other at the speed of thought [*mit Gedankenschnelle*], in no time, but rather as situations which are separated in terms of time. (Gr, 548)

Here Marx implies not only that capital appropriates the mind and body of capitalist and worker but, on a greater level of abstraction, seeks to appropriate the determination of concepts in the Idea. I have been suggesting, of course, that on a comparable level of abstraction as well as in the concretest detail of writing as work (granted such an opposition), this usurpation occurs in any construction of theory. The method of *Capital* is the method of capital (as Marx points out) not by special dispensation but because making theory has something in common with capitalization (as Derrida points out).

This is how I force my reading then; but the result is not altogether a consistency. For at the limit Marx will not grant that the definition of mind itself cannot be brought into the circuit of self-impropriety and monstrosity. The groundstone of idealism with, as it were, a small i, is still intact. Circulation being a physical process, dependent upon material exigencies, must take time. Constitutive temporality in Marx is free to side with good or evil. As I have already pointed out, it is time or rather measurement by time that mediates the susceptibility of labor-power to capitalization or valorization. In the case of circulation, time, in an older-fashioned way, declares *for* the mind by declaring its kingdom without the reach of capital. The speed of the mind is instantaneous and there capital cannot go. This incipient common-sense (what is "common sense" if not ideology at its strongest?) faith in mind over matter, this trace of idealism—which must be carefully distinguished from the vulgar rationalism that Marx is usually accused of—that pervades the *Grundrisse* will not let me force a consistent reading.

Why did Marx choose to emphasize *mit Gedankenschnelle* (at the speed of thought) with words that are in English in the original—"in no time"? Writing on the idea of the instantaneity of inner discourse in Husserl, Derrida writes of the moment (*Augenblick*, literally "blink of the eye"):

> The dominance of the now not only is integral to the system of the founding contract established by metaphysics, that between *form* (or *eidos* or idea) and matter as a contrast between act and potency . . . it also assures the tradition that carries over the Greek metaphysics of presence into the "modern" metaphysics of presence understood as self-consciousness, the metaphysics of the idea as representation (*Vorstellung*).

Derrida, reading without the ideology of a unified reading, and without the credo that consistency is the mark of excellence, finds in Husserl the wherewithal to "undermine the *im selben Augenblick* argument." If we allow the pervasive thematics of im-propriety in Marx to operate, we too might find in the Marxian text the wherewithal to undermine its own traces of traditional metaphysics. For capital to occupy (*besetzen*, what in Freud is translated as "cathect") the place of the Idea, on the one hand, and for use-value to be primordially contaminated by exchange on the other, are transgressions that Marx's text and its ostensible burden cannot come to terms with. But, "as soon as we admit this continuity between [Idea,

Capital, and Labor], . . . nonpresence and nonevidence are admitted into the blink of the *instant*. There is a duration to the blink, and it closes the eye. This alterity is in fact the condition for presence, presentation, and thus for *Vorstellung* in general: it precedes all dissociations that could be produced in presence, in *Vorstellung*."[23]

Can one, only half fancifully, presume that Marx, beset with creditors, knew that the idiomatic expression "in no time" meant, not in no time, but in the briefest possible time? Should one read the passage within the structure of *Verneinung* (denegation) where a no can mean yes and also, I need to say no so I can say yes, and so on indefinitely? Forced readings open the path of a question rather than close the door with a decidable consistency. This, too, must remain an open question.

It seems appropriate to end these musings in the middle of things, with the opening of a question. There is, in a longer version, an extended postscript to this essay, where I consider the complaint that reading Marx after Derrida neutralizes the Marxian text as a philosophy of action. I comment there upon some recent theories of practice. Here I mark the place of that postscript by summarizing what I have argued so far: there is an informing pathway of the improper in Marx's texts. If one forces a reading of Marx in order to make him consistent with Derrida, the text becomes practicable. It is a peculiar consistency, because it tries to recognize and acknowledge what is not proper to itself. If this seems the "power of puns," I refer my reader, in search of the place where the pun stops, once again to "The White Mythology."

To make "literary" in this sense, then, is to "make practicable." Not, that is to say, to expose the irreducible self-constitution of the text as self-deconstruction; but to show that the moment of the deconstruction of "philosophical" justice is the minute foothold of practice.[24] It is the peculiar case of Marx's text that no consideration of that moment, merely sketched in this essay by way of philosophy and literature, can be broached without recounting the justice-practice heterogeneity in other fields: ideology, history, political economy. And perhaps, with greater difficulty and effort, the field of sexual difference.

Notes

1. I have attempted to argue this more carefully in "Il faut s'y prendre en se prenant à elles," forthcoming in the Proceedings of *Les Fins de l'homme* at Cerisy-la-salle (Summer 1980), from Galilée.

2. Jacques Derrida, *La Dissémination* (Paris: Seuil, 1972), p. 42; Fredric Jameson, "Ideology of the Text," *Salmagundi* 31–32 (Fall 1975-Winter 1976); Edward Said, "The Problem of Textuality: Two Exemplary Positions," *Critical Inquiry* 4, no. 4 (Summer 1978): 197.

3. "Living On: *Border Lines*," in Harold Bloom et al., *Deconstruction and Criticism* (New York: Seabury Press, 1979), p. 84.

This is a pervasive possibility in Derrida. One might look specifically at "The Exorbitant. Question of Method," in *Of Grammatology*, trans. Gayatri Chakravorty Spivak (Baltimore,

Md.: Johns Hopkins University Press, 1976). This, it seems to me, is one reason why Derrida is dissatisfied with the inflation of the model of language to accommodate all structural descriptions. This, in fact, is also why he substitutes "writing" for "language." As he suggests in that book, the study of the heterogeneous writing structure cannot become a positive science because it resists reduction to verbal or linguistic textuality. I read as a related argument Derrida's warning that "what weighs upon them [two supposedly opposed philosophical traditions] both, transcending this curious chiasmus, are forces of a nonphilosophical nature," some of which get spelled out as "a terrain whose neutrality is far from certain," and "the political significance of the university" ("Limited Inc.," *Glyph* 2 [1977]). I have elaborated this reading in "Revolutions That As Yet Have No Model," *Diacritics* 10 (1980):29–49.

4. *Eperons: les styles de Nietzsche* (Venice: Flammarion, 1976), p. 89.

5. Jacques Derrida, "Speculations—On Freud," *The Oxford Literary Review* 3, no. 2 (1978):82.

6. Trans. F. C. T. Moore, *New Literary History* 6, no. 1 (Autumn 1974):14–16.

7. Karl Marx, *Grundrisse: Foundations of the Critique of Political Economy*, trans. Martin Nicolaus (New York: Vintage Books, 1973); hereafter cited as *Gr*.

8. Jacques Lacan, "The Agency of the Letter in the Unconscious or Reason Since Freud," in *Écrits*, trans. Alan Sheridan (New York: Norton Press, 1977), p. 147.

9. Jacques Derrida, "From Restricted to General Economy," in *Writing and Difference*, trans. Alan Bass (Chicago: University of Chicago Press, 1978); and "The Supplement of Copula: Philosophy *Before* Linguistics," trans. James Creech and Josué Harari, in *Textual Strategies: Perspectives in Post-Structuralist Criticism*, ed. Josué Harari (Ithaca, N.Y.: Cornell University Press, 1979). I have used this argument to describe Derrida's own accessibility to certain critical developments at the beginning of my essay.

10. Karl Marx, *Capital: A Critique of Political Economy*, trans. Ben Fowkes (New York: Vintage, 1976), 1:217. Hereafter cited as *C*.

11. For a discussion of Derrida's theory of practice, see Spivak, "Revolutions That As Yet Have No Model" (see n. 3).

12. I have attempted to discuss, at somewhat greater length, the complex position of use-value—taken by many critics of Marxism to be the unexamined arche in Marx—in "Il faut s'y prendre en se prenant à elles" (see n. 1).

13. Jacques Derrida, *Glas* (Paris: Galilée, 1974), p. 56. Hereafter cited as *Gl*.

14. Louis Althusser, "Sur le rapport de Marx à Hegel," in *Hegel et la pensée moderne*, ed. Jacques d'Hondt (Paris: Presses Universitaires de France, 1970), p. 109. Two years before *Glas*, Derrida commented briefly on Marx's project to turn the Hegelian dialectic upside down ["Hors Livre," *Dissémination*, p. 37]. It is well-known that, in the passage where he outlined that project, Marx declared that he "avowed myself the pupil of that mighty thinker"[Hegel] because "arrogant and mediocre epigones" had begun to treat him "as a 'dead dog' " and that "thirty years ago I criticized the mystificatory side of the Hegelian dialectic when it was still the fashion" (*C*, 102–3). This may be compared to Derrida's more circumspect words: "Though I am not and have never been an orthodox marxist, I am very disturbed by the antimarxism dominant now in France so that, as a reaction, through political reflection and personal preference, I am inclined to consider myself more marxist than I would have done at a time when Marxism was a sort of fortress" (James Kearns and Ken Newton, "An Interview with Jacques Derrida," *The Literary Review* 14 (18 April–1 May 1980):22.

15. "Signéponge," in *Ponge Inventeur et Classique* (Paris: Union Générale d'Editions, 1979).

16. J. L. Austin, *How To Do Things With Words* (Cambridge, Mass.: Harvard University Press, 1962), p. 6.

17. Derrida, "Limited Inc.," *Glyph* 2:243, 226.

18. Austin, *How To Do Things*, p. 123; Searle, "What is an Intentional State?," *Mind* 88 (January 1979):82.

19. Nicolaus, "Foreword," *Gr*, 7, 26.

20. Jean Baudrillard, *The Mirror of Production*, trans. Mark Poster (St. Louis, Mo.: Telos Press, 1975), p. 55. In 1973, commenting on the disappointment attendant upon May 1968 and the academic backlash to the possibility of a Left Coalition government in France, Jacques Rancière wrote bitterly about the change in the intellectual climate: "If Marx hasn't worked, try Nietzsche" (*La Leçon d'Althusser* [Paris: Gallimard, 1974], p. 14). That change can be described practically by way of the doing/knowing dyad. The asymmetry between doing and

knowing in Marx, I am suggesting, is where the opening of practice can be inserted. "After Nietzsche," on the other hand, "(and, indeed, after any 'text'), we can no longer hope ever 'to know' in peace. Neither can we expect 'to do' anything, least of all to expurge 'to know' and 'to do', as well as their latent opposition from our vocabulary" (Paul De Man, *Allegories of Reading: Figural Language in Rousseau, Nietzsche, Rilke, and Proust* [New Haven, Conn.: Yale University Press, 1979], p. 126). Even if doing is conceived of as irreducibly verbal—as, according to De Man, in Nietzsche; or if what is opposed to knowing is structured like a writing, as in Shelley's notion of the imagination, a more plausible, though still idealist model of deferred practice can be found. Writing specifically of the production of relative surplus-value and division of labor by means of technology—"a cultivation of the mechanical arts in a degree disproportioned to the presence of the creative faculty" leading to "the abuse of all invention for *abridging and combining labour,* to the exasperation of inequality" rather than "lighten[ing] . . . the curse imposed on Adam"—Shelley suggests that "we want the creative faculty to *imagine* that which we know; we want the generous impulse to *act* that which we *imagine.*" Although the "we" here is clearly elite, the imagination is nonetheless that principle of irreducible alterity housed in the Self which is directly opposed to "the principle of Self, of which money is the *visible* incarnation" (Percy Bysshe Shelley, "A Defence of Poetry," in *Shelley's Poetry and Prose,* ed. Donald H. Reiman and Sharon B. Powers [New York: Norton, 1977], pp. 502–3; emphasis added).

22. Baudrillard, *Mirror,* p. 31.

23. Jacques Derrida, *Speech and Phenomena and Other Essays on Husserl's Theory of Signs,* trans. David B. Allison (Evanston, Ill.: Northwestern University Press, 1973), pp. 63, 65.

24. Although obviously determined by European politics in the narrow sense, Derrida's remarks about an "open Marxism" can relate to what I say about the deconstructive moment in these texts of Marx: "So an open marxism is one which, without giving way, obviously, to empiricism, pragmatism, relativism, nevertheless does not allow theoretical restrictions to be imposed upon it by a particular political situation, by a particular political power, as has sometimes been the case in the Soviet Union, and in France too. It is one which does not refuse *a priori* developments of problematics which it does not believe to have itself engendered, which appear to have come from outside" (Kearns and Newton, "Interview with Derrida," *Literary Review* 14:22).

Select Bibliography

In order to keep this bibliography to a reasonable length, I have confined the listing to books. Obviously many articles are relevant; the interested reader is advised to consult the following journals, which regularly include writing on literary/philosophical relations:

Boundary 2
Critical Inquiry
Diacritics
Glyph
Modern Language Notes
New Literary History
Philosophy and Literature
Yale French Studies

Again for reasons of length, I have not attempted to list primary and secondary materials for the philosophers cited and studied in this collection. The reader should begin his research on these figures by checking the bibliographies included in *The Encyclopedia of Philosophy*.

The books listed here are helpful for an understanding of the complex and wide-ranging field of literature and philosophy; and they are also useful in describing, explaining, and evaluating the major trends and developments in literary theory. I have marked with an asterisk the books that include a bibliography. This bibliography was prepared in January 1981, and so does not include books that were published after 1980.

Adorno, Theodor, and Horkheimer, Max. *Dialectic of Enlightenment*. Translated by John Cumming. New York: The Seabury Press, 1972.

Adorno, Theodor. *The Jargon of Authenticity*. Translated by Knut Tarnowski and Frederic Will. Evanston, Ill.: Northwestern University Press, 1973.

*Allison, David, ed. *The New Nietzsche: Contemporary Styles of Interpretation*. New York: Dell, 1977.

Austin, J. L. *How To Do Things With Words*, 2d ed. Cambridge, Mass.: Harvard University Press, 1975.

Barrett, William. *Irrational Man: A Study in Existential Philosophy*. New York: Doubleday, 1958.

Barrett, William. *Time of Need: Forms of Imagination in the Twentieth Century*. New York: Harper and Row, 1973.

Barthes, Roland. *Critical Essays*. Translated by Richard Howard. Evanston, Ill.: Northwestern University Press, 1972.

Benjamin, Walter. *Illuminations.* Translated by Harry Zohn. New York: Schocken Books, 1969.

Benjamin, Walter. *Reflections: Essays, Aphorisms, Autobiographical Writings.* Translated by Edmund Jephcott. New York: Harcourt, Brace, Jovanovich, 1978.

Bishop, Jonathan. *Something Else.* New York: George Braziller, 1972.

Bloom, Harold, et. al. *Deconstruction and Criticism.* New York: The Seabury Press, 1979.

Bové, Paul. *Deconstructive Poetics: Heidegger and Modern American Poetry.* New York: Columbia University Press, 1980.

*Bradbury, Malcolm, and Palmer, David, ed. *Contemporary Criticism.* London: Edward Arnold, 1970.

Burke, Kenneth. *The Philosophy of Literary Form: Studies in Symbolic Action,* 3d ed. Berkeley and Los Angeles: University of California Press, 1973.

Casey, John. *The Language of Criticism.* London: Methuen, 1966.

Cavell, Stanley. *Must We Mean What We Say?* New York: Scribner, 1969.

Cavell, Stanley. *The Senses of Walden.* New York: Viking Press, 1972.

*Cavell, Stanley. *The Claim of Reason: Wittgenstein, Skepticism, Morality, and Tragedy.* New York: Oxford University Press, 1979.

*Crosman, Inge, and Suleiman, Susan, ed. *The Reader in the Text: Essays on Audience and Interpretation.* Princeton, N.J.: Princeton University Press, 1980.

*Culler, Jonathan. *Structuralist Poetics: Structuralism, Linguistics, and the Study of Literature.* Ithaca, N.Y.: Cornell University Press, 1975.

De Man, Paul. *Blindness and Insight: Essays in the Rhetoric of Contemporary Criticism.* New York: Oxford University Press, 1971.

De Man, Paul. *Allegories of Reading: Figural Language in Rousseau, Nietzsche, Rilke, and Proust.* New Haven, Conn. and London: Yale University Press, 1979.

Derrida, Jacques. *Speech and Phenomena and Other Essays on Husserl's Theory of Signs.* Translated by David Allison, Evanston, Ill.: Northwestern University Press, 1973.

Derrida, Jacques. *Of Grammatology.* Translated by Gayatri Chakravorty Spivak. Baltimore, Md. and London: The Johns Hopkins University Press, 1976.

Derrida, Jacques. *Writing and Difference.* Translated by Alan Bass. Chicago and London: University of Chicago Press, 1978.

*Donadio, Stephen. *Nietzsche, Henry James, and the Artistic Will.* New York: Oxford University Press, 1978.

Dreyfus, Hubert L. *What Computers Can't Do: A Critique of Artificial Reason.* New York: Harper and Row, 1972.

*Ellis, John M. *The Theory of Literary Criticism: A Logical Analysis.* Berkeley and Los Angeles: University of California Press, 1974.

Ellman, Richard, and Feidelson, Charles, ed. *The Modern Tradition: Backgrounds of Modern Literature.* New York: Oxford University Press, 1965.

Engelberg, Edward. *The Unknown Distance: From Consciousness to Conscience, Goethe to Camus.* Cambridge, Mass.: Harvard University Press, 1972.

Fish, Stanley. *Is There A Text In This Class?: The Authority of Interpretive Communities.* Cambridge, Mass. and London: Harvard University Press, 1980.

Foucault, Michel. *The Archaeology of Knowledge*. Translated by A. M. Sheridan Smith. New York: Harper and Row, 1976.

Foucault, Michel. *Language, Counter-Memory, Practice: Selected Essays and Interviews*. Edited by Donald F. Bouchard. Translated by Donald F. Bouchard and Sherry Simon. Ithaca, New York: Cornell University Press, 1977.

Gadamer, Hans-Georg. *Philosophical Hermeneutics*. Translated by David E. Inge. Berkeley and Los Angeles: University of California Press, 1976.

Gallie, W. B. *Philosophy and the Historical Understanding*, 2d ed. New York: Schocken Books, 1968.

Garvin, Harry, ed. *Bucknell Review*. Special issue on phenomenology, structuralism, semiology. Lewisburg, Pa.: Bucknell University Press, 1976.

Graff, Gerald. *Literature Against Itself: Literary Ideas in Modern Society*. Chicago and London: University of Chicago Press, 1979.

Gras, Vernon W., ed. *European Literary Theory and Practice: From Existential Phenomenology to Structuralism*. New York: Dell, 1973.

Grene, Majorie. *The Knower and the Known*. Berkeley and Los Angeles: University of California Press, 1974.

Habermas, Jürgen. *Knowledge and Human Interests*. Translated by Jeremy J. Shapiro. Boston: Beacon Press, 1971.

Habermas, Jürgen. *Theory and Practice*. Translated by John Viertel. Boston: Beacon Press, 1973.

*Harari, Josúe V. ed. *Textual Strategies: Perspectives in Post-Structuralist Criticism*. Ithaca, New York: Cornell University Press, 1979.

Hardison, O. B., *The Quest for Imagination: Essays in Twentieth-Century Aesthetic Criticism*. Cleveland, Ohio: Press of Case Western Reserve University, 1971.

Harper, Ralph. *The Seventh Solitude: Metaphysical Homelessness in Kierkegaard, Dostoyevsky, and Nietzsche*. Baltimore, Md.: The Johns Hopkins University Press, 1965.

Hartman, Geoffrey H. *The Fate of Reading and Other Essays*. Chicago and London: University of Chicago Press, 1975.

*Hartman, Geoffrey H. *Criticism in the Wilderness: The Study of Literature Today*. New Haven, Conn. and London: Yale University Press, 1980.

*Hawkes, Terence. *Structuralism and Semiotics*. Berkeley and Los Angeles: University of California Press, 1977.

Hernadi, Paul, ed. *What Is Literature?* Bloomington, Ind. and London: Indiana University Press, 1978.

Hirsch, Jr., E. D. *Validity in Interpretation*. New Haven, Conn. and London: Yale University Press, 1967.

Hirsch, Jr., E. D. *The Aims of Interpretation*. Chicago and London: University of Chicago Press, 1976.

*Hoy, David Couzzens. *The Critical Circle: Literature, History, and Philosophical Hermeneutics*. Berkeley and Los Angeles: University of California Press, 1978.

*Jameson, Fredric. *Marxism and Form: Twentieth-Century Dialectical Theories of Literature*. Princeton, N.J.: Princeton University Press, 1971.

*Jameson, Fredric. *The Prison-House of Language: A Critical Account of Structuralism and Russian Formalism*. Princeton, N.J.: Princeton University Press, 1972.

*Jay, Martin. *The Dialectical Imagination: A History of the Frankfurt School and the Institute of Social Research, 1923–1950.* Boston and Toronto: Little, Brown, and Company, 1973.

Jones, Peter. *Philosophy and the Novel: Philosophical Aspects of Middlemarch, Anna Karenina, The Brothers Karamazov, A la Recherche du Temps Perdus and of the Methods of Criticism.* Oxford: Clarendon Press, 1975.

Kaufmann, Walter, ed. *Existentialism From Dostoyevsky to Sartre.* New York: Meridian Books, 1956.

*Kennick, W. E., ed. *Art and Philosophy: Readings in Aesthetics.* New York: St. Martin's Press, 1964.

Kockelmans, Joseph J., ed. *Phenomenology: The Philosophy of Edmund Husserl and Its Interpretation.* New York: Doubleday, 1967.

Krieger, Murray. *Theory of Criticism: A Tradition and Its System.* Baltimore, Md. and London: The Johns Hopkins University Press, 1976.

Krieger, Murray. *Poetic Presence and Illusion: Essays in Critical History and Theory.* Baltimore, Md. and London: The Johns Hopkins University Press, 1979.

Kuhns, Richard. *Structures of Experience: Essays on the Affinity Between Philosophy and Literature.* New York: Basic Books, 1970.

*Kuklick, Bruce. *The Rise of American Philosophy: Cambridge, Massachusetts, 1860–1930.* New Haven, Conn. and London: Yale University Press, 1977.

Kurrik, Maire Jaanus. *Literature and Negation.* New York: Columbia University Press, 1979.

*Kurzweil, Edith. *The Age of Structuralism: Lévi-Strauss to Foucault.* New York: Columbia University Press, 1980.

Langer, Susanne K. *Philosophy in a New Key: A Study in the Symbolism of Reason, Rite, and Art.* 3d ed. Cambridge, Mass.: Harvard University Press, 1957.

*Langiulli, Nino, ed. *The Existentialist Tradition.* New York: Doubleday, 1971.

Lawall, Sarah. *Critics of Consciousness: The Existential Structures of Literature.* Cambridge, Mass.: Harvard University Press, 1968.

Lentricchia, Frank. *After the New Criticism.* Chicago and London: University of Chicago Press, 1980.

McElroy, Davis D. *Existentialism and Modern Literature.* New York: Philosophical Library, 1963.

*Macksey, Richard, and Donato, Eugenio, ed. *The Structuralist Controversy: The Languages of Criticism and the Sciences of Man.* Baltimore, Md. and London: The Johns Hopkins University Press, 1972.

*Macksey, Richard, ed. *Velocities of Change: Critical Essays From MLN.* Baltimore, Md. and London: The Johns Hopkins University Press, 1974.

*Magliola, Robert R. *Phenomenology and Literature: An Introduction.* West Lafayette, Ind.: Purdue University Press, 1977.

Miller, J. Hillis. *The Disappearance of God: Five Nineteenth-Century Writers.* Cambridge, Mass.: Harvard University Press, 1963.

Miller, J. Hillis. *Poets of Reality: Six Twentieth-Century Writers.* Cambridge, Mass.: Harvard University Press, 1965.

*Natanson, Maurice. *The Journeying Self: A Study in Philosophy and Social Role.* Reading, Mass.: Addison-Wesley Publishing Company, 1970.

———. *New Literary History*. Special issue on literary hermeneutics. Volume 10, Autumn 1978.

Nuttall, A. D. *A Common Sky: Philosophy and the Literary Imagination*. Berkeley and Los Angeles: University of California Press, 1974.

*Palmer, Richard E. *Hermeneutics: Interpretation Theory in Schleiermacher, Dilthey, Heidegger, and Gadamer*. Evanston, Ill.: Northwestern University Press, 1969.

*Percy, Walker. *The Message in the Bottle*. New York: Farrar, Straus and Giroux, 1975.

Pettit, Philip. *The Concept of Structuralism: A Critical Analysis*. Berkeley and Los Angeles: University of California Press, 1975.

Philipson, Morris, ed. *Aesthetics Today*. Cleveland and New York: Meridian Books, 1961.

Polanyi, Michael. *Personal Knowledge: Towards a Post-Critical Philosophy*. Chicago: University of Chicago Press, 1958.

Polanyi, Michael. *The Tacit Dimension*. Garden City, N.Y.: Doubleday, 1966.

Poole, Roger. *Towards Deep Subjectivity*. London: Allen Lane, 1972.

*Poster, Mark. *Existential Marxism in Postwar France: From Sartre to Althusser*. Princeton, N.J.: Princeton University Press, 1975.

*Pratt, Mary Louise. *Toward a Speech-Act Theory of Literary Discourse*. Bloomington, Ind. and London: Indiana University Press, 1977.

*Ricoeur, Paul. *The Conflict of Interpretations: Essays in Hermeneutics*. Edited by Don Ihde. Evanston, Ill.: Northwestern University Press, 1974.

*Ricoeur, Paul. *The Philosophy of Paul Ricoeur: An Anthology of His Work*. Edited by Charles E. Reagan and David Stewart. Boston: Beacon Press, 1978.

*Rosenbaum, S. P., ed. *English Literature and British Philosophy*. Chicago and London: University of Chicago Press, 1971.

Ross, Julian L. *Philosophy in Literature*. Syracuse, N.Y.: Syracuse University Press, 1949.

Ross, Stephen D. *Literature and Philosophy: An Analysis of the Philosophical Novel*. New York: Appleton, Century, Crofts, 1969.

Said, Edward. *Beginnings: Intention and Method*. New York: Basic Books, 1975.

———. *Orientalism*. New York: Pantheon, 1978.

Sartre, Jean-Paul. *What is Literature?* Translated by Bernard Frechtman. New York: Harper and Row, 1965.

Searle, John. *Speech Acts: An Essay in the Philosophy of Language*. New York: Cambridge University Press, 1969.

*Simon, John K., ed. *Modern French Criticism: From Proust and Valéry to Structuralism*. Chicago and London: The University of Chicago Press, 1972.

Spanos, William V., ed. *A Casebook on Existentialism*. New York: Thomas Y. Crowell and Company, 1966.

Spanos, William V., ed. *Martin Heidegger and the Question of Literature: Toward a Postmodern Literary Hermeneutics*. Bloomington, Ind. and London: Indiana University Press, 1980.

Stanford, W. B. *Enemies of Poetry*. London and Boston, Mass.: Routledge and Kegan Paul, 1980.

Sturrock, John, ed. *Structuralism and Since: From Lévi-Strauss to Derrida*. New York: Oxford University Press, 1979.

*Tompkins, Jane, ed. *Reader-Response Criticism: From Formalism to Post-Structuralism*. Baltimore, Md. and London: The Johns Hopkins University Press, 1980.

Vivas, Eliseo. *Creation and Discovery: Essays in Criticism and Aesthetics*. New York: Noonday Press, 1955.

Vivas, Eliseo. *The Artistic Transaction and Essays on Theory of Literature*. Columbus, Ohio: Ohio State University Press, 1963.

Weitz, Morris. *Philosophy in Literature: Shakespeare, Voltaire, Tolstoy, and Proust*. Detroit, Mich.: Wayne State University Press, 1963.

*Weitz, Morris. *Hamlet and the Philosophy of Literary Criticism*. Chicago: University of Chicago Press, 1964.

*Weitz, Morris. *The Opening Mind: A Philosophical Study of Humanistic Concepts*. Chicago: University of Chicago Press, 1977.

Wicker, Brian. *The Story-Shaped World. Fiction and Metaphysics: Some Variations on a Theme*. Notre Dame, Ind.: University of Notre Dame Press, 1975.

Will, Frederic. *The Knife in the Stone: Essays in Literary Theory*. Paris and the Hague: Mouton, 1973.

Contributors

CHARLES ALTIERI teaches modern literature and literary theory in the English Department at the University of Washington. He has published two books on modern poetry, a third book, *Act and Quality*, on literary theory, and is now working on the concept of "idealization" and its consequences for literary studies.

WILLIAM E. CAIN is an associate professor in the English Department at Wellesley College. He has published essays and reviews on Renaissance literature, American literature, and critical theory. He is general editor of the Garland Press bibliographical series on modern critics and critical schools.

EVAN CARTON is an assistant professor in the English Department at the University of Texas at Austin. He has published essays on Chaucer, Dickinson, Hawthorne, and Twain. The essay in this collection is a version of the introduction to his recently completed study, *Parodies of Possibility, The Rhetoric of American Romance*.

JEROME CHRISTENSEN is an associate professor in the English Department at the Johns Hopkins University. He is the author of *Coleridge's Blessed Machine of Language*, and is currently examining the idea and practice of "literary career" in the late eighteenth and early nineteenth centuries.

DANIEL T. O'HARA is an associate professor in the English Department at Temple University and an assistant editor of *boundary 2*. He is the author of *Tragic Knowledge: Yeats's Autobiography and Hermeneutics*, co-editor (with William Spanos and Paul Bové) of *The Question of Textuality: Strategies of Reading in Contemporary American Criticism*, and editor of a special issue of *boundary 2*, "Why Nietzsche Now?" He is currently completing a book on the aesthetic of nihilism entitled "The Revisionary Will: Critical History After Nietzsche."

TIMOTHY PELTASON is an assistant professor in the English Department at Wellesley College. He has published several essays on Tennyson's poetry, and is completing a book on *In Memoriam*.

GAYATRI CHAKRAVORTY SPIVAK is professor of English at the University of Texas at Austin. She is the translator of Jacques Derrida's *Of Grammatology*, and has published extensively in the fields of Marxist, feminist, and deconstructive criticism. She is completing a book on varieties of deconstructive practice.

GARRETT STEWART is professor of English at the University of California, Santa Barbara. He is the author of *Dickens and the Trials of Imagination*, and has also published essays on Conrad, Forster, and Lawrence, as well as numerous articles on film. He is currently working on a study of death in the British novel.

ERIC J. SUNDQUIST is an associate professor in the English Department at the University of California, Berkeley. He is the author of *Faulkner: The House Divided* and the editor of *American Realism: New Essays*. His current research is concerned with the literature of slavery.

BRYAN TYSON is a student at Yale law school.

ALAN WILDE is professor of English and chairman of the graduate program at Temple University. His books include *Art and Order: A Study of E. M. Forster, Christopher Isherwood*, and, most recently, *Horizons of Assent: Modernism, Postmodernism, and the Ironic Imagination*. He is currently at work on a study of contemporary American fiction.

Index